S0-AEB-751

feldkamp
1976

LIBRARY OF
TIS
NICOLAS J. SAMS

Not Everybody's Europe

Harper's
MAGAZINE PRESS

Edited by Fred Feldkamp

Mixture for Men
The posthumous works of Will Cuppy:

The Decline and Fall of Practically Everybody
How to Get from January to December

Written in collaboration with Phyllis Feldkamp

The Good Life . . . or What's Left of It

Not Everybody's Europe

FRED FELDKAMP

HARPER'S MAGAZINE PRESS
Published in Association with Harper & Row
New York

for Phyllis

Overleaf: Baden-Baden in Mid-Nineteenth Century

Lyrics from "At Long Last Love" by Cole Porter Copyright 1937 by Chappell & Co., Inc. Copyright renewed and assigned to Chappell & Co., Inc. All rights reserved. Used by permission of Chappell & Co., Inc.

"Harper's" is the registered trademark of Harper & Row, Publishers, Inc.

NOT EVERYBODY'S EUROPE. Copyright © 1976 by Fred Feldkamp. All rights reserved. Printed in the United States of America. No part of this book may be used or reproduced in any manner whatsoever without written permission except in the case of brief quotations embodied in critical articles and reviews. For information address Harper & Row, Publishers, Inc., 10 East 53rd Street, New York, N.Y. 10022. Published simultaneously in Canada by Fitzhenry & Whiteside Limited, Toronto.

FIRST EDITION

Designed by Gloria Adelson

Library of Congress Cataloging in Publication Data

Feldkamp, Fred.
  Not everybody's Europe.
    1. Europe—Description and travel—1972-
3. Feldkamp, Fred. I. Title.
D923.F44   914'.04'55   75-18633
ISBN 0-06-122481-2

76 77 78 79 10 9 8 7 6 5 4 3 2 1

Contents

Preface

Of the seven continental blocs on this globe (including Antarctica), the one that exerts the greatest magnetic attraction for the majority of Americans is Europe (with its off-shore islands)—where their ancestors spent all or part of their lives, absorbing the culture of their regions and enjoying the life of what has been called the most civilized of continents.

This is a book about nine places in Europe that gave me particular pleasure and provided a degree of happiness. Each in its own way is at the hub of a specialized field (art, architecture, music, literature, gastronomy, and so on)—all relating in one fashion or another to the enjoyment of life. For even in this world of unremitting disaster, famine, and crime, it is still possible to enjoy that life to the fullest, if only for a period of a few weeks or months.

National capital cities were ruled out from the start, on the ground that they have been written about in such volume and in such detail that there is virtually nothing new that can be said about them. The choices of the cities, towns, and areas that make up the chapters in this book are purely personal. Of course I have other favorites besides these (Bruges, for example), but these nine seemed to compose a balanced but mixed assortment.

Finally, a note of appreciation for the artistry and craftsmanship of the Italians (architects, sculptors, decorators) in evidence all over the continent, even in Communist countries. These creative Mediterraneans have left their mark on the noble, distinguished face of Europe, and they have not had the acclaim that is due them.

FRED FELDKAMP

New York, N. Y.

Leningrad

Despite the fact that it has been largely rebuilt following the devastating shelling by the Nazis during World War II, the result is a splendorous city with an inviolate unity, a cohesive appearance as imagined by Peter the Great before he created his capital in 1703 and called it St. Petersburg. Here the old Russia breathes still. . . .

A cultural oasis in the far north—its historic past frozen in time in this frigid climate—Leningrad is a world of its own, a living symbol of the real Russia of the eighteenth and nineteenth centuries.

"The nineteenth century is alive and well and living in Leningrad," said Donald Francis Sheehan, the amiable consul for press and cultural affairs at the new American Consulate in that city, over a bowl of cream of mushroom soup American style in his attractive apartment in Gogolya Street. He might have added that the eighteenth century is in a remarkably healthy state itself in that repository of Old Russia.

"The Russians have hit on the brilliant idea of preserving the façades of all the buildings and modernizing the interior—as in the case of this building," he added.

Despite the fact that it has been largely rebuilt following the devastating shelling by the Nazis during World War II, the result is a splendorous city with an inviolate unity, a cohesive appearance as imagined by Peter the Great before he created his capital in 1703 and called it St. Petersburg. Here the old Russia breathes still, for this is the sanctum sanctorum of the Russia of the Czars. Here, too, intermingled with Czarist palaces and shrines are the historic consecrated areas commemorating the various key steps in the Revolution of October 1917, in which Leningrad was the focal point. The many dramatic statues, of which the inhabitants are justifiably proud, pay tribute, in the same quarter, to the more prominent among the Czars and to the heroes of the Revolution, most notably, of course, Vladimir Ilyich Lenin. But even today the presence of Peter the Great is almost as pervasive as that of the revered revolutionary leader.

This remarkable, unique city of almost four million is an agglomeration of palaces, museums, theaters, institutes dedicated to various branches of science—the military, health, education, and the arts—and old churches, most of which no longer function as religious centers. In a preliminary sweep around the city, which covers an extensive area since all buildings are only four or five stories high, it was a distinct challenge to one's powers of organization to decide in which period and in which field to begin one's acquaintance with this enchanted and enchanting place.

I arrived in Leningrad on a blustery night in mid-December. The flight from Prague had been bumpy and, as we landed to the captain's announcement that the temperature was one degree above zero Centigrade (zero degrees Centigrade is the freezing point) a cheer went up from the passengers, mostly foreigners but many of them Russian. (The latter do have difficulty in obtaining permission to travel, but a trip to Prague is much easier to arrange than one to a western city.) The airport consisted of one old-fashioned weatherworn building. I had anticipated the rather thorough inspection of luggage and the questions relating to currency: do you have any rubles with you? (the answer is "no"), and make a full declaration of all paper money and all traveler's checks of any country with the exact amounts you are carrying.

It is illegal, and considered a serious offense, to take paper rubles either into or out of the country, and although the customs inspectors don't usually search the passengers, such a procedure is a distinct possibility. I had been offered seven rubles for one dollar in Salzburg, Austria, two days before, and three rubles for one dollar in Vienna the previous day, as I told the inspector at Leningrad, who unexpectedly laughed. In Russia, I found, one received 7.46 rubles for *ten* dollars. (Were those change-makers in Austria informers, I wondered idly?)

Once having wrestled with the declaration and submitted to the baggage search, I rode into town through the neon-free dark Russian night in a car with driver provided by Intourist, the government tourist agency.

My hotel, the Astoria, is considered by many—Russians and foreigners alike—as the best in town, albeit not the newest. (The shiny new Leningrad, of imitation-Hilton design, is overheated, they say, and its restaurant cannot match the Astoria's. Further, it does not have the tradition of the Astoria, a most important element in Leningrad. I was told that an Intercontinental Hotel was in the planning stage, to be built by a Swedish company.)

It was, in fact, the Astoria from whose balcony Hitler had planned to announce the capture and occupation of Leningrad in World War II, an announcement that was, happily, never made, thanks to the unimaginable resistance of the city's inhabitants during those nine hundred days of siege.

The hotel had been built, I learned, in 1903 and is considered "modern";

in the United States it would be rated as a middle-class old-fashioned hotel. But it was comfortable enough, with my bed discreetly tucked into an alcove, closed off by a red curtain, and opposite a large picture window overlooking a small park and, slightly to the right, Saint Isaac's Cathedral, claimed by an enthusiastic guide to be the third largest and most important cathedral in Europe, after Saint Peter's in Rome and Saint Paul's in London —this in spite of the fact that religious services are no longer held in Saint Isaac's. Its gilded dome, well illuminated every night, shone like a beacon throughout the city, serving especially to guide home residents of the Astoria emerging from the ballet or from a theater to find no taxis in evidence anywhere.

The windows of my sitting room were sealed against the cold nights ahead, and the heating was ideal for one who, like me, prefers a room temperature of 65 to 68 degrees Fahrenheit. The only somewhat disquieting note about my quarters, in fact, was the color of the walls, starting about a foot below the ceiling: a manic-depressive blue that had a profound effect on my morale whenever my spirits fell slightly below normal. In addition, the offending walls were far from soundproof, and it soon developed that in the room to my right (as I looked out the window at the Cathedral—a far more agreeable occupation than looking at the walls) a group of Russians assembled every evening for some gaiety around the samovar: a lot of loud talk and laughter, punctuated by songs—"la la la la la-la," many of them sang simply. It occurred to me that even in Czarist times, when the hotel had been built, eavesdropping may well have been a national preoccupation— long before electronic bugging devices were invented. The walls certainly were admirably suited to that purpose.

I vowed to make an early visit to the Cathedral opposite my window, for it was now, I was informed, a museum devoted to scientific advances. But first there were more compelling shrines to be visited.

Within the city itself the most monumental attraction is easily the old Winter Palace, which, combined with four adjoining buildings along the river Neva, constitutes the majestic Hermitage Museum today. The principal building, the old Winter Palace of the Czars, whose exterior is highlighted in a dark but subdued green, was an elongated structure with great apart-

The Winter Palace/Hermitage Museum

ments on three floors, perfectly suited to conversion into a museum for the display of a tremendous collection of art masterpieces. It has been estimated that one could spend weeks and even months in the Hermitage and still miss some of the exhibition rooms. Just to walk along the Neva the length of the buildings that comprise the Hermitage today is, in very late fall or winter, a bone-chilling experience. Even on a frigid weekend the crowds one encounters at the museum are of impressive proportions; more than three million admissions are recorded each year. At this season the Russians outnumber the foreign visitors; it was enlightening, and warmly reassuring, to note that even the peasants who had come in to town for the day from their farms outside the city headed straight to the best paintings. The French Impressionists and Post-Impressionists are still the stars of the Hermitage show: rooms full of Matisse, Gauguin, Henri Rousseau, Cézanne, Monet, Bonnard, Derain, and one particular room of Picassos, executed in his later years, that produced a strong shock impact as one walked in. Other Picassos (the Russians obviously think of him as a French painter), from his blue period, along with van Goghs, Pissarros, Renoirs, Corots, Degas, and the sculptures of Maillol and Matisse fill one entire wing of the main building, with some Légers, van Dongens, Marquets, Vuillards, and Rouaults. Still

other French painters, from an earlier period, like Watteau and Courbet, are also represented. The collection is the most staggeringly impressive and soul-satisfying that one could find anywhere in the world, at least to my mind, easily as exciting as those in the Louvre, the Prado, or the Metropolitan.

The halls are tastefully arranged, the paintings well hung—not crowded together—and the condition of the exhibits is excellent, this in spite of the fact that the Hermitage officials have unusual problems relating to humidity and temperature with which to contend: the Neva, as noted, flows alongside the buildings, and the temperature variation is considerable—the vast halls are hard to heat in the far-below-freezing winter weather of Leningrad.

The floors of the Winter Palace, which could be classed as works of art of a different genre, are in surprisingly good condition, in view of the imposing numbers of visitors and the fact that they are not asked to wear felt or cotton pads over their shoes in the galleries—a requirement in most of the other palaces in and near the city.

Most of the viewers, even the most rough-hewn peasants, walk gingerly across the floors, without any instructions on how to comport themselves. All the Russians take an obvious pride in the museum and are grateful for their access to it.

The acquisition, through agents operating all over Europe, of French art of the seventeenth and eighteenth centuries is credited to Catherine II, whose acquisitiveness bordering on greediness in the field of paintings seemed to match her appetite for a sizable collection of lovers. Whether or not it was the Czarina's own taste that was responsible for the purchase of particular works of art is debatable; several of her counselors freely took credit for selecting the canvases, although they were known for their tendency to exaggerate. The truth probably lies somewhere in between.

But the overwhelming collection of late nineteenth- and early twentieth-century French masterpieces was clearly achieved by the efforts of Sergei Shchukin and Ivan Morosov, who personally raised both the Hermitage in Leningrad and the Pushkin Museum in Moscow into the front rank of the world's art museums.

Although the Middle Ages and the Early Renaissance periods are not represented in the Hermitage, its French collection goes back to Corneille de Lyon in the sixteenth century, and continues onward with Louis Le Nain, Poussin, Ingres, Watteau, Delacroix, Fragonard, Vernet, Boucher, the sculptor Lemoyne, Theodore Rousseau, Millet, Manet, Courbet, and—among the more recent artists in the French group—Toulouse-Lautrec and Utrillo.

But while the French collection is the most celebrated in Leningrad's cathedral of art, there are plentiful examples of the work of the greatest painters of the Dutch, Flemish, Italian, Spanish, English, and German schools, among the 14,000 paintings, which form the keystone of the exhibits that also include thousands of sculptures, tens of thousands of drawings, and hundreds of thousands of engravings and prints.

The Winter Palace itself, reconstructed by Rastrelli, son of the sculptor of that name, by order of the Czarina Elizabeth, who was not greatly interested in art, was supplemented by the construction of the First Hermitage, called the Little Hermitage, in 1765 by decree of Catherine II, and a second addition, known as the Old Hermitage, in 1788 by the same sovereign. Later another building was added. Both of Catherine's Hermitage buildings were enlarged and rearranged in 1859, after her death.

The shrine was formally opened by Czar Nicholas I on February 5, 1852, a date as important in Russian cultural history as October 25, 1917 is unforgettable in the country's political annals. The public responded enthusiastically on viewing the already imposing collection, and envoys were dispatched to buy up works that had the aura of greatness about them—in Italy, Belgium, England, and Germany.

The general collection already included representative paintings by Rembrandt, Van Dyck, Rubens, and Brueghel when, in 1769, Catherine—who had caught the spirit of collecting first exhibited by Peter the Great—scored an impressive coup by acquiring, for 180,000 rubles, the collection of Count Heinrich von Brühl, Foreign Minister to Augustus III, King of Poland and Elector of Saxony; it included four Rembrandts, among them the two "Calligraphist" portraits and the "Old Man Dressed in Red"; two Watteaus, one the famous "Flight into Egypt"; a Poussin, and a variety of works by a number of Dutch and Flemish painters. The acquisition of the Crozat collection in 1772 was another notable milestone, and the museum's representation of European painters was becoming more rounded, with Italian and Spanish works of great merit being added.

Paul I reigned very briefly, but Alexander I revitalized the collection by buying a considerable number of art treasures from King Stanislas II of Poland, from various other collectors in countries all over Europe, and—perhaps his most imposing purchase—the Malmaison collection of Josephine, wife of Napoleon I, for 940,000 francs.

Nicholas I continued the tradition of moving toward the fulfillment of the dream of having Europe's premier museum. Caravaggios and Titians were added. Alexander II chipped in for a da Vinci and some Corregios. Alexander III's prime contribution was Raphael's "Conestabile Madonna," and Nicholas II found and bought an early Madonna by da Vinci, making the Hermitage the proud possessor of two da Vinci Madonnas.

All private and Czarist collections were confiscated after the revolution, and a considerable number of paintings and drawings were sold to foreign buyers. But notwithstanding this slight thinning out, the Hermitage has as it stands a truly European collection of epic proportions.

Russia itself is of course represented—there is a long hall devoted, on both sides, to head portraits of Russian marshals and other military heroes—but the principal repository of its national art is the museum in Michael's Palace, a yellow-rust-colored building commissioned in the nineteenth century by Alexander I for his younger brother, Grand Duke Michael. It's about a fifteen-minute walk on the ice down the Nevsky Prospekt, one of the city's chief thoroughfares, and a short turn to the left. It's well worth the walk, if you can't find a cab; among the painters *not* classified with the French group in the Hermitage but hung in the Museum of Russian Art in Michael's Palace is Marc Chagall, the long-time expatriate who—as Picasso did—made France his home. (The difference is of course that Chagall was born and raised in Russia, and the Soviets today still entertain a certain fierce pride for all Russians—especially talented and celebrated ones—even though they fled their native land when the Communists took over power.)

At the Hermitage, the floors of rare woods, inlaid in intricate designs, the marble staircases, the malachite room featuring the generous use of that semiprecious stone from the Ural Mountains, the ivory-and-gold décor of the doors and parts of the walls, the damask on other walls—all this sumptuousness constituted only a hint of the richness to be encountered in the personal palaces of some of the Czars and Czarinas.

In the area surrounding Leningrad some fifteen to twenty-five miles from the center lie three of the most magnificent palaces in the Western world—Petrodvorets, near the Gulf of Finland, was Peter the Great's opulent refuge; Tsarskoe Selo, a town now called Pushkin in honor of Russia's immortal poet who studied at the Lyceum there, was the site of the elaborate exercise in the sybaritic life, the palace of Catherine II; and, about twenty minutes beyond by car or bus, Pavlovsk, in many ways the most impressive of the three, built for Paul by Catherine in order to get him out from underfoot while she skirmished with her lovers on the several floors at Tsarskoe Selo.

But before embarking on sorties out of Leningrad proper, I felt it would be useful to gain a more thorough knowledge of the city, and to that end I began paying visits to several institutions, a number of museums, a theater, supermarkets, a certain railroad station, and even a fortress that had served as a prison. Further, there were some rather domestic personal problems that needed to be resolved at my hotel, where the staff was supposedly English-speaking. In reality, I encountered only one Intourist woman who really spoke English, and one *dezhurnaya* (a woman who sits at a desk near the elevators and staircase on each floor) who knew a few words.

But if you would say, at my hotel's administration desk for example: "Do you speak English?" there was always a reassuring smile accompanied by the word "yes." Then when you said or asked something, you would be greeted by a blank look. (I rode up in the elevator one evening with a furious Frenchman who was muttering to himself about the fact that no one spoke French, followed by various epithets in argot. I subsequently found a woman at the Intourist desk who spoke a little French, but by then it was too late: he had already left in disgust.)

As to my personal problems: in Prague I had mounted the rickety stairs leading up to the cabin of the Aeroflot (Russian) plane that was to take me to Leningrad. Unfortunately, I tripped over the top step of the ladder and plunged head-on into a very stocky stewardess, who looked as though she would have made a good fullback. Although she prevented me from falling, one of the pins that held my wristwatch in place disappeared, leaving the watch dangling precariously from the strap.

The flight itself was a new experience in flying. Overhead, a string of very dim nineteenth-century lights flickered uncertainly, and we took off, heavily-laden, with the aircraft—a Tupelov 104 jet—shaking all over as though it were about to disintegrate. We cleared the end of the runway, if not by much, and I began to feel that I knew how Orville Wright (or was it Wilbur?) felt on that day at Kitty Hawk, North Carolina.

The shaking continued, but the caviar was plentiful, and we arrived on schedule two and a half hours later in Leningrad, my wristwatch securely tucked in my pocket.

The second domestic problem was related to my electric shaver, which would not plug into the wall socket provided by the Astoria Hotel. It was not a question of voltage: my shaver can be switched from 110 to 220 volts with a flick of the thumb. The wall outlet had round holes, while my shaver's plug has straight vertical prongs. In Salzburg earlier in the month, the hotel had provided a special plug that accommodated both. Here there seemed to be no solution.

I talked at intervals throughout the day to the *dezhurnayas* (the floor women who take your key before you are permitted to leave the floor of your room, either by staircase or elevator), the Intourist women downstairs, the hotel's administration staff, and the porters. Only Russian came back to me. One of the porters said proudly, in English: "I speak Russian," a point that hardly needed making.

Finally I spoke to a Russian-born New Yorker, a guest, who advised me that I would never succeed in getting my watch-pin fixed, or resolving the shaver crisis, so I might just as well go into the hotel's barber shop and be shaved by one of the women barbers in residence.

I began to dream of Hiltons and Sheratons I had known where my needs would be attended to quickly. But in Russia, as everywhere, persistence pays off. The floor woman who had a little English finally said thoughtfully that she had a friend, who appeared within five minutes. He was a handyman, who of course spoke only Russian, with a case containing an assortment of old nails, screws, wire, and miscellaneous tools—all, I felt, prerevolutionary. Grasping the problem as soon as we entered my room, he constructed for me a plug with round prongs on one side and vertical slits for my shaver's plug on the other, and wound it tightly with bicycle tape. Next he filed a wire to replace the missing pin on my wristwatch. *Voilà!* The whole operation took ten to fifteen minutes. No charge, and the proffered tip was politely but firmly turned down. I found myself wondering if the service at the Hiltons would have been as quick, as efficient, and as inexpensive. My faith in Russia was restored.

But the handyman's speed was not reflected in the service in the hotel restaurant, where the waiters and waitresses felt that since foreigners had nothing really to do there was obviously no hurry in serving them. If one took the trouble to build a rapport with a certain waiter or waitress it helped matters considerably. Here again most of the staff neither spoke nor understood anything but Russian (a few words of English in some cases), so there was much pointing at the menu, which fortunately carried English and French translations of the various food and beverage items. The all-purpose phrase, which all waiters and waitresses must have been taught methodically, is "Just a moment." It's the answer to everything—"Where is my waiter?" "I am in a hurry," and, conceivably, "The building is on fire."

The order of arrival of the meal was haphazard: often the fish would be served before the soup; usually, I guessed, whenever a dish was ready it was brought out. But there were long spells when the waiter or waitress would simply disappear for twenty to forty-five minutes without explanation. A dinner companion suggested that perhaps there was a television set in the kitchen showing a soccer game in progress.

I should explain here that when one applies in the United States for a visa to visit Russia (a good month or six weeks should be allowed for this transaction) one pays in advance for hotel rent—in whichever category one picks: de luxe, first class, second class—and for meals. Coupons are issued for three meals for every day of one's stay, and one must indicate in advance exactly how many days it is desired to stay and in which city or cities, plus one's arrival and departure dates.

The breakfast coupon, I found, is worth one ruble, but it is very difficult to order a suitable breakfast for one ruble, so one must pay extra—in spite of the fact that the coupons are for "full board." Luncheon and dinner coupons are worth two rubles twenty-five kopecks each (one ruble equaling about $1.34). Again—with a very small, individual ramekin of delicious fresh black caviar costing 3.49 rubles—it was hardly possible to get by with simply the coupon. Some waitresses expressed a strong interest in having cash only —no coupons. The sturgeon and salmon were memorable, but the soups were watery and cook seemed to throw anything lying around the kitchen into the borscht (a large piece of veal, an onion, whatever), and the wine from Georgia was undistinguished and on the sweet side. Even the vodka has a taste entirely unrelated to that to which U.S. palates are accustomed.

At the Astoria restaurant it is well to dine before eight o'clock when the orchestra arrives with its multilingual vocalists often singing in English songs I'd never heard before. The music is loud, putting an end to all table conversations, and the Russians seem to enjoy jitter-bugging and doing the fox-trot to the simple rhythms. The dinner service slows down even more.

I also discovered early in my stay that the telephone in my room was more of a symbol than an instrument to be used for its implied purpose. When I tried to find the number of an American journalist I know in Moscow, I was told by the hotel, in answer to my question, that they had no telephone directory—that they had once had one some time ago but hadn't seen it lately. The woman at the reception desk seemed very suspicious when I admitted I didn't know the number. As for information, it proved to be impossible even to induce her to call information, if indeed there is such a service. I entered Russia on a tourist's visa; if I had applied to go as a writer, I was told, it would have taken at least a year to acquire a visa, with a good chance of failing to be granted one at all; if they finally issued one to me as a writer, they would have been even more suspicious of any unusual request.

The fact is the Soviet officials simply don't want tourists contacting anyone on business, even just to make or renew an acquaintance. Any business appointments, I learned, must be cleared on a ministerial level before the foreigner ever enters Russia, and a special visa is issued for that particular purpose, after a number of appropriate Communist functionaries have reviewed the request for the appointment, what is to be discussed at the meeting, what results might be expected, and so on.

So even though I simply wanted to say hello to my journalist friend in Moscow, that call proved to be impossible to make. (The word "journalist" evoked an especially dark look on the part of the woman at the desk.)

But these peccadilloes of the hotel staff were soon understood and taken into account. After all, the bulk of one's time is spent away from the hotel, and there is, I'm happy to say, no attempt to restrict one's movements, as in former times. The biting cold of winter, along with the icy streets and sidewalks, weakens one's resolve to walk around town, undoubtedly a delight in summer. But even in the setting of leaden gray skies, Leningrad is a surprisingly bright city, thanks to those light, gay colors—yellow, light green, pale rose—of many palaces, institutes, theaters, and museums which keep it from being somber.

The alternative to walking is the bus or trolley or subway (very impractical for a non-Russian-speaking visitor with no knowledge of the city) or a taxi, nearly as difficult an adventure. (The spotless subway is said to be the deepest in the world, lying in places beneath beds of Cambrian soil, but nowhere can one find the answer to the question "how deep?" Obviously a state secret.) While it is possible to order a taxi at the hotel, and set forth after a wait of usually twenty to thirty minutes—taxis being in very short supply—armed with a slip in Russian giving one's destination, the return journey is something else again, since one almost never sees an unoccupied taxi on the streets. In the one case that I was lucky enough to find one, on an especially bitter-cold morning, my words "Astoria Hotel" produced no reaction at all in the driver, although it is a well-known institution to all citizens of the city. I finally had to resort to hand motions at each intersection; when we finally pulled up in front of the hotel the driver nodded knowingly. Taxis—when available—are one of the best bargains a visitor can find in Leningrad; one can travel a considerable distance across town for twenty-five or thirty kopecks.

But generally the return trip from a museum or theater involves walking, as I discovered on my first night at the Kirov Ballet. The performance was sold out, so the two taxis that were parked in front of the theater as the first wave of patrons emerged into the cold night were taken promptly. Thus it was off on foot over a route half-remembered from the ride over (during which I had been deep in conversation with the Russian-born New Yorker mentioned earlier); unfortunately, my companion had not been born in Leningrad—in fact, this was his first visit to the city, too. We crossed a canal, called the Fontanka River, and walked parallel to that until we could see the golden dome of Saint Isaac's a fairly short distance ahead.

It was snowing heavily—as it did on almost every day of my visit. Even the snow seemed Russian—silent, deep, and with a melancholy air. We reached the hotel without acquiring a case of frostbite; naturally a fur hat and fur gloves are *de rigueur* in Leningrad in December.

The snow was never allowed to pile up; the city has a most efficient re-moval apparatus. These machines glide smoothly along, stacking the snow for the truck that scoops it up and mashes it. The machines that do the piling move along in formation, one behind the other and slightly off the path of the one preceding, followed finally by the "baboushka brigade"—a group of elderly women with scarves covering their heads, working with brooms made of thin tree branches. The snow is off the streets promptly, but the ice alas remains.

I am forced to report that, in the matter of maps of the city, Intourist is completely deficient. Thanks to the kind woman at the Intourist desk who obtained second-row-center tickets for the ballet for me when the house was sold out (I had given her a carton of American king-sized cigarettes bought in a duty-free airport shop en route to Russia), I finally became the possessor of an old German map of the city—which she had brought from her home.

Leningrad is really two cities, superimposed one on the other, like a composite of two color plates. One is the city of Peter the Great and the Czars who succeeded him, the other is the city of the Communist Revolution. The sites of the history-making events of both are intermingled, making it possible to walk in a few minutes from one epoch into 'another.

The Czarist shrines are, in general, the easiest to spot; their magnificence, curiously, has not been allowed to deteriorate under the rule of the regime that overthrew them.

On a particularly cold, windy morning I set out from my hotel by cab for a small islet adjoining Aptekarsky island in the Neva where the Fortress and the Cathedral of Saints Peter and Paul are situated. I had decided in advance to wander about by myself and trust to luck that I would come upon the most interesting areas of this spacious enclosure, the location not only of the ornate Cathedral where most of the Czars are buried but the site as well of the famous prison where Dostoevsky and Lenin's brother, among many, were incarcerated.

Once in the compound it seemed even colder; in spite of the protecting walls of the fortress, the island on which it sits is in a completely exposed position to the winds whistling down the river, and the area is too extensive for the walls to be of much help. I was beginning to wonder if I would find a way to a door leading to a heated interior when a tour group of about fifteen to twenty led by *two* guides invited me to walk with them, at no cost to me. I readily agreed (by hand motions), for the guides seemed to know where everything of interest was and also presumably were headed indoors.

I suddenly realized that this was an extraordinary tour group I had joined. At the same moment I understood the reason for the presence of *two* guides, and why one of them wore no gloves in the below-zero cold. One guide (both were women) gave, in Russian, the running commentary of what we were seeing, plus some background—the other translated into the language of the deaf-and-dumb, transmitted to this unusual tour group by her freezing fingers. The deaf-and-dumb language and the Russian tongue that the first guide was using are equally incomprehensible to me, but at least I had made contact with a sympathetic group, and I was being led to the places I had come to see.

The Cathedral, which like most such edifices in the country is no longer consecrated to religious purposes, is perhaps the most opulent of the many gilt-trimmed buildings I visited in Leningrad and its surroundings. This

Fortress of Saints Peter and Paul

overpoweringly impressive house of worship was built by an Italian-Swiss architect, Domenico Trezzini, over a nineteen-year span beginning in 1714, just over a decade after the city's creation. The Russians who crowded into the Cathedral during my visit looked about with great curiosity mixed with awe, especially at the coffins of the Czars and Czarinas. The final resting place of Catherine II drew special attention, with Peter the Great a close second.

The sepulchres, of marble and burnished jasper, of all the Czars from Peter the Great to Alexander III with members of the royal families, except for Peter II, are placed in rows. They were suddenly there, to be touched, and they seemed a bit unreal in the light of the crystal chandeliers that glanced off the gold leaf of the great iconostasis. The sarcophagi of the dead despots lost, I thought, some of the aura of theatricality they should have had by being simply too close to the viewers. The storied gold vaults were not part of the tour.

The elaborate religious paintings that adorned the walls were inspected closely and, though no one blessed himself, were accorded great respect. This reverence for the religious Czarist past on the part of the Russian visitors was noticed in all the former churches I entered.

My unusual tour of the Fortress of Saints Peter and Paul moved on to the prisons where we were to visit the cell blocks that housed the celebrated out-of-favor dissidents of the moment. The translator's hands were turning blue with cold, in spite of the rush of words she was transmitting to her audience. This, I thought, must be a specifically Russian deaf-and-dumb language, or could it be international? Just as I was feeling especially inept concerning the language, we passed a few signs in English—the first I'd seen since arriving—identifying some of the prisoners who had been in residence within—Gogol, Gorki, Dostoevsky, and even Peter the Great's son Alexei.

The cells, on the ground-floor level, were dark and dank—a few had very small windows high on the wall near the ceiling; certainly no place to spend twenty to thirty years. My tour-mates wept openly at the recital of the names of those who had died in those cells, after years of confinement.

After we had inspected a long line of cells—roughly eight by about ten or twelve feet—I took leave of my comrades, and comrades they were, with a wave of the hand, the most appropriate form of farewell I could think of. They waved back. Some were still sobbing.

Walking across the bridge to the left bank of the Neva, where I was quartered, was no delight on this bitter, windy morning. Once on the mainland, appalled at how much of a walk still lay ahead, I was lucky enough to spot that unoccupied cab, stopped for a light.

In the swiftly running river, some small distance from the Winter Palace/Hermitage, lay the cruiser *Aurora*, today a shrine of the Revolution, surrounded by the world and creations of Peter the Great. It was the *Aurora* that fired a round of blanks pointed toward the Winter Palace, giving the signal that finally started—after several abortive attempts—the real revolution of October 25, 1917 (Julian calendar date) by launching the attack on the Winter Palace. It was the beginning of the revolution that changed Russia and changed the world. Today everywhere in Leningrad one sees pictures of its leader, Vladimir Ilyich Lenin—huge posters, and of course framed photographs in every office and every home in the city. When he arrived at the Finland Station (which looked to me like a typical suburban train terminal, with no historic atmosphere), not far from Peter's Fortress of Saints Peter and Paul, Lenin expected to be taken at once to that very fortress, he has confessed; instead he was met by an enthusiastic citizenry ready for a revolution and desirous of an end to bungling attempts at one. (I was struck by the fact that Lenin's mission began in Zurich, where he had lived in self-imposed exile—the same city to which Alexander Solzenhitsyn repaired after being expelled from his native land nearly fifty-seven years later.)

The *Aurora*, which fired the blank round that gave Communism its start, is berthed today a few hundred meters from where she lay in the Neva in 1917 on that memorable day.

At the airport coming into Leningrad I had purchased a paperback brochure—no sex-laden novels for sale here—titled "Lenin: Problems of Building Socialism and Communism in the U.S.S.R." and noted, on the evening of my visit to the Fortress and the Finland Station, and a drive past the *Aurora*, that by December 25, 1922, just five years after the founding of the Communist state, Lenin was having second thoughts about some of his personnel. About Joseph Stalin, a future Communist czar, Lenin had this to say on the day of Father Frost: "Comrade Stalin, having become Secretary-General, has unlimited authority concentrated in his hands, and I am not sure whether he will always be capable of using that authority with sufficient caution. Comrade Trotsky [finally to be murdered in Mexico by Soviet agents], on the other hand . . . as has already been proved, is distinguished not only by outstanding ability. He is personally perhaps the most capable man in the present Central Committee, but he has displayed excessive self-assurance and shown excessive preoccupation with the purely administrative side of the work.

"These two qualities of the two outstanding leaders of the present Central Committee can inadvertently lead to a split, and if our Party does not take steps to avert this, the split may come unexpectedly."

Then, a few days later, on January 4, 1923, Lenin added a footnote: "Stalin is too rude and this defect, although quite tolerable in our midst and in dealings among us Communists, becomes intolerable in a Secretary-General. That is why I suggest that the comrades think about a way of removing Stalin from that post and appointing another man in his stead who in all other respects differs from Comrade Stalin in having only one advantage, namely, that of being more tolerant, more loyal, more polite, and more considerate to the comrades, less capricious, etc. This circumstance may appear to be a negligible detail. But I think that from the standpoint of safeguards against a split and from the standpoint of what I wrote above about the relationship between Stalin and Trotsky it is not a detail, or it is a detail which can assume decisive importance."

But Stalin persevered, was certainly not more considerate to the comrades, and seized absolute power, while Trotsky, the brilliant administrator, was forced to flee the country. Stalin and Trotsky, the two promising young comrades about whom Lenin was beginning to have doubts as early as 1922–23, certainly did split; Trotsky was considered important enough as a potential threat to warrant the sending of a group of killers to Mexico where he was in luxurious residence to obliterate him for good.

But, after all, Lenin prevailed in the end: today there is no physical evidence of either Stalin or Trotsky in Leningrad and both have become unmentionables, while Lenin—"our founder"—is everywhere and spoken of with great reverence.

As I exulted in the warmth of the cab, I marveled—as we passed through street after street of buildings that had been rebuilt in the original spirit after being bombarded and reduced to shells by the German artillery during the nine-hundred-day siege of the city—at the artistry and meticulous craftsmanship that went into the restoration of virtually the entire city.

One of the most spectacular examples of this unexcelled craftsmanship is the Kirov Opera and Ballet Theater, formerly—under the Czars—the legendary Maryinsky Theater. Within the city limits of Leningrad proper, the Kirov Theater was, I think, the grandest, most elegant building I visited during my stay. The reincarnation of the old Maryinsky—renamed after Secretary Kirov of the Communist Party in Leningrad, killed by a terrorist—is a miracle of splendor in gold leaf and crystal. The Czars' box—a cozy but commodious vantage point directly facing the stage on the first tier—is still assigned to honored guests and top-ranking comrades; it is, I understand, virtually unchanged from Czarist days save for the absence of the golden double eagle that adorned it when the theater was called the Maryinsky.

But not all visitors were as impressed as I. An English-speaking Japanese man to whom I spoke while drinking my Russian "champagne" during intermission did not really find the Kirov to his taste. When I registered surprise, he said simply: "Too much gold," flashing a wide, typically Japanese smile that revealed at least eight gold teeth.

I was lucky enough to acquire tickets for two performances—both of which were said to be sold out—thanks to the English-speaking woman to whom I gave the carton of cigarettes. Late in the afternoon on the days of the performances I wished to attend the tickets magically appeared. And considering that the theater was really sold out—I judged by the Russians begging to buy tickets on the sidewalk in front of the theater, in the stinging cold—I was amazed to find, on one occasion, that I was being ushered to a seat in the second row on the aisle in the orchestra.

Not only the Czars' box is ringed in gold; gold is everywhere, setting off the silver candelabra. My chair was covered in sapphire velvet. And the Kirov may be the one building in town where the sculptures (colorful cherubs, sprites, and such) do not depict the heroes of the revolution.

Giselle was a masterly blend of superb dancing (a very pretty Rumanian girl danced the leading role), gossamer costumes, and a brilliantly performed score. The corps de ballet was incomparable—far above and beyond its counterparts in the Bolshoi, any American or Canadian ballet troupe, or for that matter the old Ballet Russe de Monte Carlo imported to the United States by the late Sol Hurok in the thirties and forties. The Bolshoi in Moscow is currently specializing in more modern ballets, the Kirov in Leningrad the classical. Though, as its adherents claim, the Bolshoi may have a vibrancy unchallenged in Russia, or throughout the world, the Kirov has undeniably achieved the apogee in delicate elegance.

Swan Lake was, unfortunately, not on the program during my stay in the city, but I did return—thanks again to my devoted cigarette-loving friend at the hotel—for *The Sleeping Beauty.*

Again I found myself in a strategic position in the orchestra, this time not quite so close to the stage. Again every seat in the orchestra, parterre boxes, and the four circular balconies above was taken, and there were some standees at the rear of the boxes. Some down-front spectators used binoculars, in the best tradition of the old burlesque houses in New York.

During the intermission at each performance I made my way to the buffet for an oversized canapé and a glass of highly touted Russian "champagne," which tastes not at all like its French model. It has a strong, somewhat sweet flavor with a strange, musty taste that made it a disappointment. Certainly it is not dry. Most of the customers were hungry, and bought up most of the assortment of heavy "snacks" for sale. The women behind the showcases were kept busy at their abacuses during the brief flurry of business before it was time for the next act. In a well-lit room just off the stairway on my way down to the orchestra, behind the dress circle, there was a kind of promenade in progress. Russian balletomanes dressed in their best were stepping gingerly along a runner of carpet barely two feet wide covering the delicate inlaid wooden floor along the walls of the room. No one set foot on the graceful marquetry of the exposed floor. It was difficult to imagine this circumspect stroll taking place in quite this respectful manner in any theater in the United States.

Studying the gilt-covered walls of the interior, in the moments before the curtain was rolled up, it was hard to believe that this impeccably beautiful structure had suffered extremely heavy damage by Nazi shells during the siege some thirty years before.

Once again a memorable performance, with many curtain calls and shouts of "bravo" from the addicted balletomanes. But this *Sleeping Beauty* was the long, uncut version, and it was eleven twenty-five before I lined up at the cloak room for my coat, fur hat and gloves, and galoshes.

I had taken a late tea at the hotel, planning to have dinner on my return. (As a diabetic, I must pay special attention to the spacing, and regularity, of my meals.) I realized that the dining room closed at midnight, but eleven fifty was the fastest arrival time I could manage, after walking quickly but carefully over the ubiquitous ice.

"Finish" was the announcement that greeted me at the dining-room doors at ten minutes to twelve. I was so hungry I was beginning to tremble, and I started to worry that an insulin reaction was imminent. Neither the women at the administration desk nor at the Intourist counter understood my need, nor did they understand the word "diabetic" on the bracelet I wear, adorned by a red cross.

"Morning eight o'clock" one said when I pleaded for something to eat. "Dining room all closed." Room service also shut down at twelve; outdoors it was snowing heavily, and the prospect of searching for a restaurant still open, in my current condition, was not a reassuring one.

From my room I telephoned and asked for the manager, who unfortunately had gone home. The woman on the floor was not much help either, and by now I was fully prepared for the onset of the coma—brought on by a combination of no sugar in the blood (from not having eaten) and therefore nothing to counteract the insulin I had injected into my thigh that morning.

I phoned back to the administration desk and heard myself saying: "By tomorrow morning I may be dead. DEAD," I almost shouted. "I must eat something—anything. But FOOD."

Then I gave up and lay down to try to sleep, hoping I would wake up in the morning. But somebody must have understood something of my plight; at two fifteen just as I was dozing, still trembling and dizzy, there was a loud knocking on the door. I opened it to two of the administration women with a tremendous tray bearing a huge repast: soup, fish, brown bread and butter, a beet salad, and tea. I thanked them profusely—it was the first time I felt like kissing anyone in Leningrad—and started quickly on the meal that ranks among the most appreciated I can remember. It was consumed in record time.

My sleep was untroubled, and promptly at eight o'clock I was awakened by another knock on the door—this one a bit softer than the tattoo performed during the night.

It was one of the regular room-service waitresses, blond, ruddy-cheeked, stocky, and undeniably Russian. She bore a large breakfast—much larger than I usually had or was accustomed to. Evidently, the idea that I needed *food* had filtered through to the staff.

The young woman looked at me anxiously to determine whether I seemed all right or whether she should call a doctor—another word I had used during those early morning hours and one that had apparently hit its mark. In any case I was deluged with food and drink, to the point where I was obliged to return to the dining room with the sleepy service and order smaller meals. The Russians, it seems, can be a compassionate people.

Directly opposite the entrance to the dining room in the hotel lobby one came upon the "news" stand. Laid out neatly in a row was a fine selection of Communist papers—including *The People's World*, of San Francisco, and *L'Humanité*, of Paris—and Communist magazines, a few in English. One headline trumpeted news of a plot involving J. Edgar Hoover of the F.B.I., long since resting in his grave, on a day when terrorists were blowing up a plane in Rome and attempting to hijack another, I later learned.

It wasn't until my last day in Leningrad that I discovered that the stand had the American paper the *International Herald Tribune*, published in Paris, under the counter. It was, however, possible to buy copies—at a price— four or five days old. The aged woman behind the counter pulled them out quickly for my inspection and with equal speed replaced those that were not wanted to a shelf below, out of sight. She obviously regarded the paper as subversive and not fit for a good Russian comrade to see.

This newsstand was one of the few facilities to divert the guests in the lobby who were waiting indoors for a taxi or for friends or were just killing time. Besides the Intourist desk, which arranges tickets for guided tours, admissions to the Hermitage, tickets for the theater, and taxis, there is a cashier's cubicle whose occupant changes rubles, at their very stiff rate for visitors, in exchange for hard currency or traveler's checks from other countries; this transaction was then recorded on the declaration form filled out on entering the country, listing all the visitor's currency and traveler's checks. A hard-currency bar nearby is open for business from eight P.M. until two A.M., with drinks of all kinds for sale at elevated prices, rubles not accepted. A hair-cutting salon featuring women barbers completed the opportunities for diversion on the ground floor.

But one flight up the grand staircase on the first floor (it would be the second in the U.S.), hidden away along a passageway, is the Beriozka store, specializing in souvenirs (a staggering array of dolls in bright peasant dresses), a few books in English, French, and German, Johnny Walker Scotch and a few varieties of gin, and a large selection of knick-knacks, all for sale to hard-currency customers only, at prices that must be called high.

Although the Soviet government is most anxious to have tourists visit the U.S.S.R., it is not really organized to handle them. There is an obvious lack of hotel space, and precious little guidance for those unfamiliar with the city (the unavailability of street maps, for instance). The currency restrictions should be simplified somewhat, so that it doesn't take a major effort to exchange a bit of foreign money for a few rubles. And the presence of some English-, French-, and German-speaking personnel is sorely needed.

Soviet officials have caught on to the efficacy of the guided tour by bus, throughout the city and to the summer palaces of the Czars some twenty to twenty-five miles outside. (In the latter case, it is virtually the only way to see these magnificent monuments to the eighteenth century.) Also, by tour bus the visitors' movements outside the city proper are controlled: they see only what the authorities permit them to see.

And though one hears little English or any other foreign tongue in Leningrad, the young women who are guides on the tour buses have learned their linguistic specialties well; the ones on the buses I rode speak a purer English than can be heard at random at Piccadilly Circus—with the most proper accent. The French- and German-speaking guides on whom I eavesdropped were equally proficient.

The palace and estate of Catherine II—who the guide reluctantly admitted was sometimes called Catherine the Great—known as Tsarskoe Selo, or the Czar's Village, is situated in the town today called Pushkin, where that famous poet went to school in a building adjoining the palace, and where he composed some of his more memorable poems. Brutally battered by the Nazis, who occupied the town, the palace has been all but completely restored: every silk drapery redone to match exactly the exquisite work in the original, every molding, every painting reproduced so that it would have been impossible for Catherine herself to detect any difference. Labor is relatively cheap in Russia, but it cost a fortune nonetheless in salaries to her most skilled artisans to return this lovely, spacious palace to a state almost identical to the original.

Catherine's palace was designed by the same Italian architect, Rastrelli, who rebuilt the Winter Palace in Leningrad. It was done in the style that has come to be known as Russian baroque, with countless splendid, high-ceilinged rooms. One large hall is 1,000 square meters in floor area, and is decorated with large gilded cornices. (The formal balls were usually given here.) There was a Chevaliers' dining room, a waiters' room done by Cameron with eighteenth-century parquet floors. For the mistress of the establishment there were a dining room in green, with the doors slightly darker, in Cameron's neoclassical style, a blue living room, a Chinese room in blue, a Chinese parlor featuring Chinese art works, carved lacquered pieces, and Oriental vases,* an amber parlor, a picture hall, a Turkish room,

* All a gift of the last Chinese Emperor to the last Czar of Russia, long after Catherine's death.

a Pheasant room, decorated by original silk drapes of pheasants and swans (these were sent to the Urals and saved from Nazi desecration), a huge White Hall in gold, white and red, with gilded molding, and a chapel that seemed more like a church. Everywhere there was gilt, even gilt chairs, gold leaf and decorations painted with gold, amber chests, malachite from the Urals, cabinets in marquetry, parquet wood in chestnut and birch, Delft tiles and Delft tile stoves, and crystal glass in the form of raindrops, a particular favorite of Catherine's.

The palace was finally nationalized by the Russian Royal Family, and after the revolution it was opened as a museum. The first peasants entered this holy of holies in July 1918; before that date they had never had a look inside.

On June 22, 1941, the palace was destroyed and set afire by Nazi hordes. When one inspects the black-and-white photographs of each room, as well as the overall shot, of the condition in which the Nazis left them, one is staggered again by another careful appreciation of the present, artfully restored state of this unique museum.

Back on the bus, we waited for the one German tourist with his very own Russian girl guide. As the time passed in the cold December evening, one Russian-born American guessed aloud that he must be in the chapel, asking God's forgiveness.

The pretty young girl with our English-speaking group—who was from Irkutsk, deep in the interior—went on in her precise manner of speech about Peter I and his accomplishments. "For the first time," she admitted, "the Romanoffs united the country. Peter needed an outlet to the Baltic Sea, and the site he chose for the city he was to call St. Petersburg suited his purpose admirably—on the Neva River which flows into the Gulf of Finland, which in turn empties into the Baltic. From there a ship has access directly to the North Sea and the Atlantic Ocean. In the other direction the Neva goes across country, connected with canals linking it to the Volga River and the Caspian Sea."

Peter actually called his dream city Sankt Pieter Burkh—the Germanic name for St. Petersburg, which was given a more Russian flavor during World War I by being christened Petrograd (still the city of Peter, without reference to the Saint). In 1924 the Soviets renamed it after the founder of the new Russia, Vladimir Ilyich Lenin. (I am reminded of the story about the man applying for a position in the Soviet Union. He filled in the form thus: Born, St. Petersburg. Educated, in Petrograd. Current residence: Leningrad. And all, he told a friend, without moving from the house in which he was born.)

The palace of Peter, called Petrodvorets by the Russians, was almost completely demolished by the Nazis, leaving only a shell standing. Here work was progressing, but at the time of my visit just two rooms had been restored, and since it is quite a drive from the center of Leningrad I went instead to the palace of Paul, Catherine's son, of whom she was not overly fond. To move him out of her own palace she built him his own, somewhat farther from Leningrad.

On the bus to Pavlovsk (Paul's palace) still another young Russian woman from the provinces gave a running commentary in what was really quite excellent English. Paul, we learned, considered himself the true successor of Peter. During his mother's reign he held the title of Grand Duke; to escape her heavy hand, he traveled to France during the last few years of

Main dining room, Pavlovsk Palace

her rule. There he picked out Gobelins tapestries, as well as some French rotating clocks. The palace he was given by his mother was designed by England's Charles Cameron, who fashioned an impressive Italian hall, featuring second- and third-century busts of the Roman Emperors, and a reception room remindful of the thirteenth and fourteenth centuries in white and blue, with of course plenty of gilding—the colors of the Russian Orthodox Church of the time.

We passed next through a Greek Hall and a Guards Vestibule, before reaching the boudoir of his wife Maria, decorated by a priceless Gobelins tapestry. Many of the palace's treasures were successfully evacuated—shipped to the Ural Mountains and beyond to Siberia—before the Germans arrived in the area during the Second World War.

Paul, being a naturally suspicious, insecure type, had spent countless hours drilling his troops. From the beginning of his reign he feared a coup d'état, and he proved to be right. After living only forty days in his sumptuous palace he was killed by his own guards.

The profusion of stunning rooms featured inlaid woods of mahogany and red birch, French chandeliers, stucco walls covered with a marble crust, porphyry vases from the Urals, silk hangings executed in the same technique used by the eighteenth-century silk houses of Lyon, France (the silk in the royal bedroom was successfully evacuated during World War II), malachite, a Sèvres toilet set presented by Marie-Antoinette, paintings by the so-called small Dutch painters, a smattering of French paintings, early nineteenth-century bronze, Russian crystal with its distinctive bluish tint, an eighteenth-century English clock, and one of the first pianos. The dining room, in bronze and crystal, was of a tremendous size, and an Antique Hall contained some impressive, original Greek statuary.

After Paul's death, Maria inhabited the palace for a while, but their son Alexander, who became Czar Alexander I, used it only occasionally.

On the ride back to town in the early dusk, we passed mile upon mile of flat land being put to no use; during my several tours in the environs of Leningrad I saw only one good-sized building under construction, small relief for the population of four million who are forced to live in the same quarters they have inhabited for decades. Most newly married couples must move in with the parents of the bride or groom. As we lumbered on toward town we passed a stretch of ground completely free of buildings of any kind. Our guide explained that this was "the green belt of glory," the former front line during the Nazis' siege of the city they never captured. The enemy progressed to within 15 kilometers of the center of the city and 5 kilometers from the city limits.

With all its problems, Leningrad—even in late fall and winter—is a jewel of a city, bearing no similarity to any other I have visited anywhere. This northernmost metropolis in the world, with its forbidding gray December skies, still manages to be cheerful and light-hearted with those pastel rose, blue, and yellow exteriors of many of its buildings, not to mention the distinctive green of the Hermitage Museum, giving the city a lilting gaiety that is accentuated by its many gilded interiors, and by its great paintings, frescoes, mosaics, and by its icons.

Its classical statues add to the atmosphere one feels of Leningrad's past. Just to the left on leaving the Astoria Hotel, in the vast square that faces the City Hall, is an equestrian statue of Czar Nicholas I, with his mount rearing; it has the distinction of being the only major sculptured work featuring man and horse in which there are only two points of contact with the base. (The steed's two hind legs.)

Peter the Great rates two notable statues: the more famous one by Falconet has his horse trampling on a snake, representing the enemy (Sweden). The other, begun by Carlo Rastrelli, father of the Rastrelli who reconstructed the Winter Palace and left his mark on the stately appearance of Leningrad itself, was first commissioned by Peter I, but its completion was delayed by a series of politically motivated maneuvers over a long period. Finally Rastrelli's architect son supervised its casting in bronze and eventually, after yet another series of orders and counterorders, it was put into place opposite the stunning Engineer's Palace, formerly named the Mikhailovsky Palace. Critics of classic statuary have said it was ahead of its time, as an argument to account for the great deal of criticism of the work at the time of its inception. It has now taken its place as "one of the best specimens of European monumental sculpture." Rastrelli's *chef d'oeuvre* presents Peter as a conquering warrior in the epic mold, following his victory over the supposedly invincible Swedish Army.

I was taken to see the Rastrelli statue of Peter by Don Sheehan, the Consulate's press and cultural attaché, on a final drive around the city prior to my departure from Russia from what would prove to be a fresh, new, ultramodern airport building, where nothing yet functioned except for customs and immigration clearance facilities. I was already familiar with the Falconet equestrian statue of Peter and the one of Nicholas I, near my hotel. But this was my first view of Rastrelli's Peter, again on horseback and with the most warlike mien of all. Sheehan considered the Rastrelli the most interesting of the three. My American "guide" made a short detour to drive by the wide-angle expanse of symmetrical columns at the center of which rests the domed Cathedral of Our Lady of Kazan, another deconsecrated house of worship which now serves as a "Museum of the History of Religion and Atheism."

I regretted the lack of time that made a stop impossible, as I have no acquaintance at all with the History of Atheism. As for the History of Religion, in this irreligious land, Sheehan remembered some especially spectacular icons and various instruments of torture allegedly used in the Spanish Inquisition that were on exhibit inside. It was quite an idea, I thought, to combine the histories of Religion and Atheism under one roof —and in an unfrocked cathedral at that.

On the way back to my hotel we passed the house where Lenin once lived. And while waiting for a traffic light to change I noticed an arresting plaque on a building just across the pavement; my volunteer driver-guide-interpreter, well-schooled in Russian, promptly advised me that it proclaimed that "Lenin was in the habit of dropping by here from time to time" or words to that effect. (The Russian equivalent, I mused, of George Washington Slept Here.)

Before packing and leaving for the airport, I worked in a brief visit to Saint Isaac's Cathedral, across the small park from my hotel. Its exhibits are related to scientific achievements especially in the hydrographic field, but their impact is dwarfed by the large frescoes of Christ, the Christ child, and Mary in this really tremendous church. The Russian men in attendance all removed their hats on entering and were obviously very impressed with the religious artwork in a dazzling golden setting, reflecting the resurgence of interest in religion and the country's religious heritage in this atheistic state. One Russsian standing alongside and gazing raptly at the frescoes muttered something in Russian, which translated into "And they say there is no God."

Saint Isaac's was constructed under the guidance of still another foreigner, French architect Auguste Montferrand, and was completed in 1858. It is another testimonial, if more were needed, to the opulence of the years under the Czars, who spared no expense on their palaces and churches.

But in spite of foreign architects, sculptors, designers, and decorators (Italy's two Rastrellis, Quarenghi, Rossi, England's Cameron) and its French, Italian, Dutch, and Flemish art masterpieces, Leningrad is unmistakably Russian in flavor. For this Czarist capital is, after all, the city of Tchaikovsky, Rimsky-Korsakov, Shostakovich, Dostoevsky, Gogol, Gorki, Tolstoy, Pavlov, Stanislavsky, Chaliapin—even Rasputin lived here—and the birthplace of the formalized ballet, home of the Imperial Ballet School and its hundreds of graduates, a number of whom later gained international reputations— among them Mikhail Baryshnikov, Rudolf Nureyev, Natalya Makarova, Valery Panov, Galina Ragozina, Alexander Minz, and Alexander Filipov. Some in this Kirov group defected to the West, others emigrated; most studied under the late, legendary Aleksandr Pushkin, a descendant of the poet and classed as one of the greatest ballet teachers of all time. All the dancers and teachers mentioned above are now in the Western world, but all owe their success to their years in Leningrad.

A cultural oasis in the far north—its historic past frozen in time in this frigid climate—Leningrad is a world of its own, a living symbol of the real Russia of the eighteenth and nineteenth centuries. The visitor from abroad will discover that it takes a little getting used to, but be assured he will find it is well worth the effort.

Granada

There is ample testimony to the aptness of the accolade to the supremacy of the Muslim art and architecture to be found in Granada, the finest examples in all Spain. The masterpiece, of course, is the Alhambra; even though parts of it have had to be restored, it remains the stunning centerpiece of Mohammedan artistic achievement. One is soon aware that the Arabian palace is the heart and soul of Granada. And it is still today, materially as well as spiritually, the Alhambra of the Caliphs.

*T*here is something about Spain that sets a writer's juices in motion. It has a primitive quality not exactly matched in any other European country of my acquaintance; nowhere else—in Europe, at least—is the twentieth century at such a remove. There are, of course, innumerable evidences of the past—and the distant past—to be found throughout the continent, but in Spain one is alive *in* the past: in no other country are the past and present compressed into one entity as they are in Spain. The future is a condition that does not impinge on one's consciousness.

In the nineteenth century there were, among others, Washington Irving, Alexandre Dumas, *père et fils*, and Théophile Gautier who became fascinated with the Spanish experience; in the twentieth, the compulsion to write about this brooding, mysterious land seized such masters of their craft as Rose Macaulay, V. S. Pritchett, Sacheverell Sitwell, and, of course, Ernest Hemingway.

In the last century Stendhal voiced the conviction that it was in Spain that the manners and customs of medieval Europe had been preserved and, for all its bloody wars, a certain continuity of civilization had been maintained there. "I regard the Spanish people," he wrote, "as the living representatives of the Middle Ages. They are ignorant of many small truths of which their neighbors are childishly vain, but they know deeply the great truths, and they have the character and intelligence to follow them out to their most remote conclusions. Spanish character forms a fine opposition to French intelligence; hard, brusque, scarcely elegant, full of savage pride, not concerned with the opinion of others, it is exactly the contrast of the fifteenth century with the eighteenth."

Perhaps the extreme difference—in spirit, in the quality of life, even in the character of the light—between Iberia and its neighbors to the north is partly accountable for the premise stoutly maintained by many that Spain, while geographically European, can actually more logically be considered a part of Africa. Racially, Spain today is composed of a high percentage of

African strains, but this observation can be made of other areas on the northern periphery of the Mediterranean. Spain has a uniqueness.

Whether or not Europe stops and Africa begins at the Pyrenees, it is certainly true that the farther south one penetrates from the French border the deeper the quality of Spanishness. By the time one reaches Andalusia, in the extreme south of the country, one is totally immersed in Spain—its culture, traditions, prejudices, and in the most colorful aspects of its dramatic history.

The recurring popular dream of Castles in Spain reaches its zenith in Granada, where the most romantic and historic of all Spanish castles, the immortal Alhambra, still stands watch over the surrounding countryside. For generations the Muslims and the Christians fought bitterly for possession of this so-called Moorish fortress, the last and most cherished bastion of the North Africans on the Iberian peninsula. Today the tourists are in control —Americans, Germans, Swedish, English, French, and Japanese; they have come to feel the strong spell of history in an atmosphere that has changed hardly at all since the fourteenth century.

Coming into Granada, keenly anticipating the treasures in store, the first-time visitor will be surprised by the swift transition from dusk to dark; the ice blue of the sky just before nightfall turns into a solid, "profound" blue —the word of one of the city's partisans—a stark, shrieking blue without warmth that produces the same shivery feeling as a cry for help in the night. (A European visitor has termed the Andalusian sky at dusk "frightening.") The atmosphere is crystal clear—no pollution here—and one can see for many miles across the vega.

Washington Irving, who arrived in 1829, and Dumas and his son, in 1846, made the overland journey by pack mule, a trip that usually involved encounters with bandits, who took advantage of the clear nights to descend on travelers of all persuasions. Today the bandits have been replaced by the gypsies who prey in their own fashion on the successors to those sturdy nineteenth-century tourists. (There are gypsy beggars in all quarters of Granada today; one ingenious individual followed me into a bank, stood patiently in line behind me, and, when I had cashed a check and received the money, extended his upturned palm in the classic gesture. An enterprising practitioner of the ancient calling who should go far.)

Some of the more vivid impressions gleaned on my trip by rail to the southern city of Granada, still fresh in my mind, are the flatness of the sun-baked countryside, the mile upon mile of groves of olive trees, not large enough or sufficiently luxuriant to give any degree of shade, and the interminable stretches during which I did not see a single living, moving being, either human or animal. A good week had gone by before I spotted, in the center of Granada, a dog actually walking; until then the few dogs I had observed had been stretched out in a motionless state. (Doubtless the expression "Let sleeping dogs lie" was first uttered in Spain.) Although my view across the tableland was unobstructed, I saw no roads, and the familiar warning signs indicating a railroad crossing were invariably planted adjacent to what probably had once been dirt roads several generations ago.

Spain is, of course, one vast tableland—dotted with mountains in some areas—extending right to the sea, where the land plunges to water level, leaving only a relatively narrow shelf to support the coastal cities and towns that have become havens for sun-worshipping, beach-loving tourists. Modern high-rise apartments and hotels on this coastal ledge have very little relation to the interior of the country, which begins at the edge of the tableland; in these coastal population centers along the Costa del Sol, the Costa Blanca, and the Costa Brava, the visitor is in territory that is more or less international—Spanish will be heard no more often than English, French, German, Swedish, or Japanese. The result is Spain superimposed with, and almost buried by, Beverly Hills, Chicago, and London, or a mixture of all. For the real Spain, one must not hug the coast.

Two-thousand-foot-high Granada, only about thirty miles from the southern coastal sea-level strip—but decades away—exists in a different age. Thought of as Valhalla by many, it has been variously described by well-traveled assessors as "a dead city" and "a living ruin." The former description was written by Edward Hutton, an ambulant British author, in 1906 in an appraisal of "The Cities of Spain"; the latter is included in a 1901 edition of Baedeker's *Spain and Portugal*—one of the series of early guidebooks, which are still, in many departments, the best in the field.

In that first decade of this twentieth century, Hutton found the city "utterly fallen from her high estate, without learning, without self-respect, without trade, and full of vanity." A few years earlier, Baedeker's emissary noted that "the side streets are full of filth and decay, and some of the more remote are not even lighted at night. A large proportion of the population subsists by begging alone. When all is said, however," he concludes, "Granada still remains as the culminating point of a journey in Spain, not only for its magnificent views of the great snow-clad mountains to the southeast, but also for the glimpse it affords of the past, the remains it has to present of a strange and exotic culture and art."

Some seventy years after those opinions were set down, I found Granada an immensely exciting place, deeply rooted in the past, a city that perpetuates itself as the years go by and the world around it changes and grows ever more modern.

Spaniards are alleged to have been brutalized—first by the Inquisition and more recently by the Civil War; nowhere in Spain did the fearsome purge of the populace in the fifteenth century strike as heavily as at Granada, and the Civil War in the latter 1930s took a devastating toll of the city's civilian inhabitants. Some twenty thousand were simply taken out and shot, among them the revered poet Federico García Lorca, and their bodies thrown into a common pit.

Today the physical evidences of the Civil War are not readily visible to the visitor, but it still evokes vivid, painful memories in the minds of the older generation. It was, after all, the first experience of modern warfare, in which that new weapon, the airplane, although it had been used in World War I, was for the first time employed offensively against cities and their populations, in a dress rehearsal for the Second World War, which followed the Spanish conflict after a very brief intermission.

Neither is the city filthy or decayed; it seems rather to lie immobilized as if it had been arrested in time by a spiritual lava flow at some remote period in its long history.

On all sides certainly there is ample testimony to the aptness of the accolade to the supremacy of the Muslim art and architecture to be found in Granada, the finest examples in all Spain. The masterpiece, of course, is the Alhambra; even though parts of it have had to be restored, after a lengthy period of neglect, it remains the stunning centerpiece of Mohammedan artistic achievement.

One is soon aware that the Arabian palace is the heart and soul of Granada.

And it is still today, materially as well as spiritually, the Alhambra of the Caliphs. True, there are now a few souvenir shops, photo supply stores, wood-workers, lace-makers—even a small bar—tucked away in the recesses of the walled hilltop spoken of generally as the Alhambra. (More exactly, the Alhambra is the castle itself.) It is even possible, if one reserves some months in advance, to stay within the confines of the Alhambra preserve, in a small, modern hotel housed in a reconstituted part of the complex of buildings adjoining the palace of the Sultans. Its modern interior—which compares favorably in cleanliness and freshness with the newest Hilton—boasts impeccable plumbing, thus achieving for American visitors the ultimate dream: fascinating history unsullied by change combined with twentieth-century comfort and functional, pristine plumbing. The Parador Nacional San Francisco, as this gem of a hostelry is called, is only two stories high, and has but twelve guest rooms, which are occupied throughout the year. (Altogether there are four or five hotels within the expanse of the broad hilltop called the Alhambra; most others lie on the sides of the hill that is surmounted by the palace.)

But except for these carefully camouflaged evidences of modern life, the pulse of the historic past beats with a measured, almost audible cadence. Without much difficulty, one can re-create in one's mind the images of the battles for this strategic fortress, vital to the successful occupation of a large part of Andalusia—dominating as it does the plains and rolling hills that stretch as far as the snow-capped Sierra Nevadas, twenty-five miles distant.

The first sight of the Alhambra is even more arresting than one anticipates. Climbing up the steep incline to the heights of the hilltop, one catches a glimpse, on the sharp turns, of part of the reddish clay wall and then one or another of the towers, first line of defense for the occupying powers. The Alcazaba, the first building to confront the visitor, is a ninth-century ruin. Its tower is still in a tenable state of preservation, but the structure itself —which served as the soldiers' quarters—has not survived the centuries; where it stood, wildflowers grow in profusion.

But it is the Casa Real, the Arabian Palace, that is the heart of the Alhambra, the magnet that attracts visitors from every major country on earth. This *Calat Alhambra*, the red castle, was the seat of the Royal Court of the

Sultans, who ruled the area until they were dislodged from power finally by the Spanish Catholics in the fifteenth century.

"These people came from Mauritania, in Africa, so they were first called Moors," said my informant, a good-humored, erudite Spanish scholar who calls himself Pepe. "Although many came by way of Mauritania all right, they were not all Moors; it would be much more accurate to call them Arabs, or better still Mohammedans or Muslims," he went on. "Since there were no papers and no TV in those days, the correction of the error was never circulated and the name stuck. Today it's still called a Moorish castle."

We began a centimeter-by-centimeter exploration of the splendors of the Casa Real, and as we entered the first chamber that could properly be called a room, Pepe at once grew lyrical. "This is a castle for poets," he said with some elation. "You know, archeologists come here and examine every inch of wall, to see whether it's in its original state, or has been restored. That's all they're interested in. But then," he added deprecatingly, "archeologists have no soul."

Pepe, I should add, was most enthusiastic about the opportunity to give me a detailed tour of the Palacio Arabe, and apologized for having to accept money for his services. At the moment, he explained, there was a bitter argument in progress between the government—in the person of the education minister—and the teachers. Some of the latter had been fired for expressing their ideological sentiments, even though not in class—others were tolerated but suspended without pay, until the issue of what exactly was permissible for the students to hear was resolved. I recalled reading in the Paris *International Herald Tribune* on my ride down from Bordeaux that some of the suspended teachers had been granted the privilege of teaching during this period, but without pay! (Pepe was apparently in this latter group.)

He seemed delighted to have fallen on a fellow writer—and someone who was genuinely interested in more than a superficial run-through of the palace and its history. He filled in as many details as he could remember in the time we had together.

The Alhambra was built during the late thirteenth and fourteenth centuries; its spiritual architect was the ruler Alhamar, who first dreamed of constructing a Muslim palace on the hilltop site of the Roman fortress. "When the Romans looked at the High Sierras, they saw only snow," Pepe continued. "But Alhamar saw water." By bringing it down from the mountains (11,000-feet-plus altitude), he made it possible for the walled town to be built on the hilltop and to function.

We were now standing squarely in the middle of the Palace of Justice, the least ornate of the official rooms of the Sultan's domain. "In the desert, before coming here, the Mohammedans erected tents and sat on pillows," Pepe related. "Here they built a tent, with walls and a roof, and they still sat on cushions."

In this chamber, the Mexuar, where Arab justice was meted out, I had my first close-up look at the filigreelike Arabesques carved in the stucco walls, a combination of leaves, flowers, and geometric designs, in addition to Arabic script quotations from the Holy Book and other learned works. This grouping—sometimes supplemented by an Arab shield—is to be found in all the rooms of the Sultans' Palace. "The Mohammedans are permitted no idols," Pepe advised, "so you will find the theme of leaves, flowers, and geometric patterns used constantly." The script quotations, I learned, usually record some of the deeds of the Sultan who built the palace as well as bits from the Koran. Since three grand sovereigns—following Alhamar—had a hand in constructing the truly fabulous Palacio Arabe, there is a profusion of deeds chronicled on its interior walls.

After the Palace of Justice one comes next on an antechamber where the resident Sultan prayed, possibly for guidance in the administration of justice. At one extremity of the small room, the east end, a niche (Mihrab) with five panels was used as the repository for the Holy Book, the five panels representing the five commands of Mohammed—relating to fasting, prayer, charity, unity ("there is only one God"), and the admonition to "go to Mecca." And, of course, when one faces the niche, one faces east—toward that Muslim spiritual capital. (From Granada, Mecca is almost due east, a fact in which the local Arabs place special significance.)

While my enthusiastic companion launched into a recital of the races that successively ruled Granada (Iberians, Celts, Phoenicians, Greeks, Romans, Visigoths, and Arabs, before the current occupants took over), we moved on into a splendid, typically Spanish patio, featuring a long rectangular pool, flanked by rows of myrtle bushes cut symmetrically, positioned between the pool and the walkways around the four sides of the patio. The Court of the

Myrtles, the plant that symbolizes love, was the one the Sultan looked out on from his throne, often with no love in his heart. Adjoining the main chambers off the court are what must surely be the most spectacularly decorated sentry boxes in all history—of marble, artistically colored tile, and delicately engraved scripture on their stucco walls. During the era of the Sultans' residence, the guard was mounted by some of the many eunuchs in the reigning ruler's service.

"The barbarian Visigoths, who came after the Romans, built nothing, and had trouble controlling the area," Pepe said, doubling back to the period before the Arabs arrived. The Byzantine Visigoths, a singularly tolerant people considering the times, are given credit by some for having introduced the horseshoe arch, which the Arabs bent to their own purposes, and they were drawn to sculpture. But Pepe gives them credit for nothing. They finally called in the Arabs for help, but when the Muslims arrived from North Africa in answer to the plea they asked themselves: Why should we help? Why don't we simply take over the place?

Pepe peered at me intently here, to be sure I appreciated the logic of their reasoning. "You would have done the same thing, no?" he asked finally, not certain that I was sympathetic to this line of thought. Like many Spaniards, Pepe has strong feelings for the Arab rulers.

It was hard to imagine oneself taking over this handsome fortress, but it was an interesting idea. I considered the suggestion, looking out at the distant Sierra Nevadas across the irrigated plain, as the ghost of Walter Mitty put in a brief appearance.

"I suppose so," I said at last. "It would be hard not to want to take it over."

"Exactly," Pepe said triumphantly, satisfied that he was conversing with someone who shared his own common sense.

This wish, on my part, was based on an inspection of the least impressive parts of the palace. We were now about to enter the Sultans' royal throne room, at one end of the pool in the Court of Myrtles. The two rows of carefully trimmed myrtle bushes flanking the long, narrow pool extending almost the length of the court and the walkways that bounded the whole furnished the Arabs the three commodities they most missed in the desert: water, greenery, and shade.

From the court, we proceeded first into the throne room's antechamber, where the ambassadors once waited for the call to present their credentials or for other audiences with the almighty monarch. The ceiling of this rectangular room is shaped like the hull of a round-bottomed boat, and was known as the Hall of the Boat. The overturned boat-bottomed ceiling—like many throughout the palace—is of cedarwood.

The throne room, in the Tower of Comares, once had stained-glass windows; its ceiling is also of cedarwood, but inlaid with gold. On all its walls one notices the same inscription in delicate carved script; in its Arab syntax, it translates "Only the Conqueror is Allah," a reply by Alhamar to his subjects who chanted his praises after a military victory. "The English equivalent," Pepe added, "would probably be 'The Only Conqueror is Allah,' or 'The Only Winner is God.'"

In almost any corner of the preserve known as the Alhambra one can picture in one's imagination the figures of the court and even conjure up some of the events that occurred there. But in the throne room even the most phlegmatic types will find it difficult not to be stimulated by the historic moments that had passed in this room.

I was reminded of a conversation, some years earlier in Paris, with the late Preston Sturges, who, searching for an idea for a television series, proposed one based on the premise: It Happened Exactly Here. He planned to start the series in the Place de la Concorde, not far from the Hotel Crillon, in Paris, where Marie-Antoinette was guillotined. For several reasons, the series was never done, partly perhaps because the spot in the Place where the execution took place—if you can wait until the early morning when the traffic lets up and you have a chance to see it—is hardly dramatic, indistinguishable as it is from any other spot on any *place* in the French capital.

But here in the throne room of the Alhambra in Granada, Mr. Sturges could have begun one installment of his series in highly dramatic fashion. Here in the exact center of the room—one can pull back the tattered mat and examine the original tiles of the square marking the center of the chamber— sat Queen Isabella on February 19, 1492 to receive Cristoforo Colombo and give her backing to his planned voyage to the Indies.

And from the gracefully arched window behind the spot on the floor where the rulers sat one has a superb view of the valleys, hills, the plain, and a part of the city—a view that must have set even a monarch to dreaming, perhaps of the golden riches that her emissary would lay at her feet upon his return.

The oneness of the palace, in style as well as spirit, is a testament to the good judgment of the sovereigns who collaborated, in turn, on the construction of the building that ranks in majesty with the Taj Mahal and the Parthenon. Alhamar (Mohammed I), having moved into the Alcazaba, began modestly to expand his residence. His building program was continued by his son, Mohammed II, but it was Abul walid Ismael who began work on a small palace, most of which was later torn down by Abul Hacha (Yusuf I)—all but the Patio del Mexuar. He began the construction of the Court of Myrtles, with its Tower of Comares, containing the throne room of the monarch, and the baths. Mohammed V completed the Court of Myrtles and contributed the elaborate Court of the Lions, toward which Pepe and I were proceeding.

Except for a small area, notably a chamber in one tower inhabited by Washington Irving in the nineteenth century—given a Renaissance flavor by Charles V in 1526, complete with a fifteenth-century painting of his grandparents, Ferdinand and Isabella, attributed to Francisco del Rincon—the architecture and décor of the palace have a remarkable unity well preserved during the intervening centuries.

Throughout, the stucco walls are composed of ground alabaster, ground marble, and plaster-of-Paris. The ceilings in the more important chambers are of cedarwood, sometimes inlaid with gold; in one slightly smaller room the ceiling is decorated by a painting on leather, executed by Spaniards, picturing in its center the man who conceived the plan for the palace, the inspired Alhamar.

From the ceilings and arches, in the rooms giving off the Court of the Lions, where Pepe and I now stood, stalactites in profusion appear to drip down, clinging one to another. These clusters of honeycells accentuate the stunning symmetry of the whole—the court and the chambers adjoining it; looking across the Court of Lions from one side to the other, one is struck by the succession of arches, each carefully delineated one within the other although in actuality they are separated one from another in a perfect row, receding from one's point of view.

England's Sacheverell Sitwell found that, "apart from the view down over Granada from the *mirador*, the most beautiful sensation of the whole Alhambra is to look from one side to the other across the Court of the Lions, because the stalactitic arches are at different levels and there is a moment when you see all four of their arabesqued outlines one against the other, which is the intended climax of this Oriental poetry."

Another interesting angle from which to view the stalactites and honeycombs is the one provided by the fountains; by looking into the clear water of even a small pool from a certain position one can see reflected the dazzling intricacies of the ceiling opposite.

If the area surrounding the Court of Myrtles was the official, or business, headquarters of the reigning Sultan, the Court of the Lions, just a few steps away, was the focal point of his private life. Here the Arabian Nights atmosphere prevailed, with the Dance of the Seven Veils a favored form of entertainment. It is easily the prettiest quarter of the palace.

This patio of the Harem was constructed by Mohammed V with a profound understanding of the needs of the occupants: adjoining the court there are a gossip room, dancing room, a room for the Sultan's favorite to display herself in provocative poses, and, above the gossip room, the women's sleeping quarters.

Salon of the Ambassadors

Court of the Lions

The centerpiece of the grand patio is a stone fountain resting on the backs of twelve stylized lions of Byzantine appearance—looking more like dogs than lions—facing the arcades and their 124 columns supporting exquisite arches, and the chambers that give on the court. The two principal salons are the Hall of the Abencerrages and directly across from it the Hall of the Two Sisters (the name refers to two slabs of perfect white marble that form part of the pavement).

Here, in the complex of chambers surrounding the Court of the Lions, Boabdil—the last of the Muslim sovereigns—had thirty-six Muslim knights of the clan of the Abencerrages, an Oriental Muslim tribe, executed, with their collective blood flowing into the fountain—an act occasioned by Boabdil's suspicion that his harem favorite was trysting with the chief of the Abencerrages, one Hamet. The story goes that the blood of the victims is still visible on the floor of the hall, but the faint pinkish stains are usually viewed with some skepticism.

Below the level of the Court of the Lions, an impressive series of rooms devoted to the bath reaffirms the high degree of civilization reached by the Muslims resident in Granada. A steam room, massage room, another bath for washing after a stay in the steam room, and still another chamber for relaxing afterward were available to all the members of the seraglio, who then treated their skin with paraffin and oil. The floors of the bath are of tile and marble, and were heated from beneath by a large copper boiler, no longer in evidence on the premises. This early sauna was decorated with stained-glass windows, and the solarium, whose skylight caught the rays of the sun at every angle, was enhanced by tastefully arranged flowerbeds.

The balconies that ringed some of the concubines' bathing chambers were occupied by singers and musicians who provided agreeable background melodies. On orders of the Sultan, only blind entertainers were chosen for this desirable duty.

In warm weather the girls preferred to bathe in the outdoor pool in the meticulously designed garden adjacent to their quarters. This natural solarium overlooks some of the Alhambra's clay towers and a stretch of jagged, sawtoothed defensive wall; beyond lie the incomparable gardens of the Generalife, the Sultans' summer palace, perched on a neighboring hilltop.

But before following a winding path that would take us to that objective, we passed through the unfinished Palace of Charles V, constructed in a high Renaissance style by the orders of that Spanish Christian monarch in the sixteenth century. The colonnaded court was finally completed in 1616, ninety years after work was begun, but the structure, set off by Ionic pilasters and a Doric cornice, was never finished. Nor was its central court ever covered; today it is utilized as an amphitheater for an annual music and dance festival.

Mohammedan Spain was known throughout the civilized world as the land of gardens and water. Here, on the hilltop occupied by the Sultans' blindingly white summer palace, the Spanish garden reached its apogee.

The stucco building itself was undergoing repairs at the time of my visit; the gardens are, in any case, the most noteworthy aspect of a visit to the Generalife, termed by my companion and volunteer guide "the Castel Gandolfo of Muslim Spain." This trellised sanctuary, with a spectacular vista of the valley and the Alhambra Castle on a lower hill, inspires in one a feeling of isolation, of profound peacefulness in which the concerns and worries of one's personal life seem to drop away like the veils falling from a houri. The British writer and scientist Havelock Ellis found the Generalife gardens in 1908 to be "an ideal spot for devout or philosophic meditation on the problems of the world." An avid sampler of formal gardens throughout Spain, he rates the gardens of Granada, and specifically those of the Generalife, the most admirable in the country.

Certainly the variety of forms of plant life, the conception of the design, and the meticulousness of its execution combine to make a visit to this preserve infinitely more memorable an experience than an inspection of, let us say, the mundane gardens at England's Hampton Court or the more conventional gardens of the Pavillon de Bagatelle in the Bois de Boulogne in Paris.

Though the impression of the Generalife gardens is one of size, their physical proportions are in fact quite limited. The ruling Muslims were partial to small, almost dainty, effects. Part of the deceptive feeling of spaciousness is doubtless attributable to the expanse of countryside that greets the viewer from the terraces at one extremity of the gardens. Aside from an abundance of blooms in precisely arranged flowerbeds, there is a plenitude of other decorative plant life—cacti, carefully clipped hedges, and graceful cypress trees plus a sprinkling of orange, lime, and quince.

Everywhere, it seems, there is water—some running, in channels of inverted tiles along the tops of semicircular balustrades paralleling flights of steps from one level to another, some quiescent, in pools placed to reflect and intensify the delights of the arboreal area. And the quite penetrating mood of solitude is accentuated by the ever-present sound of the fountains; the rippling melody of gurgling water underscores the quality of enchantment one feels in those bewitching gardens. Simply to sit for a time on one of the benches enclosed in a pocket of perfectly shaped hedge is a soul-satisfying experience.

"The greatest beauty of Granada must be, indeed, one of the supreme beauties of the whole world," Sitwell writes with impassioned conviction. "If all other memory of Spain were dead and gone and there was to be nothing else left to indicate what meanings and implications are attached to the 'Spanish' adjective in every language, then the gardens of the Generalife would be one of the objects that must be saved."

Here, looking out toward the red towers of the Alhambra on the height below, Ellis concluded that Granada "represents the victory of the least amiable moment of Christianity over the most exquisite moment of Islam. We are amid the relics of one of the finest civilizations the world has known, a civilization we can only learn to know perfectly in the pages of 'A Thousand and One Nights.' "

Whatever the reasons, perhaps the combination of the unexcelled view, the delicately designed gardens, and the feeling of solitude, I found that one's perceptions grew more acute; one had the sensation of understanding hitherto puzzling, unfathomable mysteries. In this truly Mohammedan setting, it was quite fitting to ponder on the Divine spirit—more appropriate perhaps than in the once grandiose, desecrated Christian church of San Geronimo in the city itself. Here in the gardens even a confirmed atheist might well pause to reconsider the possibility of the existence of God.

For the dark-skinned immigrants from North Africa were no less devout in their regard for Allah than their Christian antagonists were for their own God. Aside from the difference in the image of their Supreme Powers and their lasting disagreement over who should rule in Spain, the Muslims and their eventual Christian conquerors had much in common. The Spanish poet Calderón noted that a Moorish knight was in every respect like a Spanish knight, except that the former calls on Allah instead of Christ.

There are many Moorish types to be seen on Granada's streets and avenues today; whatever differences there may once have been are blurred or erased entirely by intermarriage and the passage of centuries. It has been said that the visitors from North Africa became Spanish during the nearly eight hundred years they occupied southern Spain; for their part the Spaniards have acquired many characteristics of the Muslims. Certainly it is incontestably true that Spain has benefitted tremendously from the Muslims' refined taste in art and architecture

My first visit to the Alhambra and the Generalife was concluded some three hours after it was begun, but it was followed by repeated return journeys up the hill to the Arabian Palace and its preserve. Throughout my stay in Granada scarcely a day passed without an urge to call again at the Muslims' sublime monument.

(Incidentally, during my stay in the city a package tour operated by one of the U.S. airlines and aptly named its "Getaway Tour" descended on my hotel late one afternoon; the group visited some gypsies in a cave, returned for dinner, and early the next morning left for Toledo. They never paid a call on the Alhambra, an omission comparable to going to Niagara and not seeing the Falls.)

Before quitting the hilltop on my first visit, I was told by Pepe that there are a few other debts that must be acknowledged: to the French, who rescued the Alhambra from the neglect that had turned it into an incipient ruin, and to the Duke of Wellington, during the period of the Napoleonic wars—he had planted the trees that transformed the approach to the hilltop into a sylvan glen, rendered more magical in the spring by the songs of nightingales.

After the Alhambra, as Sitwell found, "it is an anti-climax to come down the hill." But even though no nightingales were singing, the descent on the sharply sloping road to the city under the canopy of enveloping English shade—a deep pall reminiscent of Berkeley Square—was a pleasant interlude for which I was grateful in the still hot October afternoons.

Americans will find a visit to Granada more of a "foreign" adventure than a stay in most other European cities. English—or French, for that matter—is not generally spoken or understood, and the little luxuries that are taken for granted in the United States are not always at hand. One American lady sitting down to breakfast in a middle-ranked Granada hotel rattled off her order without pause to the Spanish waiter assigned to her table—grapefruit juice, two eggs boiled for exactly three minutes and twenty seconds, whole-wheat toast, lightly buttered, and American coffee. The waiter listened with his jaw sagging slightly; he returned after a short interval with two doughy rolls and coffee (Spanish)—the same collation he brought to everyone.

But these minor inconveniences can also be welcome at times. An Englishman encountered in a shop specializing in classic mantillas and shawls declared that this was his most enjoyable vacation in memory simply because none of the jukeboxes in restaurants and coffee bars featured English or

American recordings; in fact, he had not heard one familiar Anglo-Saxon melody since his arrival in the country. On reflection, I decided that this condition would not prevail in any other European city of any size. Of such unexpected small delights are great vacations made.

For my part, I was intrigued—if a bit hungry—by the practice of serving dinner at eleven P.M. And it took a while to become accustomed to the fact that nothing at all happened in the city between about one and four thirty in the afternoon, except for lunch, of course. All the shops closed for siesta, so the continuing search for the best mantillas, shawls, slippers, castanets, and other gifts had constantly to be postponed till the end of the afternoon or early evening.

I often had luncheon in the Nevada restaurant attached to one of the downtown hotels. Here English was understood, after a fashion, by certain waiters and waitresses—at least it was possible to order a chicken sandwich, which often arrived complete with bones, and a Yogurt Fresas (strawberry), served in a tall, thin glass. Spaghetti, of the canned variety, was also a specialty; here they did not serve the Spanish dishes anchored in rice that were to be found in the little restaurants on the side streets and alleyways. But the sangria was delicious, the service was good, and the Nevada's atmosphere was sympathetic—the more attractive waitresses flirted a little—and there were absolutely no gypsy fortune-tellers interrupting the meal. It was also located just around the corner from the central Post and Telegraph Office. (Sending telegrams or cables in English from the hotel was a gamble—that the message would arrive in nongarbled form; cabling in French was a better bet, as the chief concierge had worked in France and French-speaking Switzerland.) The surest course, as always, was to use the central Telegraph Office and write out the message.

Across the wide intersection from the Post and Telegraph Office, at a café-restaurant whose tables spilled out onto the sidewalk and into the street, the gypsy fortune-tellers who buzzed around the tables like bees in a flower garden seemed to outnumber the waiters. As one of them went inside, into the kitchen with his orders, a gypsy woman would advance, and since the diner was in no position simply to walk away he would often succumb to the persistence of the seamy seer, who invariably predicted a great future in the field of love. As the waiter returned with his dishes, the gypsy would move away slightly, only to return with more blandishments for more coins. They advanced and receded like the waves on a beach—always governed by the waiters' whereabouts. It was quite evident that the gypsies had made a thorough study of their victims and the situations in which there was a maximum chance of success, such as a queue leading up to a bank teller's window or a restaurant table during the serving of a meal. It reminded me of the technique of a press agent I had once known in Paris who frequented an expensive hotel and rode up and down in the elevators all day, since that was the only place he could be sure his unwilling listeners would not be able to get away.

After lunch, with the siesta already well under way, the choice lay between a trip up the hill to the Alhambra or, if a nap back at the hotel wasn't a necessity, a quiet few hours in the city's parks. Even from a bench in downtown Granada the view of the snow-topped Sierras was an uplifting delight.

This was certainly a city operating at a slow pace, and there are some, I suppose, who might even class it as backward. A two-and-a-half-mile taxi ride from the railroad station to my hotel, after all, cost only seventeen pesetas (63.08 pesetas to the dollar, at the time of my visit), and the banks are open for business on Saturdays until two P.M., so the advances of modern civilization have obviously not yet hit home here. (At a mom-and-pop-type grocery-general store slightly larger than a phone booth just up the hill from my hotel, I bought a large, strong Spanish cigar, a box of matches, a large bottle of mineral water, a package of razor blades, shaving cream, and six magdalenas—madeleines—for 36 pesetas.)

I found Granada a fascinating place, but it is by no means a center of excellence in the field of the arts in which Spaniards are most accomplished —architecture. Still, one of the prime examples of the plateresque style is the formidable Granada Cathedral, the final resting place of Ferdinand and Isabella (the Catholic). It was constructed during the first phase of the Spanish Renaissance in architecture and decoration. The ornamental quality of the style, based on the work of the Italian Renaissance, suggests by its delicacy the craftsmanship of a silversmith, from whom it derives its name. But besides Italian Renaissance forms, this new Spanish style also drew on Moorish and Gothic designs, resulting in a singular mode with a heavy emphasis on imaginative details.

The imposing structure, intended as a memorial to the Catholic conquest of southern Spain, was begun in the Gothic manner, from the design of Enrique de Egas in 1523, just thirty-one years after the final expulsion of the Muslim sovereigns from Granada. But after two years the project was turned over to Diego de Siloe, who continued in the plateresque style and who receives most of the credit for the structure's arresting appearance. After his death, a pupil, Juan de Maeda, added the first stage of a tower (north) in the Doric manner; its second and third stages, in Ionic and Corinthian styles, were contributed by Ambrosio de Vico, who also added a fourth, octagonal stage on top, but this later was removed as a concession to the safety of worshippers and passersby. A planned south tower was never built. The west façade was the work of Alonso Cano and José Granados, in a manner quite at odds with de Siloe's intentions. The interior wasn't completed until 1703, one hundred eighty years after the building was begun. Altogether, the result of this disjointed collaboration is somehow, amazingly, a cohesive whole.

The burial chamber of Ferdinand and Isabella, the Capilla Real, is really a chapel attached to the Cathedral. The celebrated monarchs are in the company of the parents of Charles V, Philip the Handsome and Juana la Loca, the Infanta Johanna, whose sarcophagi are alongside. Before coming to rest here, Philip's coffin had been carried about by his demented wife.

At least the Cathedral contains enough evidences of the delicate and restrained plateresque style, far removed from the debased and capricious use, as one expert put it, of Renaissance motives in the churrigueresque manner, which—about a century later—was to become the distinguishing feature of the landscape in other Spanish cities.

Granada's principal example of the style that was popularized by Churriguera is the Castillo di Bibataubín, a barracks, the design of Pedro Ribera. It has been called "a distorted echo of the parade grounds at Potsdam."

But perhaps the most noteworthy piece of Christian Spanish architecture in Granada, after the Cathedral, is the Cartuja, a monastery whose two halls were intended to boast a décor rivaling the arabesques of the Alhambra. The doors of the Sacristia were done—by a Carthusian monk, Fray José Manuel Vásquez—in cedarwood, inlaid with ebony, mother-of-pearl, tortoiseshell, and silver. Théophile Gautier was said to be especially appreciative of this hall

Sepulchres of the Catholic rulers

with its pilasters of red marble with white and pink veins.

However, the architecture that prevails in Granada and has become synony-
mous with the very name of the city is Mohammedan. Even under the terra-
cotta roofs of the Albaicín, the old Muslim quarter, Pritchett notes, one can
still find modest houses "where one would find a horseshoe arch of the
Moors in a bedroom or a few delicate Moorish tiles."

The hillside of the Sacro Monte offers still another aspect of Granadine
construction: the modernization of the gypsy caves that have been a part of

the countryside of Andalusia for hundreds of years. The narrow rooms, illuminated by garish, unshaded electric light, provide just enough width, between the plaster walls, for an aisle and two rows of straight-backed chairs for the spectators who troop in throughout the night to watch Mamma, aunts, daughters of all ages beginning at about eight, and even Grandma perform their wild, stomping gypsy dances to the accompaniment of general hand-clapping and perhaps a lone guitar. A group of fifteen or twenty visitors supplementing the eight or ten gypsies waiting their turn to dance makes for quite a stifling atmosphere. Of course there is always a collection. The Granada gypsies are reputed to be the most prosperous of their brood in the land, and I find no reason to doubt this claim.

The gypsies are more abandoned in their primitive gyrations than the more controlled movements of the formal flamenco specialists who perform in the city's nightclubs, such as the Jardines Neptuno.

Flamenco is, of course, indigenous to Andalusia and, in particular, to Granada. The form and attitudes of the dance reflect a number of the attributes of the native Andalusian; fierce pride, determination, grace, and—on the part of the male—the will to dominate. The staccato heel-pounding and the abrupt movements of the dancer's arms and head are as stylized as the body motions of the matador in the bullring; neither ritual has changed in centuries, nor is there any likelihood that they will.

Flamenco, which means Flemish, is probably an allusion to the Flemish court of the Spanish monarch Charles V, who thought those members loud and exuberant. Both the dancing and singing that go by the name flamenco are all of that. The chanting that sometimes accompanies the highly dramatic dancing, in which the legs of the performers pound the floor alternately at incalculable speed, is loud and punctuated by sudden exclamations. Flamenco singing, which features considerably more tones than the normal Western tempered scale, was considered lowbrow, and almost beneath contempt, until 1922, when the talented Spanish composer Manuel de Falla conducted a congress of flamenco singers in Granada, devoted to the history and growth of Spanish folk music. Since that time even Spanish grandees have regarded flamenco with respect.

If dancing is a manifestation of the Spanish character, the bullfight is even more a reflection of the Spanish psyche—the overriding preoccupation with rigid form and graceful movement and the obsession with the exhibition of courage and, perhaps strongest of all, with death. Two of these basic concerns —with the dance and with death—are united in the spectacle of the corrida. The *pas de deux* performed by man and bull can be described as a Dance of Death; it is, after all, the Spanish Danza de la Muerte of the fourteenth century that is claimed to be the oldest known Macabre Dance legend, although some, including Émile Male, consider the Dance of Death a French conception.

Besides the ritual bullfight, in which the bull usually does the dying but which encompasses the titillating possibility that it just may be the other way round this time, there are examples on all sides of the Spanish obsession with death. The quadrangle of buildings called the Escorial, not far from Madrid, is a veritable Palace of Death, built by King Philip II to house his own deathbed.

And as Ellis points out, "In Barcelona Cathedral, the most solemnly impressive model of Catalan architecture, the broad and stately entrance to the crypt, the gloomy house of death, is placed in the center of the church. . . . Every Spanish sacristan seems to possess a well-polished skull and a couple of thigh-bones, with which to crown the catafalque it is his duty to erect— a task in which we may sometimes find him engaged in the silent church at twilight, preparing for the funeral ceremony of the morrow." And Spanish painters and sculptors seem to have vied with one another in their works on the Crucifixion to represent the pain and suffering of Christ as vividly and realistically as their media permitted.

Above all, the chivalrous Spaniard, raised in the romantic tradition, is a stoic, with a monumental indifference to pain—his own or that of others. Nor is he concerned with animal pain, as a great many English and American men and women are. The Spaniards who do not go to the Plaza de Toros for the important bullfights—usually held on the most sacred religious holidays—absent themselves not out of any sense of outrage or disapproval of the goings-on but out of boredom with the familiar ceremony at the arena.

Sitting in the Club Taurino on Granada's Plaza del Carmen, one would never suspect that the country's national sport of bullfighting no longer has the place in the hearts of all true Spaniards that it is reputed to have. This haven for aficionados—festooned with mounted heads of impressive bulls and decorated with posters proclaiming memorable days in the arena—is the Spanish equivalent of baseball's off-season Hot Stove League in the United States. The talk here is still of the great days of the classic performances of the matadors who have become legends—Belmonte and Manolete; some attention is also given to the recently retired El Córdobes, who appeared from time to time in this city's arena, today the scene of some twenty-five corridas each year.

But outside the privacy of this club, the talk is somewhat different. "Ernest Hemingway would be a very sad man today," said Rafael Caro, a *hostelero* who was once as devoted a bullring fan as anyone. "Let's face it, the national sport today is football [soccer]. Only about forty percent—if that—of Spain's sports fans still go to bullfights on their own. The rest don't care. They go only on a big religious holiday, if they have nothing better to do and somebody else pays for the tickets.

"It's all publicity anyway, and always has been to a degree. Bullfighting just doesn't appeal to a great many Spaniards, and never has. Today there are many thousands more who are just indifferent." He paused to order a glass of sherry. "Here we once had the impression that everyone in Chicago was a gangster. That story still circulates," he continued.

"To listen to the peña [composed of persons who get together regularly to talk about bullfighting] you'd think things were the same as always. But it's not so. The art and elegance that bullfighting once had are on the decline. And the matadors aren't as good as they once were."

An English friend of Caro's, resident in Spain, agreed. "It's a bloody mess these days," he put it succinctly.

Finishing his glass of Jerez, Señor Caro delivered his final words on the subject. "If it weren't for the tourists—especially Americans—bullfighting would die out completely. Why at Málaga on some days you'd swear all the spectators were foreign tourists, mostly Americans. In the U.S. they say the sport is too cruel. But here Americans love it."

It is soon clear to any visitor to these shores that bullfighting, like flamenco dancing, is a prime tourist attraction, and is being scheduled, in the various cities and towns, to coincide with the peak tourist season. But in the cigar-smoke-filled rooms of the Club Taurino, it was apparent that the knowledgeable members in this sanctuary had not yet had the word. And even if they had, it would not have mattered, for to these aficionados bullfighting is not a sport at all but the ultimate art form—an art that is beyond dying.

Throughout the centuries—since the early Muslims first brought the bullfight, in a less stylized form, to Spain—it has been a particular passion of the Andalusians. Pritchett was impressed with the Spaniards' strong stomachs. "They do not flinch when the blood gushes out of the bull's mouth as he goes down heavily to his death, but in their eyes one sees that proud, frightening brilliance of the conqueror who has emerged from great emotion, who is elated by victory and satisfied by performance. Spanish religious art and the work of Goya reveal a people who do not shy from strong feeling or from the tragedies that fall upon the human body. Above all, they are caught by the drama and the supreme dramatic moment. Undoubtedly, they experience the tragic purgation. Undoubtedly," he feels, "there is something savage in it. All historians and the soldiers who have fought against them in the great ages have mentioned the lack of all fear of death in the Spaniards."

During the notorious *autos-da-fe* of the Spanish Inquisition—the burning of the heretics—it was not the Spaniards but the foreigners present who averted their eyes during the fetid ceremonies at Valladolid.

Ellis describes the Spanish character as savage, Pritchett as barbarian. As to the Granadinos, the consensus alleges that they are proud, stiff, superior, with an unsmiling appearance. Conceited and avaricious are sometimes added.

But in spite of the somewhat harsh judgments that have been made, Granada remains an eminently satisfying experience. It is difficult to find a place that is at once European and at the same time almost totally unrelated to the Western civilization of the late twentieth century, with its accelerating anxieties.

In Granada no one hurries, as far as I could determine, either on the sidewalks or in the banks and shops; I am reasonably certain that the incidence of ulcers and heart attacks, on a percentage of population basis, is very low compared to New York or even Des Moines, Iowa.

A measure of the spell Granada exerts can be found in the feelings of the people who lived and ruled there over a span of seven hundred and eighty-one years. Boabdil, the last Muslim monarch on the Iberian peninsula, evacuated the city in 1492, leaving the Palacio Arabe and his Andalusian domain to Ferdinand and Isabella. It is reported that he paused in his flight, some twenty-odd miles from the city's gates, for a last look at Granada's spires and the red castle on its hilltop, and wept.

(The exact spot in the Sierra Nevadas where his tears fell, suitably marked, is called El Ultimo Suspiro del Moro. Baedeker and most other authorities credit Aisha, mother of Boabdil, with telling her son, "Weep not like a woman for what you could not defend like a man." James Michener, in his heavyweight tome *Iberia*, has her saying: "You do well, my son, to weep as a woman for the loss of what you could not defend as a man." Since her words of advice were uttered in January 1492, it's difficult to prove who has the right version. We may never know what she really said. Either way, it appears he did shed some tears, or at least his eyes were a bit misty.)

More recently, some four and a half centuries after Boabdil's departure, Sacheverell Sitwell quit Granada and proceeded to North Africa. In Marrakesh he exchanged a few phrases in halting French with a caíd, an old Moor with a white beard. When the word Granada was mentioned, the Muslim turned his eyes to Heaven and murmured: *"Ce que nous Maures appelons la terre promise."*

The late Cole Porter added a footnote. In his lyric for a song called "At Long Last Love" he translated the Arab vision of the promised land into a westerner's soaring dream:

> Is it an earthquake
>   Or simply a shock,
> Is it the good turtle soup
>   Or merely the mock.
> Is it a cocktail—
>   This feeling of joy,
> Or is what I feel
>   The real McCoy
> Is it for all time
>   Or simply a lark,
> Is it Granada I see
>   Or only Asbury Park. . . .

Baden-Baden

All other European resorts pale by comparison with Baden-Baden, the most sublime place for complete relaxation in utter, blissful comfort. . . .
For if it is still possible to enjoy life as it was once lived, and meant to be lived, it is here in the rolling countryside of the valley of the Oos that one can exist in a most benign state.

$\mathcal{R}$esorts are where you find them, or these days where you make them. To some, the ideal is a small ski colony nestled in the lee of a Tyrolean Alp; to others, a community of scuba divers in the Caribbean is preferred. As for more general resorts, their life span is limited in this age of accelerated obsolescence. Mexico's Acapulco, for instance, considered by some a late arrival, is already on the downhill slide.

But when one is discussing classic resorts—the Greats—that have prevailed at their superb best for at least a century, all too few come to mind. Marienbad, Carlsbad (now Karlovy-Vary, Czechoslovakia), Bad Gastein. Deauville, on the French coast of the English Channel, certainly qualifies, having been created in the 1860s. But Deauville was built in imitation of another great European spa that had reigned as queen of the Great Resorts for many years before that. That perfect pearl is Baden-Baden, in West Germany, on the edge of the Black Forest, in the valley of the Oos, and quite close to Strasbourg and the French border.

And still today all other European resorts pale by comparison with Baden-Baden, which is at once a masterpiece in miniature as a town, the most completely equipped spa in the world, boasting the most luxurious, most elegant gambling casino on earth, plus one of the most tradition-laden racetracks to be found anywhere, with a grand prix that is still one of Europe's most sought-after prizes, and finally the world's greatest de luxe hotel, bar none, in my view.

The Ritz in Paris is, of course, on everyone's list of great hotels, and justifiably so; London's Savoy is on most, and London's Claridge is on some. The Swiss "Riviera" hotels along the north shore of Lake Geneva, like the Beau Rivage-Palace in Ouchy-Lausanne, might provide some nominees, and the old, second Imperial—the Frank Lloyd Wright Imperial—in Tokyo and the Miyako in Kyoto could be considered great in a different style. (The Imperial in Tokyo was opened in 1922 and proved its mettle in the following year when it survived the Great Earthquake.) All of these I have known and enjoyed.

I have always regretted never having experienced a stay at Shepheard's in Cairo when that monumental edifice was still functioning; nor have I ever been privileged to know the Raffles in Singapore, extolled by some as one of the greatest and described by S. J. Perelman as utterly commonplace, with "the most odious cuisine in Asia." (In the lexicon of Perelmania, these slurs may well constitute a lavish accolade—it's hard to tell. Since it is his fancy to lay about him with heavy shafts of criticism, a relatively light reprimand like this one may well indicate three-star value.) Most individuals have their own favorites: Kaiser Frederick III once observed: "Of all the hotels I have visited I like the Insel Hotel best." He was referring to the Hotel Insel on an island in Lake Constance, Germany; it was a sweeping, generous compliment, but it would have meant more if he had indicated how many hotels he had visited.

I am not including in this brief compendium such *outré* temples for the serious sybarite as L'Hôtel in Paris and, to a lesser degree, the Negresco in Nice, with at least one room, I vividly recall, in Turn-of-the-Century-Bordello décor: blood-red damask walls, black-and-gold frames, and a liberal supply of mirrors. (The screaming walls kept me awake all night.) When in Nice, I much preferred the Ruhl, which though less imposing and less exotic and definitely not a "great" was at least comfortable and restful. It no longer exists, unfortunately. Deauville's Normandy deserves to be on any list of Europe's better hotels.

Of all the greats, and with a special, lingering nod to the Ritz in Paris, I would give Brenner's Park Hotel in Baden-Baden full marks in every department that comes into consideration in assessing a great hotel. It is the scrupulous attention to every detail in the preparation of the meals, of the service generally (the attitude of the staff is still in the best nineteenth-century tradition), and to the luxurious appointments that make the Brenner's Park truly the headquarters of the unabashedly hedonistic life. But while it has a rich, *luxueuse* appearance in all its quarters, it is subdued rather than ostentatious—the epitome of good taste, with not one jarring note. The staff is solicitous and thoughtful, considerate without coming close to obsequiousness. In fact, never—this late in the twentieth century—have I encountered an establishment in which the relationship between staff and guests is so harmonious, so delicately balanced, and at the same time so comfortable.

And for one who is weary of, and bored with, mass-produced hotels and motels, identical even to the reproductions on their wafer-thin walls, and to their perfunctory impersonal "service," the Brenner's Park will quickly re-acquaint one with the joy of living, and restore one's faith in the time-tempered principles of dedicated innkeeping.

The whole team—director, maître d'hôtel, chef, concierge, waiters, cooks, busboys, barmen, maids, and porters—really *cares* about the guest and his feeling of well-being. He is not simply the faceless person in room 412 who checked in this morning; he is a very special person with his own tastes and desires.

Personalized service is an essential part of the mystique of Brenner's Park; the guest's slightest wish is regarded by the management and staff as a command. An arriving guest who is paying a return visit after more than a decade and a half will have his previous stay gently recalled by the concierge, who consults a list of all former visitors, their individual preferences—their favorite wine and year, their favorite vintage champagne—along with any dietary restrictions (no sugar, no salt, etc.), and even pure whims. While many guests who live fairly close by in Germany and France often arrive at Brenner's Park for a stay of several days while their laundry is done (so pleased are they with its condition on being returned to them), there is only one guest who asks to have his shoelaces pressed. This request is honored just as seriously as any other. An accomplished tailor has always been a part of the Brenner team; his ministrations to well-made but aging garments have been an inducement to those who, finding themselves and their wardrobes in a state of disrepair, check in for a stay at the Brenner's Park to set themselves, their clothes, and their shoes and boots right.

It was the most comfortable and most satisfying room, or brace of rooms, I had ever inhabited. I remember quite a few years ago an Austrian film actress was brought to New York to help promote one of her motion pictures —Elisabeth Bergner, I think it was—and she fell so deeply in love with her room, or rooms, in the Plaza Hotel that she refused to leave throughout her stay. It was her first trip to New York but she wouldn't budge, day or night. Her newspaper interviews were, of course, held in the sitting room, and her food and drink were sent up. She was heartsick when it was time for her to board ship for Europe. Now I know how she felt. My rooms at the Brenner's Park had a personality that suited me perfectly. (I have forgotten the number of the apartment, but it doesn't matter as the management knows.) A long narrow hall led in from the door, with gold-plated hooks for overcoats or whatever in a row along the far wall. At the end of the hall a small but memorable sitting room overlooked the park, the Lichtentaler Allee, and the slim stream called the Oos, which winds its way down toward the Casino and the Drinking Hall, where one imbibes the mineral waters. The décor was distinctly nineteenth century, or older, and so too were the various pieces of furniture—notably a handsome, two-centuries'-old secretary-desk. The adjoining bedroom, with its ample twin beds and tremendous closets, was flanked on the other side by the bathroom, a huge affair in which one could certainly have held a cocktail party or installed a putting green. The windows of the sitting room covered almost one entire side of the room; outside all was blanketed in snow—the balcony, the park, the buildings opposite, and the allee that parallels the Oos.

The "river," a stream of sparkling blue water of uniform width, looks like nothing so much as the result of a heavy rain in the nearby mountains. It is something between ten and fifteen feet wide, and remains at a level just an inch or two below the greensward of the park through which it flows. I have always felt that it should be possible to leap across it without much difficulty. It reminds me of a stylized painting in which the artist, after covering his canvas with bright greensward, added a narrow, even band of a medium blue as an afterthought, without bothering with riverbanks or patches of plain brown earth between the water and the lawn.

The Brenner's Park faces on the river and the park, its ample porch unused and snow-covered in late fall and winter. Actually the main entrance to the hotel is at the "back"—an unprepossessing doorway giving onto narrow Schillerstrasse.

I first became acquainted with this superb hostelry some sixteen years ago in the course of returning overland from the Austrian Alps to Paris. My wife, who was grippé, retired immediately after arrival, to become the first of the family to discover the most comfortable beds ever experienced, covered by fluffy eiderdown quilts. While she slept blissfully, I set out in the newly fallen snow along the Lichtentaler Allee through the park the hotel faces to the Kurhaus, which includes the most magnificent casino in the world—

Chess, Baden-Baden style

Marlene Dietrich is one among many who regard it as the most beautiful gaming house in existence. My original plan called for only a short visit of inspection, but since I was there I decided to bet a few marks just for the fun of it. I selected a table where the game was something called roulca, a version of roulette. Within an hour, I had miraculously won enough to pay for my family's entire vacation in Austria and the trips to and from Paris, where we lived at the time.

Back in our rooms at Brenner's Park I found my wife studiously downing a hot grog (for her grippe) and only vaguely aware that I had been gone.

It was with these pleasant memories in mind that I returned recently to Baden-Baden and, of course, to Brenner's Park Hotel. My mind was not playing tricks on me, I discovered with relief; the hotel, its appointments, and the staff (at least its spirit) were just as I remembered them. I noticed a few new buildings on the way to the hotel (no skyscrapers) but all was virtually unchanged—the great park outside my balcony window was as beautiful in the new snow as it had been, and the mountains behind it were as clean and bright in the clear air as though they had just been laundered (at the Brenner's Park).

A prompt visit to the Casino—a pleasant short walk in the snow through the park, across one of the graceful small, arching footbridges over the Oos —was called for even before I unpacked. But this time, though I found myself ahead of the house briefly, I did not have the touch I had on my first visit. Perhaps it was the game: this time there was no longer any roulca so I found myself at the roulette table. But my modest loss did not diminish in the slightest my exhilaration at being back in this impressive place.

The high-ceilinged rooms are adorned with mirrors, tapestries, and sculpted friezes; their furnishings have a certain heavy feeling of opulence, in spite of the fact that they were designed not by Teutonic but by Parisian architects. The oversize crystal chandeliers add just the ornate touch to dazzle the first-time visitor. Between turns of the wheel, while some of my neighbors were collecting their chips—solid gold ones on weekends and holidays—I reflected on the fact that the peerless Russian writer, Fyodor Dostoevsky, spent some time here gambling away his precious, hard-earned rubles. The contrast between this lavishly splendid recreation hall and the dank cells in the freezing fortress of Saints Peter and Paul in Leningrad, where he spent many unforgettable days and nights as a prisoner, must have been numbing.

These days the Casino is administered by Baron Hartmann von Richtofen, nephew of the world-famous Red Baron, World War I flying ace, immortalized by Snoopy in the comic strip "Peanuts." This engaging thirty-five-year-old Direktor has graduated to that post following a term as legal adviser to the Casino administration.

"I have the feeling you are going to ask me about 'breaking the bank' and whether it has ever been done," he said one morning, before checking over the previous day's (and night's) take. "Well, it is not possible to 'break the bank' here, since the Casino Company has sufficient resources to pay whatever sum one may win, regardless of the wagered amount."

In response to another unasked question on my part, he volunteered: "Half a million marks, approximately, has been the highest amount ever won here." (About $200,000.)

I did pose a question about systems-players and whether the systems ever worked, over a long period. "Generally speaking," the Baron replied, choosing his words carefully, "winning is a matter of luck. However, some gamblers do use certain systems, but the Casino is not able to give any definite information with regard to the winning chances."

He regarded me evenly, as I suspect he does in the case of all or most visitors to his establishment. To my next query he said, with a disarming smile: "We have a blacklist, of course, as all Casinos do—of persons who are denied admission to the premises. But one of our biggest problems is spotting the businessman who is playing with his company's funds—an embezzler, in other words." Any loss on the part of such a player apparently falls into a cloudy legal area in which the determination of the final ownership of the money in question (by the Casino or by the victimized company) is a troublesome matter.

This awkward situation led the Baron into his next statement: "Students, bookkeepers, and cashiers are not allowed to gamble in the Casino, nor are residents of Baden-Baden. Twenty-one years of age is the minimum for visitors who are permitted into the gaming rooms."

Brightening somewhat, he continued: "This is the largest Casino in Germany, and has the highest turnover of receipts." There was just a tinge of pride in his voice as he mentioned this. "Roulette is by far the most popular game, with vingt-et-un ["21" or blackjack] second." Baccarat also has its dedicated adherents, who are permitted to continue after the two A.M. closing —until seven A.M. if their reserves hold out.

I had heard somewhere that the Casino "lived on the spa," and asked if this was so. "The Casino does not live 'on the spa,'" he answered emphatically. "Quite to the contrary, it contributes materially to employment and the general welfare of Baden-Baden.

"I'm happy to say that our business is good, and increasing—we're earning more money." He paused. "Will I see you this evening?" he asked solicitously. I decided there was no connection between the accelerating profits of the Casino and his implied hope that I would return for another evening at the tables. In any case, I was not prepared to buy enough chips to contribute materially to the welfare of Baden-Baden. (I was still well ahead of the Casino—as a result of my earlier trip—and I hoped to keep it that way.)

The Casino, which was designed in imitation of Versailles, became part of the Kurhaus in 1827, when it passed into the hands of French lessees, headed by Monsieur Edouard Benazet, who transformed not only the gambling establishment but the whole of the town as well, giving it an international glitter that attracted such illustrious visitors as the Emperor Wilhelm I, Bismarck, Alfred de Musset, Berlioz, Brahms, and the already mentioned melancholy Russian, Dostoevsky. In more recent years this coterie was supplemented by the Emperor and Empress of Persia, King Ibn Saud, the Duke and Duchess of Windsor, and the Begum and the late Aga Khan (III).

In fact, it was the Parisian Benazets, Jacques and Edouard, father and son, who gave this medieval town just the right international ambiance to achieve the status of unparalleled watering place and "summer capital of Europe."

That ambiance is strongly reinforced by the Brenner's Park Hotel. Its thirty-nine-year-old Managing Director, Richard Schmitz, always knew he wanted to be a hotel man in the classical mold. His progress, from the bottom rungs, has been swift and steady; in its course he has learned the business from all standpoints. Starting as an apprentice in a Konditorei (confectioner's shop), he worked next in the kitchen at the Hotel Petersberg, above Bonn, then moved on to Switzerland, where he attended the esteemed French-administered Lausanne Hotel School, which he found to be strict and difficult. Armed with his diploma, he gained a position as a headwaiter at the Grand Hotel Alpina in the Swiss resort of Gstaad, where his *patron* was equally strict. Then on to Paris, and a post with the reception at the fashionable Hotel Bristol, followed by terms at the Ritz in London, the Dom-Hotel in Cologne, and—as cashier and receptionist—at the Zonnenberg in Zurich, where he later served as assistant manager for two years. In 1968 he became second manager of the Brenner's Park in Baden-Baden, and two years later rose to Managing Director.

Seated in the salon of his impeccably well-ordered establishment on a late November afternoon, with the fading sun supplying a faint pinkish tint to the snow in the park beyond the wide picture windows that extend along the entire front of the building, Herr Schmitz reminisced about his own philosophy of innkeeping.

(At thirty-nine I calculated, Schmitz had been eight years old when Adolf Hitler perished in his Berlin bunker in the dying hours of World War II in Europe. Schmitz is typical of many Germans of his generation who find it hard to believe that Nazism could have gripped the country as it did, causing such a trauma and leaving its mark on future generations of Germans.)

His goal in his current post as the head of the Brenner's Park is to run the hotel as well as it always has been, perhaps make it even more luxurious. "In 1980 it will be quite different than it was in 1930," he predicted. "Service is the most important single element," he said firmly. "But we are not succeeding 100 percent, although the basic staff is good."

He looked about him with the roving eye of an experienced expert auctioneer. With some relish he said: "I've left the chandeliers, but I've taken out some of the tapestry-covered chairs—which looked old—and without losing any charm." Rare tapestries—some more than three hundred years old —and matchless carpets—among them one from China—are among the many antique pieces that line the walls and corridors.

"Most of our rooms—like yours," Schmitz said, nodding at me, "still have a nineteenth-century atmosphere. But we've made eight or ten modern, with curtains, chairs, and carpets in the English style—gay but conservative.

"But in general the décor is still in the spirit of the last century. The more Hiltons there are, in my opinion, hotels like this one will have more and more reason to survive," he said. "The key word here, after service, is *Gastlichkeit*" (hospitality).

Managing Director Schmitz works a fourteen-hour day to keep the Brenner's Park at its exalted position at the top level of the world's great hotels, and still manages to spend a part of every evening with his guests. Since the last Brenner departed eight years ago, the hotel is now privately owned— by Rudolf August Oetker. Alfred Brenner, the last surviving member of the dynasty, is over eighty and retired as this is written.

Baden-Baden had already been celebrated as a spa of international renown for two centuries when the first Brenner—Anton Alois—acquired the Hotel Stephanie-les-Bains for 171,200 florins in 1872. The town's colorful "French era" ended abruptly with the start of the Franco-Prussian War in 1870, and it was Brenner, a tailor or, more precisely, garmentmaker to the Margrave's Court, and especially his son Camille, who guided the town on a course leading to an ever more finely polished image of the ultimate in grand luxury living.

Named for Stephanie Beauharnais, Napoleon's adopted daughter and mistress, who was also the wife of Charles, Prince of Baden, the Stephanie-les-Bains was changed to the Brenner's Hotel Stephanie by Anton Brenner, who a decade later sold the hotel and its lovely grounds to his son, a textile merchant in London with a good sense of business, for half a million marks.

Local historian J. Loeser wrote at the time, in his *Geschichte der Stadt Baden*: "The interior of this magnificent building fronted by a garden includes every comfort of modern times and satisfies the most extravagant demands. Architecture and the crafts cooperated in producing something which may be called model in every respect."

This unusual hostelry was soon attracting such gilded guests as Emperor Dom Pedro of Brazil, the Grand Duchess Olga of Russia, tennis-playing Gustav V of Sweden, the Sultan of Johore, the Maharajah of Kapurthala, and King Chulalonkorn of Siam, for whose royal convenience Camille Brenner erected the exclusive Villa Stephanie and Villa Imperiale, as annexes connected to the main hotel by bridges.

It is notable that a small hotel immediately adjacent to the Stephanie, the Minerva, was rented at about this time by an aspiring young innkeeper named Cesar Ritz; he and Camille Brenner became friends and shared opinions on how to make their establishments more appealing to their guests. Ritz of course persisted in following his calling and went on to found the world-famous hotel bearing his name on Paris's Place Vendôme. Thus two of the greatest hoteliers of modern times furthered their fledgling careers side by side along the banks of the Oos in Baden-Baden.

Ritz gave each of his rooms on the park side a private bath, an innovative idea in those days. On the street side were rooms for the servants of his upper-echelon guests. Camille Brenner adopted the practice when he enlarged the Stephanie. The hotel moved with the times; in 1898 a property bordering on the hotel was acquired from Rumanian Prince Stourdza—it included a villa, stables, manège, and 8,000 square meters of land. Within two years a five-story wing had been added on the new property to Brenner's main building, and soon more guests from North America were arriving; they shortly constituted half of the total number of residents.

A spacious ballroom was added to the Stephanie in 1913, but that new American adjunct, a bar, was not provided until the Roaring Twenties. (Camille Brenner had died in 1914, his hotel an unqualified success. Before his passing he had installed telephones in the rooms, a pneumatic postal network, electric clocks, refrigeration, and the hotel's own electric plant. With a keen sense of intuition he built a large garage on some of the land he had acquired from Prince Stourdza—the first German hotelkeeper to anticipate the age of the automobile. Finally, not long before his death, Camille Brenner took over Ritz's Minerva and transformed it into the Sanatorium Stephanie

—and Baden-Baden took another step forward toward becoming an even more enjoyable spa.)

But with the commencement of World War I, Camille's son Kurt, who took over from his father, gave up the idea of a sanatorium with the conveniences of a luxury hotel, named his establishment the Brenner Park Hotel, and concentrated on catering to the pleasures and comforts of his guests without specific regard to their health. That was something for the guests to decide, he believed, and the baths were after all close by.

In 1968, just before his departure from the scene, Alfred Brenner wrote, in his reminiscences *Origin and Development of the Brenner Hotel Establishment*:

"The hotel and grounds my father left me comprised an area of 2.5 hectares in the most beautiful section of the Lichtental Allée, and blended delightfully into the landscape. The property, including neighboring estates acquired in the course of years, was worth nine million gold marks. This meant that each of the 400 hotel beds was worth 22,000 gold marks. If one translates that into present money value [1968] it comes to 100,000 Deutschmarks per bed and that is just about the worth of a bed in a luxury hotel today.

"After World War I, in 1922, we turned the property belonging to my mother and to us five brothers and sisters into a family corporation. This was done to facilitate possible future sale for members of the corporation who wanted to dispose of their share, and to insure good business management. During the inflation years both hotels did so well that we could do the necessary repairs, make the renovations, and better the maintenance neglected during the war. In addition to this we enlarged our premises by buying adjoining real estate: in 1922 we acquired the house on Ludwig-Wilhelm-Platz 4, and in 1924 the Villa Knorring, formerly Plessen, which, surrounded by a large park, lay between the hotels so that we had wanted to include it in our property for a long time."

The spiritual legacy of Stephanie Beauharnais remained: this latter villa, which today is known as the Park Villa and is connected with the Brenner's Park Hotel, was reconstructed in 1924 as the Casino Stephanie and decorated in the modish Japanese style. Here thés dansants became the height of fashion.

Throughout Baden-Baden, as in the United States, the Blues and the Charleston supplied the background for those highly charged years of the Twenties. But in spite of the continued gaiety, the 1914–18 war years had had their effect: the devaluation of the currency and the political upheavals contributed to a strong feeling of uncertainty about the immediate future. The gaiety continued, but on a day-to-day basis; every night was New Year's Eve.

While the jeunesse dorée amused themselves with their frantic antics, the hotel owners sat in their offices and pondered on the melancholy financial news. The New York stock exchange crash in 1929 provided the climactic exclamation point to the era of wonderful nonsense.

In his memoirs, *The World Is My Guest*, Conrad Hilton points out that the international traveling on which European luxury hotels depended had come virtually to an end. Since the cost of maintenance did not decline in the new financial climate, many elaborate hotels entered a period of great difficulties. Besides these tangible setbacks, a general feeling of resent-ment of the wealthy began to spread—especially against the ostentatiously wealthy—sparked by a dramatic rise in unemployment throughout the world.

The Brenner's Park Hotel and the Stephanie suffered less than most, but it was not until 1937 that they again had as many guests as they had in 1930, and by that later date the room rental was one-third lower.

But if royal personages and their retinues became less visible during this somewhat more Spartan period, their places were taken by a limited coterie of diplomats, bankers, industrialists, the military, scholars, artists, and some wealthy flaneurs who were somehow unaffected by the economic situation and cared little about the ill-concealed hostility on the part of the less fortunate. Henry Ford, W. L. Mellon, William K. Vanderbilt, and Daniel Guggenheim came to know the Brenner's Park well. The moneyed giants were represented by the Rothschilds and the Thyssens, show business by Mary Pickford and Lillian Gish, Elisabeth Bergner and Yvonne Printemps, the world of music by Irving Berlin and Franz Lehár, and even literature— not the most remunerative of professions—by Georg Kaiser. And politicians were most flattered by the hospitality they were extended at the Brenner's Park—among them, Nobel Prize winner Gustav Stresemann and Sir Neville Chamberlain, along with many members of foreign embassies in Berlin.

Beginning with Hitler's invasion of Poland and continuing through the war years of 1939 to 1945, the Brenner's Park went through three distinct phases, with a fourth following in the postwar years of 1945 to 1950. For the war's first two years the hotel was closed, then it was reopened and served, among other capacities, as an internment "camp" for U.S. embassy personnel from Berlin. In the war's last two years it became a refuge for fugitive Vichy politicians, escaping the wrath of the Free French and the bulk of the French citizenry as the Nazis were being driven out of their country.

During the five years of occupation following the war, Baden-Baden and the Brenner's Park were host to a different breed of Frenchmen—the strongly anti-Nazi garrison forces. The hotel itself was headquarters for the military government of the area, and the Stephanie was used as its office building. When it was finally returned to its owners (during the war the Brenners, Kurt and Alfred, sold the plurality of their shares to a family named Oetker, involved in a multiplicity of versatile business operations), the once plush hotel was badly in need of refurbishing. The main part of the old hotel was sold, resulting in the transformation of the former wing of the Stephanie into a guesthouse for those taking the cure.

But with the advent of the air-travel boom, and soon afterward the jet age, it was a certainty that the Brenner's Park would somehow be restored to its former brilliance, with a patina that rivaled the sheen of its most glittering nineteenth-century years. A few prominent public figures continued to be faithful visitors—the old Aga Khan (III), Marshal Tito, and Aristotle Onassis, among them—but a new class of jet travelers was emerging. It was no longer considered advisable for the celebrated to parade evidences of their wealth—there were always some exceptions to this code—but less well-known tycoons replaced the former publicized group, and the Brenner's Park is more than ever at the apogee of its orbit. And it seems that even the budget-minded traveler of moderate means is pleased to stretch things a bit for a week or so of unexcelled luxury living.

So is a really top-class hotel achieved, with infinite attention being given to the most minute details of all facets of the establishment's operation. And nowhere, in my experience, is such painstaking care taken as at the Brenner's Park.

During the winter months, from November to March, Managing Director

Schmitz and his town colleagues have instituted a new anti-stress program for overtired businessmen and women or for those who have been indulging a bit too enthusiastically in the Good Life. Those suffering from fatigue of the brain or fatigue of the liver may select an all-inclusive package that includes several types of baths, massages, medical checkups, special diets, exercises, and all hotel accommodations for either an eight- or fourteen-day period.

My most recent visit to the Brenner's Park was made, as noted, in November and December, and although I certainly considered myself eligible for an anti-stress treatment, or series of treatments, my own conception of anti-stress therapy is somewhat at variance with the currently advertised program. I did work in a few visits to one of the baths, and every day I made a point of sipping the mineral water in the Trinkhalle (Pump Room), a rectangular community meeting hall of Grecian proportions— easily the length of an American football field. But my idea of anti-stress is an existence of deep and abiding comfort, preferably stretched out on down pillows and with periodic trips to the bar and dining room for food and drink and of the most delicate yet Lucullan persuasions. Leave the Spartan *régimes* to others; this is really the only anti-stress program for me. And the Brenner's Park is singularly well equipped to accommodate me.

The bar, an intimate corner just off the principal salon, and adjoining the formal restaurant, is stocked with all the stimulating liquids appropriate to that locale and many not usually found in the average beverage dispensary. Luncheon or dinner in the main restaurant is an exercise in the pleasures of self-indulgence. The meals are exquisitely prepared and served; the menu is not perhaps as formidable as that at a French three-star restaurant, not as crowded with dishes of the most refined of gustatory sensations. But for me they are among the most pleasurable I can remember; I placed no restrictions on my choices, for I felt it was sinful to dine at Brenner's Park on a salad of lettuce leaves without dressing, stress or no stress. Well, each to his own taste, as the French say, and I like something a little more satisfying than dry lettuce leaves. (Seriously, I understand the diet is a bit more liberal than that, but I would never consider stopping at the Brenner's Park in order to diet, so I didn't bother examining the anti-stress menu.)

The regular menu, which I gather must have been shielded from the eyes of those on the *régime* (the headwaiters must have carefully synchronized lists of which guests are handed which menus), includes a garland of tantalizing dishes in the categories of game, roasts, and fish, sufficient to have tempted Henry VIII half an hour after one of his royal repasts. The trout that come shooting down the Oos, just outside the hotel's front door, at certain seasons can be taken by hand, so plentiful are they in the narrow confines of the clear mountain stream. The trout I was privileged to dine on at the Brenner's Park were the tastiest I had sampled since some memorable Loire river trout I was once served at Amboise.

The inducements to stay in the hotel are many, but Baden-Baden is an interesting town, with its roots in the Roman Empire, and one must be firm and tear oneself away from the delights of the hotel from time to time.

The baths, it might be said, are the principal business of the town. The cure patient is offered Roman-Irish baths, thermal baths, saunas, the Kneipp Bath, carbonic acid baths, Stanger baths, Fango (mud-pack) baths, underwater jet massage, and a variety of inhalation treatments, plus a series of massages—the pushing and pounding of the flesh by masseurs with hands like steel grappling hooks. Still, after it's all over, I'm told one feels in a euphoric state—with a sensation of flying at 50,000 feet without the assistance of a plane.

The Friedrichsbad is a good place to start one's health program. A splendid Renaissance building with a green dome and two corner towers, it was constructed in the 1870s to cater to Russian duchesses and other nobility.

The baths in the Middle Ages

But it is popular with visitors of all classes; the Grosse Gesellschaftsbad (Great Communal Bath) is a particular favorite of noninvalids as well as of those requiring treatment in the waters.

The Friedrichsbad is situated over the main source of Baden-Baden's springs; the waters, first discovered and tapped by the Romans, come bubbling into the air at a temperature of 69 degrees Centigrade (156 degrees Fahrenheit). This area was a Roman recreation center; evidences of the Roman period are still fairly plentiful, including ingenious walls devised by the Romans to retain the heat in the baths. More than a score of springs supplied them with all the health-giving thermal waters they could possibly desire; the baths for privates were separated from those for officers, which latter were located under the Catholic Church.

Of the Roman baths, Karl Baedeker writes in a short guide: "Representing only a small portion of the whole lay-out, they consist of a hot air sweating bath (sudatorium) with a small dressing room, a pre-heating room and heating stoves, the parallel hot bath (caldarium), a warm air bath (tepidarium), and swimming pools. The baths probably date from circa A.D. 117. . . . The Imperial Baths, more spacious and lined with marble, were discovered under the market place and Stiftskirche in 1816, and more particularly in 1846–48, but they have been covered up again."

The *anciens habitants* of the town found the waters especially effective for use in diseases of the joints. In the Middle Ages, the baths were indulged in mostly for the fun of it, although it was thought at the time they were especially useful for those suffering from syphilis.

The Celts were devotees and may have instituted the fango (mud bath); they advocated no more than twenty-five minutes in the bath, followed immediately by massage and extended rest. For rheumatic ailments and inflammation of the joints, they prescribed no more than ten minutes in 35-degree-Centigrade water.

Even then it was not the effect of the spring water alone that was alleged to achieve remarkable cures, but—as today—the philosophy of the patient toward the beneficial possibilities of the cure.

After a brief sample of the waters of the Friedrichsbad, I returned to the hotel, experiencing a pleasant glow, and topped off the morning with a few glasses of a superb Riesling. (Drinking at midday is not permitted to serious anti-stress types.) But I kept firmly in mind, throughout my stay, the slogan of this area on the Black Forest's edge—it centers on three "w"s: wood, water, wine. A fourth "w" has been omitted with perhaps due deliberation.

Besides their importance in the quest for health, the baths have also provided—throughout history—a focus for the social life of the community. The earliest tribes derived great joy from participation in the communal bathing, and meals were often served to both sexes indulging in the baths.

Whether moving from hot room to hotter room and being sprayed down, pushed, pulled, and tugged until the body rebels or wading knee-deep in troughs on alternately hot and cold smooth stones followed by a good scrub, the final result is always a state of well-being hard to come by in any other way.

Meanwhile, the serious anti-stress types are checked at intervals by their special doctor (there are nearly a hundred working in the program); many ailments seem to improve under this regimen of water applied externally and internally. The mineral water one drinks is not really medicinal-tasting, although it is not to be compared to a good dry champagne, and there is a certain friendly, conspiratorial air shared by those imbibing at the spacious Trinkhalle, as though all there had discovered a secret not known to the world at large. The small talk is the same as anywhere: last night's play, the afternoon's concert, or the weather, but it is conducted with more zest than usual—a result of the state of mind induced by downing the mineral water. I'm certain the feeling of instant well-being is psychological rather than physical, but it does give one a wonderful lift and produces the gratifying conviction that one is doing the right thing for a change.

The Augustabad is an extremely modern establishment of seven stories with great expanses of glass that let the sun do its work, a roomy communal pool, which one must use sparingly—ten minutes is the time allotted for immersion in the warm, chemically prepared water. All the treatments involved in the anti-stress program are given here. It is also equipped with every balneological and medical facility that could conceivably assist the spa directors in their determination to make theirs the greatest health resort the world has ever known.

Paracelsus, the revered Swiss physician and alchemist, and thousands of doctors since—many of them unsurpassed in their fields—have stated flatly that the waters from Baden-Baden's springs, originating some 2,000 meters in the earth, are without question the most formidable health-giving liquids to be found on this globe.

Discounting the Roman occupation, Baden-Baden really became an international spa in about 1650, and its reputation has accelerated steadily since then. Today it is at its all-time peak.

At a Sunday afternoon concert in the Kurhaus, given by the Baden-Badener Orchester, I noted a sprinkling of elderly listeners with crutches. But these, I was reminded later, were persons who would not be walking at all, were it not for the waters. Some of these partially crippled cure regulars are invalids from the last world war, others are victims of traffic accidents. But the highest percentage of those invalids who regularly take the waters are those suffering from diseases of the joints.

The most curative thermal springs in the world, whose origin is in the Paleozoic era, lie within an area of about 110 by 90 meters, stretching from the Collegiate Church in the west to the western façade of the Convent of the Holy Sepulchre with the contour of the Florentiner Berg in the north, to the ruins of the Roman baths in the south. They produce an average of 770 cubic meters of spring water each day.

That the thermal treatments are beneficial is probably undeniable. Beyond that, there are the cases of persons who could barely move who, after a relatively few weeks, were reported walking briskly along the streets of the town. The desired result in Baden-Baden as in Lourdes, France, where the believers in miracles assemble, is the same in each case; only the avenue pursued is different. There seem to be no figures available relating to the numbers of crutches discarded at Lourdes and at Baden-Baden, but the therapeutic effects of the spring waters have doubtless worked many more cures than the relics of the saints. The canes one sees in use on the streets of Baden-Baden are commonly said to belong to those who have just arrived and are just beginning the treatments.

But the baths are not the only part of Baden-Baden with their roots in antiquity. Beneath the Catholic Stiftskirche, the most prominent church situated in the marketplace in the town's center, are Celtic remains said to be as much as 1,500 years old. After the Roman baths, the castles of the Margraves of Baden are perhaps the most historically interesting. The *new* castle, whose current resident for at least a few weeks a year is the Duke of Baden, nephew of Prince Philip of Britain, was built about 1437, was partially destroyed by the French armies in 1689, and was thereafter restored. (The *old* castle, now simply a picturesque ruin, dates from approximately 1100, and was burned with heavy damage in 1600.)

Baden-Baden seems to have exerted a strong attraction for, among others, Russian writers of the pre-Communist era. Across from the Brenner's Park Hotel on Schillerstrasse is the charming house where Turgenev lived and worked. For German artists and composers Baden-Baden was a popular place to visit. Johannes Brahms spent long stretches of nine rewarding years in what he regarded as an ideal place to live and work. In two attic rooms in the house on Maximilianstrasse that is now a small museum (containing memorabilia) and a residence for an approved music student, Brahms composed some of his best works: the Requiem, popularly known as the German Requiem, the Rhapsody, and the "Song of Destiny."

But there is more to the city than old houses, baths, and castles, hotels, and casino. Throughout the town one is greeted with a profusion of restaurants with varied bills of fare, but I much preferred the colorful, cozy *stube*—small bars which serve some food—where one will fall into easy conversation with the customers and proprietors. Such a one is the tiny, *gemütlich* Bürgerstübel, on a small side street only a short walk from the park and the Casino. Invariably the habitués—who drank mostly beer—were singing, laughing, and joking throughout the length of my visits.

Of the restaurants—excluding for the moment both the formal one at the Brenner's Park Hotel and its decorative grill room, called the Schwarzwald Grill, both incomparable—I much preferred some of those in the nearby Schwarzwald itself.

One is barely outside the streets of the town before finding oneself in the Black Forest, that storied mountainous terrain studded with pine, fir, and maple that contributes so strongly to the salubrious climate of the area. Many of the towns and villages of the Schwarzwald, which overlooks the Rhine plain, have preserved their medieval appearance: a great number of the farmhouses have thatched roofs and some have attached stables under sheltering hip-roofs. The inhabitants often dress in the costumes of centuries past.

At an altitude of 3,600 feet, high in the snow-covered pines, it is refreshing to enjoy that second natural commodity of Baden-Baden, after its mineral spring waters—the clear, invigorating, pine-scented air; here there is no time limit for the inhalation treatment.

Psychological or physical, the simple fact is that one does feel much more alive in Baden-Baden and its environs; without a doubt this condition is attributable to the waters and the air and their almost instant tonic effect on the body and the psyche.

Returning from the Schwarzwald one evening, heady with good health, I plunged into a tremendous German meal in the old tradition. It was delicious but the courses were far more plentiful and more sizable than I was accustomed to. I had planned an evening at the theater, but *Macbeth* in German on a full stomach was a bit much, I felt.

After that ponderous meal starting with *markklosse suppe* and ending, some two hours later, with *kuchen mit schlagsahne*, I had no appetite for a heavy drama, and after the dinner I had just consumed all those umlauts would certainly have been indigestible.

I postponed my visit to the Schauspielhaus until the next night, when my dinner was to be of more manageable dimensions, and the evening's divertissement was announced as *Der Talisman*, a play by Johann Nestroy, acted—as it turned out—with uncommon zest and completely free of murders and dark deeds.

While shopping in the late afternoon preceding my visit to the theater, I came upon a vignette that caught my attention: a policeman taking out his ticketing book as he noted that a parked car had run out of meter time, and simultaneously a stockily built man, presumably the owner of the car, sauntering in a very leisurely manner up to his vehicle. He nodded to the policeman, then waited without a word while a ticket was written and handed to him. A case of *Deutsche Ordnung* (a German sense of order), I suppose. Certainly it would have been inconceivable for such a calm, mannerly scene to take place in the United States under similar conditions. Not a word of protest, no attempt to forestall the writing of the ticket. It is said that one can judge the nationality of a person by his shoes and the way he walks; it may well be that it is also possible to identify a person's country of origin by his reactions in a given set of circumstances.

With all its attractions—elegant casino, nonpareil baths, fine hotel, warm-and cold-weather sports facilities, Black Forest trails—Baden-Baden is "nothing without the races," in the somewhat prejudiced view of Doctor Erich Teuscher, Secretary-General of the International Club, the parent body of Baden-Baden's horse-racing activity. At the tastefully decorated club headquarters facing on the park, opposite the Brenner's Park Hotel, Dr. Teuscher told me that the house had been built, in 1822, as a palace for Queen Frederika, the last Swedish Queen before Bernadotte, and gave credit —for the founding of racing in Baden-Baden—to Edouard Benazet, the Frenchman who provided the impetus for the resort's nineteenth-century renaissance.

Benazet brought artists in all fields of the arts—particularly great opera singers—and celebrities and royalty from all corners of Europe and beyond. England's Prince of Wales—later as King Edward VII to become a living symbol of the Good Life—was a strong booster of Baden-Baden, and was particularly taken with the races and the milieu.

To be sure, even Dr. Teuscher admitted, there isn't all that much racing in Baden-Baden over the course of a year: one meeting in May and another in August, sometimes extending into the early days of September. A few weeks in all. The most important, and most elegant, day of both seasons is the last Sunday of August or the first Sunday of September, when the Grand Prix of Baden-Baden is contested. This race, which carries a purse of 250,000 Deutschmarks, bears the same cachet it has had since the days in the mid-nineteenth century when Baden-Baden was known as the "summer capital of Europe."

Iffezheim, where the track is located, is only a short drive, and even though there was snow on the ground and not a horse in sight, Dr. Teuscher tempted me with the offer of a drive out to see the facility. The track itself is a complex arrangement of courses, so that races can be, and are, held at any reasonable distance and with a variety of combinations of turns and straightaways. A bit like those displays of model railroads at Christmas time, with a number of tracks and many switches.

For Baden-Baden, which is usually slightly warmer in winter than the rest of northern Europe, it was a cold day, and the caretaker's offer of a Schnapps was gratefully accepted.

The track at Iffezheim, 1861

Back in town at the International Club, the paintings and photographs on its walls gave evidence of Iffezheim's colorful history and its roster of distinguished visitors; just about everyone who is in Baden-Baden at the end of August and early September, at the height of the high season, finds his or her way to Iffezheim to see the Grosser Preis von Baden, in which some of the best thoroughbreds in Europe compete, among them horses from France, England, and occasionally even from America.

As at Deauville, France, the running of the Grand Prix caps the season; directly afterward the town becomes less crowded, and it is possible to enjoy the resort in a more intimate atmosphere—as many visitors prefer to do. Unless they close down completely, resorts have always appealed to me more in the off-season; even without horse racing, Baden-Baden in fall and winter—with its other splendid attractions functioning in full fig, for the benefit of groups of modest proportions—is my idea of the right place to be at the right time.

In the park a number of warmly clad figures were to be seen scurrying about in the early, dramatic dusk, but not a footfall could be heard in the soft, silent snow. A three-minute walk across the park brought me back to the warmth of the Brenner's Park, where Herr Schmitz promptly offered me a restorative drink, eagerly accepted. We raised our glasses in a silent toast standing alongside the fireplace in the comfortable lounge, under the striking canvas of a Dutch harbor scene (filled with sailing vessels) by the seventeenth-century Dutch artist Jan van de Capelle. (Most of the distinctive paintings hanging on the walls of the hotel's rooms, public and private, seem to be Dutch, of the sixteenth and seventeenth centuries.)

"Our aim," Herr Schmitz said with quiet determination, "is to retain the best of what is old and include what is good of the new. For we must change somewhat, we must prepare for the future.

"Our guests in the days ahead will be not only royalty but leaders in the fields of culture, business, and so on."

He sipped his drink thoughtfully. "This presents a challenge for our top management. We would like to continue making the good life available, and in the spirit of the times."

A perfectionist of the old school, despite his youthful thirty-nine years, Herr Schmitz is obviously striving for the ultimate for his tradition-soaked hotel.

In the view of this recent guest, who does not even request that his shoelaces be pressed, Schmitz has already achieved it. Following visits to many countries throughout the world, I am convinced that the most sublime place for complete relaxation in utter, blissful comfort is Baden-Baden and the Brenner's Park Hotel. For if it is still possible to enjoy life as it was once lived, and meant to be lived, it is here in the rolling countryside of the valley of the Oos that one can exist in a most benign state.

It is ironic that this incandescently beautiful area, lying on the rim of a nation that withdrew from civilized society for a dozen years of madness, and precipitated a global war during the latter half of that period, finds itself in the position of being a last bastion of a civilization we once knew and enjoyed and that may one day be just a memory.

Tralee and the Dingle Peninsula

The feeling of isolation is overwhelming, but it is felt in all parts of this primitive southwestern area of Ireland. The land itself at this extreme end of the peninsula—a few windswept mountainous humps and a series of bluffs hanging over the sea—has not changed since refugees from Ireland's interior, caught in the famous potato famine of the mid-nineteenth century, made their way along the peninsula to the sea. . . . The natives have long since become accustomed to the eternal beauty of their land and sea. There is no other corner of Europe I know that possesses the same haunting, lyrical, soul-cleansing quality.

The Irish way is not the direct way. No local ruler would conceivably have replied in the manner of Czar Nicholas I of Russia to the engineer father of painter James McNeill Whistler when asked what route he wanted his proposed St. Petersburg-to-Moscow railroad to take. The crusty czar is said to have taken a ruler and drawn a perfectly straight line between the two cities, ignoring all considerations of terrain or other problems.

It could never have happened that way in Ireland. My target on this lush, romantic island was the town of Tralee, at the base of the Dingle Peninsula, on the wild southwestern coast; the closest and most convenient point of entry into the country by air is at Shannon, some eighty miles to the north. A visitor from the western hemisphere would have thought that this should be a short, quick journey, without complication. But one must first take into consideration the fact that one is now in Ireland, and life in all its multifarious facets is quite a different matter here.

First there is a leisurely second breakfast, after landing, with a hospitable Mr. Tobin, of the Shannon Airport Company; over eggs, sausages, toast and marmalade, juice and coffee there is time for a brief discussion of the current state of Irish literature, obviously a topic of great moment. The Irish are so concerned with the flow of artful prose and poetry that writers in Ireland (including foreigners resident on the island) are not required to pay income tax.

Although one thinks of the average Irishman as rough-hewn, he has a certain inherent literary grace that is not common among other English-speaking and -writing peoples. The English, of course, use their language brilliantly, but the Irish, I have always felt, have added a certain zest to the tongue that is, for them, really an adopted one.

Asked finally about choices of transportation to Tralee, Mr. Tobin off-handedly remarked that he would be driving to Limerick by and by, and why didn't I accompany him that far.

The first stop was a good eight miles from the airport, at Bunratty's, a fifteenth-century castle in good condition, that specializes in medieval banquets, done in the manners, dress, cuisine, and spirit of the times. A trencherman in Tralee, a sage who was to give me the benefit of his wisdom later in my stay, and who periodically takes off on the medieval banquet circuit in this woolly western country, described to me one particularly memorable, Valkyrian night at Bunratty's when the lads who had drunk too deep of the mead and had become somewhat disorderly—himself included—were thrown into the ancient dungeon and locked up, to add a special touch of verisimilitude to the proceedings.

Of course since it was still morning, it was a mite early for the mead to be flowing at Bunratty's, so we repaired to a small, somewhat broken-down pub just next door, called Durty (sic) Nellie's. In the two-hundred-year-old pub's dark recesses, seated next to a voracious fire, we indulged in one of the land's gastronomic delights, the most delicious smoked salmon ever tasted, accompanied by a pint of stout, an Irish coffee, or a glass of good Scotch whiskey, whichever seemed most tempting.

We continued comparing notes on Irish writers, past and present, but during occasional pauses I was able to learn a bit about our battered, but picturesque surroundings. Nellie, whose name is now immortal in the area, was a zealous serving maid who in her enthusiasm to dispense the bitter that flowed in a nearly continuous stream from her taps airily refused to wash the glasses between customers. She has been paid the supreme tribute; to all appearances tradition has dictated that her philosophy prevail in the operation of Durty Nellie's today.

She will go down in local history along with the eighteenth-century poets who sat in a pub not far away, in County Limerick along the banks of the Maigue, and between drinks composed the doggerel now identified throughout the world by the name of the county in which they drank and versified —Limerick.

Proceeding by easy stages in a roughly easterly direction, Mr. Tobin and I moved cautiously on the city of Limerick, another seven-mile stage from Durty Nellie's. En route we made the bridge from writers to poets to limericks.

The background of this verse form is shrouded in mystery and misinformation, I learned. One version has it that the verse form was brought *to* Limerick by the returning veterans of the Irish Brigade attached to the French army for nearly one hundred years after the siege of Limerick in 1691. But there is no proof that any of these veterans ever returned to Limerick.

So some consider it more likely that the French copied an old Irish form of verse brought into France by the Jacobites, and that the French verse form returned to Limerick clothed in the English language. But this is all sheer speculation.

The Oxford English Dictionary and the Oxford Companion to English Literature, I learned over a pint of bitter in Limerick itself, state categorically that the first instance of the type of rhyme known as the limerick occurs in "Anecdotes and Adventures of Fifteen Young Ladies" and "The History of Sixteen Wonderful Old Women" published in 1820. Edward Lear, who popularized the limerick, came even later.

But likeliest of all is the belief that the place of origin of the first limerick was in the County of Limerick along the banks of the Maigue well before the Oxford English Dictionary's and the Oxford Companion's "birth"— in fact, in the middle of the eighteenth-century. Before I even heard the limerick involved, I felt there was, after all, a certain logic in the notion that the first limerick should have been composed in County Limerick.

The tavernkeeper John O'Tuomy was a genial host with a penchant for composing drinking songs, as the spirit moved him. One of his poet-customers, a broth of a boyo named Andrew McGrath, known as the Merry Pedlar, was wont to reply, in a kind of poetical jousting competition.

Here, then, is O'Tuomy's first drinking song composed in a now familiar meter, and which is hereby proclaimed the first authentic limerick:

> Do b'ait liomsa ceolta na dtiompan
> Do b'ait liomsa sport agus brandan
> Do b'ait liomsa an gloinne
> Ag Muirinn do lionadh
> 'S cuideachta saoithe gan meabhran.

It has not been translated into English in the limerick form.

His adversary McGrath, never at a loss for words, replied almost at once.

(It was translated into English freely, as follows, long after his death.)

> O'Tuomy you boast yourself handy
> At selling good ale and bright brandy
> But the fact is, your liquor
> Makes everyone sicker,
> I tell you that, I your friend, Andy.

This was followed by five additional verses, all rendered into English and all maintaining the limerick rhythm.

O'Tuomy died in the city of Limerick in 1775, aged sixty-nine—McGrath sometime later, rather mysteriously. In spite of the Oxford English Dictionary and the Oxford Companion, the place of the Maigue poets in history is secure.

A ceremonial side trip to the treaty stone commemorating the pact violated by the British in the Siege of 1690–91 was necessary before Mr. Tobin deposited me and my luggage at the Limerick rail station. Tralee now lay only about sixty miles to the southwest, but the train followed a semi-circular course that must have covered more than a hundred miles, a trip punctuated by a number of long, inexplicable stops. Finally arrived in Tralee, after a full day of effort, I was surprised to find the station completely dark at an hour well past dusk; still, everyone seemed to be going about his business normally. My taxi threaded its way through a totally blacked-out town, with the shops open for business in murky candlelight. All the towns-people behaved routinely.

I was well aware, before my visit, that this is the oldest, most undeveloped part of the island, where peat is still used for heating; where marriages—though presumably made in Heaven—are arranged here on earth, with the bride often never seeing her husband-to-be until the wedding; where it is still risking a court case of substance to place twelve eggs in a circle in a farmer's field, thereby bringing him unremitting bad luck. But I was unprepared for this Stygian atmosphere.

It could not, I reasoned, be a matter of war having been declared suddenly, precipitating a blackout, for the headlamps on the cars were not dimmed. The possibility of an electrical workers' strike never occurred to me, though I had several times experienced in France a few of these guerrillalike operations in which the current was cut for a few hours without warning, as a reminder to the officials of the power companies of the workers' grievances.

Driving toward my hotel just outside the town of Tralee, I couldn't bring myself to ask the driver if they had never heard of electricity in the area, not wanting to appear the overcoddled foreigner sneering at the simplicity of life in this faraway corner of the world.

When I reached my hotel, a low-slung modern building, and found a reception room lighted only by two small candles, my astonishment was profound. Before long, of course, I had the answer to the puzzle, and in the suddenly brilliant light when the electricity came on, I could begin to take stock of my surroundings.

The town of Tralee lies at the base of the heretofore little-known Dingle Peninsula; it is a compact community of old stone houses and shops, remindful of similar towns in northern Nova Scotia and in the farther reaches of the South Island of New Zealand. In Dingle town, not far from the tip of the peninsula that bears its name, the distinctive odor of burning peat permeates the atmosphere, an odor that evoked instant images of Antigonish, Nova Scotia, and an unidentified town near Christ Church, New Zealand. These three far-flung places have now acquired, in the inner recesses of my memory, a kinship that will never be dissolved.

I have called it the *heretofore* little-known Dingle Peninsula for, thanks to a film named *Ryan's Daughter*, featuring the stark beauty of this part of the country, the area has achieved a certain recognition among a particular group of filmgoers. David Lean, the accomplished and meticulous director, spent more than two years on the peninsula working on the film, employing many of the local inhabitants in an assortment of jobs including performing as extras and working in the crew. It is apparent after a few conversations that the filming of *Ryan's Daughter* was easily the biggest event hereabout since the Spanish Armada's bullion ship sank off the western tip at land's-end. (Some adventurous English divers penetrated the hull a few years back and surfaced with various souvenirs. A ship picked them up in the deep of night on one of the uninhabited Blasket Islands just off the peninsula, and the local skeptics are convinced they made off with a fair amount of bullion they never mentioned.)

Proud of their land and its location, the locals enjoy telling one that Slea

Head at the southwestern tip is the closest point in Ireland to the United States, and that this is where Europe begins. In a reference I only dimly recall, Sacheverell Sitwell wrote of the western end of Ireland being the edge of the world, beyond which stretches only the mighty Atlantic.

Both he and the locals seem to have overlooked the Blasket Islands, a group of half a dozen currently uninhabited bits of earth lying just off Slea Head. If the Blaskets, not to mention the great hulk of Greenland, are to be disqualified because they are islands, how does Ireland—itself, of course, an island—qualify as Europe proper? This bit of Jesuitical reasoning escapes me.

This is presumably just another facet of the chauvinism that pervades Ireland. On reflection, most island nations tend to be extremely nationalistic —England among them—an attitude fostered by the insular life of its citizens. I am reminded of that unforgettable headline in the London *Daily Mail* some years ago when a heavy fog over the channel made all transportation across it by sea or by air impossible. The *Mail*'s head read: "Fog over Channel. Continent Cut Off."

Even in Tralee, considered a good-sized town by Dingle standards, the feeling of being out of touch with the world is with one constantly. The radio—when the electrical workers permit one to listen—concerns itself chiefly with news of the region, occasionally with Irish national news, and almost never with anything that may be happening beyond the limits of the island. Once, while shaving, I thought I heard a short sentence to the effect that there was some sort of trouble in Greece involving a curfew, but the announcer did not elaborate.

The newspapers are even more chauvinistic, if that is possible. Throughout my recent stay I read no Washington news, even though there were some scandalous revelations being made there at the time. For that matter I saw no international news to speak of; in spite of Ireland's membership in the European Common Market community, an Irish reader seems interested only in what happens in Ireland. The only U.S. item I saw was a front-page picture of Senator Edward Kennedy and the son whose leg had been amputated some time before. There was no real reason for the use of the picture at that time, but then the Kennedys have always been big news in Ireland and doubtless always will be.

As to Irish literature, David Marcus sums it up neatly: "To produce stories of vibrant authenticity they had only to write about themselves. This, too, suits them perfectly because an Irishman is obsessed with Irishness. You will not find the main stream of Irish literature releasing even the tiniest rivulet of writing about the outside, non-Irish world."

All this gave me the curious sensation of being somehow "outside" the world. For those who want to "get away from it all" without having to resort to outer space, this may well be the perfect way to do so—and a very agreeable way it is, too. What better system for relaxing than to return to the hotel for a bracing tea and a good read on the lively debate on why the election posters haven't yet been removed from the lampposts in town. Of course, the undeclared war in northern Ireland was a daily story, but somehow the troubles in northern Ireland seemed rather more remote on the Dingle Peninsula than it had in the United States.

Tralee, a typically Irish community of fourteen thousand, is the largest town in County Kerry, whose attractions also include the lakes of Killarney and the 110-mile tour that is known, even abroad, as the Ring of Kerry. It's a quiet town that changes little; originally the chief seat of the Desmond clan, it passed—with its Great Castle—from the Desmond to the Denny family. After a siege lasting six months in 1641, the garrison of Tralee Castle surrendered to the Irish forces. Then, after being rebuilt the castle was reduced to ruins in the later Willamite wars.

The area directly surrounding Tralee is well endowed with golf courses, modest-sized mountains to climb, and a country racecourse, which unfortunately holds only a very limited number of meetings each year. Fishing, both fresh- and salt-water, is unexcelled.

As the "gateway to the Dingle Peninsula," Tralee is the focal point for a certain amount of coming and going to and from the western tip of land at Slea Head. Its most renowned inhabitant—even more famous than Roger Bresnahan, who emigrated to the United States, became a major-league catcher, and is credited with the invention of shin guards—was a local girl named Mary O'Connor, in whose honor a certain William Mulchinock wrote a musical love-lament, which he called "The Rose of Tralee." The true story concerns a local youth, smitten with Mary's charms, who went off to the United States to make his fortune, succeeded, and returned to his one love in Tralee, only to encounter, on his arrival, her funeral procession winding down the road. A very sad song indeed.

It is still played and sung regularly in every Irish bar from Tralee itself to Boston, New York, and points west. It came around without fail at the cabaret at my hotel on the outskirts of Tralee, and on my return to the United States I walked into a bar-restaurant in Ardmore, County Montgomery, Pennsylvania, to the strains of the same song, sung by an unmistakably Irish tenor. Thanks to its popularization in the United States by singer John McCormack, "The Rose of Tralee" has taken its place among the hardy perennials which include "San Antonio Rose," "Mexicali Rose," "The One Rose," "The Yellow Rose of Texas," and for that matter "Sweet Rosie O'Grady," "The Rose of Washington Square," "Rose-Marie," and even "La Vie en Rose."

The home of composer Mulchinock, Cloghers House at nearby Ballymullen, has the same standing and attraction for visitors as the film stars' homes in Beverly Hills, and is approached with much the same reverence. These days, more than a century after the song was written, the town of Tralee annually holds an international Rose of Tralee contest for girls who are Irish or of Irish descent. The Rose of Tralee for 1974 was Miss Margaret Flaherty, of Norfolk, Virginia.

Towns are often more interesting to browse in than large cities, since every place one may want to explore is closer at hand. After visiting a number of shops, the post office, a few well-stocked bookstores, and the principal hotel in town and its well-patronized bar, I dropped by to see a local printer and photographer named Padraig, his wife, and a number of their children. Every square inch of space in the living room of their town house was taken up with maps, photographs, printing work, and a shale of assorted like material. (The press, I understand, was in the basement.)

Padraig, a chain smoker who uses the hearth as his ashtray, has a finely chiseled aristocratic head, but he would not talk about his own antecedents. When asked about the background of this part of the world, however, he began with the flat assertion that it was the ancient Egyptians who had first settled in this area. "When you go out on the peninsula, just look at some of the profiles in Dingle town. Exact replicas of the heads of the Pharaohs you'll see in the good museums. Exactly the same noses, the same foreheads. There's no question about it. And since most Dingle persons don't marry outsiders, that classic head will continue here through the ages."

A connoisseur of sagas and an amateur archeologist, Padraig roused my appetite for a trip down the peninsula by describing the fine array of clohans (beehive-shaped buildings), Bronze Age stone forts, ogham stones, Celtic crosses, ancient stone churches and oratories, sheila-na-gigs (fertility symbols), dolmens (megalithic monuments), and assorted stones and mounds dating back to the paleolithic era.

"I don't know which route you plan to take," Padraig said, lighting a fresh cigarette from the expiring one, "but by making only a small detour you will find at Annagh quite a good piece of sculpture of a headless horseman —his head was never carved. And then in the valley Gleann-na-gealt you will come upon the Glen of Lunacy.

"In the third and fourth century," he continued with hardly a breath, "the going cure for lunacy was a residence of a certain period in the Glen. To live in the valley for one month and eat its watercress was often enough for a complete cure."

The secret of the cure? "A combination of the climate in the valley and the watercress, which contained traces of certain minerals."

More coffee was brought, and Padraig, warming to this discussion of the area he loves, plunged on: "You'll be wanting to go over the ridge—the spine of the peninsula—at Connors Pass. The view is not believable. And of course the tiny church at Gallarus, the oldest—seventh century—Christian church still standing as built. And the Gap of Dunlow.

"Out near Ventry you'll find a whole network of tarred roads that lead nowhere—just stop in the middle of a field. That was the result of a work program the government laid on at one time."

He was becoming a bit breathless by now, and he was smoking faster. "Out at the tip you may be lucky enough to see a chough or two—they're jet black birds with orange beaks and feet, and they're very nearly extinct. Around Dunquin is the only place you'll find any. What you *won't* see is the old Dingle Railroad, which ran from Dingle town back this way. Its track was only thirty inches wide, and it could never make the hills. The little railroad's instructions to passengers went like this: 'First-class passengers get out and walk; second-class passengers get out and push.' . . . God how I wish I were going with you, but I have a printing job I'm behind on and I must catch up on so you'll have to excuse me," he finished warmly, then pressed on me the names of various old residents in different towns and villages who would presumably regale me with some of their experiences, as well as some of the legends that have been passed down from generation to generation.

"You might take along some whiskey," he advised me. "It might help get the talk started. Offer them a little, but not too much," he said emphatically.

"By the way," he said, as I prepared to leave, "in parts of Dingle no English is spoken, particularly by the old folks." He offered no suggestions on how to overcome this obstacle. (Gaelic is not a dead language, but from the standpoint of general use it is not exactly robust—even though all street signs and many others are studiously bilingual.)

As I edged out toward the door, giving my thanks, he showed me some of his photographs of the peninsula's topography and one shot of a clohan, the beehive-shaped structure, that had been built a thousand years before Christ and was still in exactly the same condition as the day it was completed.

Fortified by an Irish coffee at the candlelit bar of the Benners Hotel in the heart of Tralee, I set off on my trip around the peninsula in an archeological frame of mind. Ireland is one of the few regions of Europe that missed occupation by the Romans; as a direct result, many ancient remains have survived in a state far more pristine than would otherwise have been possible. Besides having been denied the "advantages" of Roman occupation, Ireland alone among her British and European neighbors did not benefit from the industrialization process; thus, her streams and lakes are pollution-free, the countryside is more verdant, there is an absence of clouds of polluted smoke from industrial plants, and the air is as pure as one will find in any civilized country today.

There are still other differences between Ireland and its English and European neighbors. As is the case with many islands that are separated from the nearest land mass by a sizable body of water—New Zealand is a good example—the flora and fauna of the island bear little resemblance to those found in nearby countries. Irish plants and animals are not the same species as those in England; curiously, a plant group called Cantabrian, indigenous to Ireland, is related to a similar strain found in Spain, and a few North American plants are in evidence in Ireland.

Common English animals are not to be found in Ireland; there are of course no snakes on the Emerald Isle, but a variety of wood lice exists that is native to the Pyrenees, as well as a small fresh-water sponge that flourishes in North America.

The remains of such animals as the mammoth reindeer and the giant Irish deer dating back to the paleolithic era have been uncovered in cave excavations, but the beginnings of Irish civilization may be placed in the Mesolithic Age.

Just who it was who inhabited Ireland during the late Stone Age, the Bronze Age, and the Early Iron Age has still not been established. (My friend Padraig's theory about the Egyptians as the first settlers has not been universally accepted.) The sect commonly known as the Druids is popularly supposed to have populated parts of Ireland in ancient times, a belief strengthened by the numerous dolmens (a form of megalithic tomb, consisting of a heavy flat capstone supported by three or more stone uprights); they are also known as Druids' altars, and are especially prevalent in the wild western part of the country, which seemed to be the center of Irish prehistory. But sometime before the arrival of Saint Patrick and the introduction of Christianity, the Celts had drifted onto the lush green island from mid-Europe and grouped themselves into five kingdoms.

When the Christians gained control of the island, some of the priests— my friend Padraig had told me—simply suggested that the Celts change the names of their gods and unite them all in one. To make the transition to Christianity easier, many Catholic bishops allowed Celtic crosses and monuments to stand—sometimes within the new Christian church. Even a sheila-na-gig (fertility symbol) was permitted to remain in the nave of one Catholic church.

My driver knew the locations of some of the more celebrated sights on Dingle, but he was no match for Padraig, who was of course not with us. We had driven some distance from Tralee before we were to come on the first clohan, but then the ancient stone structures and markers seemed to proliferate. A Celtic cross, with the circle ringing the point where the two

An ogham stone

Stone fort, County Kerry

stone spars met, bore an inscription in an unfamiliar alphabet; later in Dingle town I was told it said simply "This cross was built by Fergil."

A few miles farther on we saw our first ogham stone, with inscriptions composed of combinations of vertical lines, up to five in a group, bisected by a horizontal line—bearing a strong resemblance to the system used by prisoners today to keep track of the days served. This form of writing dates from the very beginnings of Christianity and is peculiar to the southwestern part of the island.

The view from the spine of the peninsula—in all directions—was as spectacular as Padraig had promised, and on the way down to Dingle town we came upon one of a number of stone forts we were to find scattered over the area. Although the island did not experience wars on the scale of the ones raging on the continent from medieval times onward, Ireland did suffer its share of invasions: by the Vikings, the Danes, the Normans, and of course the English.

Lying at the foot of Mount Brandon (all of 3,127 feet), Dingle town is a cozy seaport overlooking Dingle Bay, just twelve miles from the western tip of the peninsula on its southern shore. Dingle was the principal port of County Kerry during the years when trade with Spain flourished; I was reminded of Padraig's admonition to keep an eye out for Spanish tiles of the fifteenth and sixteenth centuries, similar, I supposed, to those I had seen in Granada, of Moorish design.

Considerably smaller than Tralee, Dingle town can be traversed and inspected in short order. We stopped at several shops, including an excellent bookstore, with native authors well represented, where I made several purchases, followed by a sandwich-and-bitter lunch at a local pub. Asked about the legends of the area, the barman took the popular stand that they had been preserved for the ages by being recited orally from generation to generation.

This is the belief shared by the late Gerard Murphy, a scholar of Irish myths and sagas; he held that the legends preserved in written form originally were traceable to the oral recitations, and cited as "proof" the fact that the stories in these manuscripts seem to peter out toward the end, an indication to Professor Murphy that the person reciting, in the original version, was simply growing tired of talking.

Opposed to this view is Professor James Carney, who believed that the early Irish sagas have their roots not in ancient oral tradition but in the literature of the period in the literal sense of the word—composed by Irish monks well acquainted with the classical and Christian literature of the early days of Ireland and only to a small degree based on oral tradition.

This debate on the origins of Irish literature and legend—a matter of some concern even to the average Irishman, who is acutely aware of the background of his native language and culture—is still raging in the universities and in the pubs of this stimulating island. Professor Murphy was so biased in his view that he regarded "the manuscript versions of the tales as recorded lore, any artistry in the stories he attributed to the oral story-tellers, any defect to the monastic scribes."

In support of this contention, Professor Murphy added: "The stories are very imperfectly narrated in the manuscripts and not infrequently in a way that definitely suggests recording from an oral source"; and, "a poorly-narrated manuscript version is often a mere summary of incidents rather than a tale meant to hold the interest of an audience by its artistry."

Replying to Professor Murphy's categorical position, Professor Gearóid S. Mac Eoin is equally positive: "The theory that these stories, in any form, were written down from dictation must be abandoned. It is altogether un-necessary, for there were in the monasteries, from the eighth century on, men well versed in historical traditions. These could have written the sagas in the form in which we have them without recourse to a narrator."

Professor Proinsias Mac Cana supports the latter view in an essay in *Irish Literary Tradition*: "It is abundantly clear that they [the Christian clerics] were far from being mere amanuenses in the service of oral tradition."

In an attempt to sum up this troublesome question, Professor Cecile O'Rahilly, in an introduction to a new edition of *Táin Bó Cúailnge from the Book of Leinster*, ponders the question of oral tradition in the heroic saga in general with special reference to the national epic, the *Táin*. She notes that heroic traditions preserved by scribes of a later age are inevitably influenced by the literary attainments of the compilers, a rather self-evident conclusion. "If, however," she says finally, "we may postulate, as most scholars believe we can, a highly developed oral art of saga-recitation before the stories took literary form, then despite any influence on the saga-writers' technique or matter from written sources, we may conclude that the inspiration of the sagas is ultimately oral."

If all this professorial backing and filling seems to be making too much of an issue of a small point, be advised that in Eire today this controversy is still very much alive and a matter of great importance to the average man. It is also advisable not to make light of the *Táin* within the hearing of a native Irishman.

There are two principal versions of the classic *Táin Bó Cúailnge*, one mainly Old Irish, based on ninth-century oral tellings of the tale, and another Middle Irish, known as the Book of Leinster version, which—Professor Murphy points out—is an almost purely literary composition based on the manuscript form of the mainly Old Irish version, probably first written about the year 1100 and compiled in the Book of Leinster in 1160.

The mainly Old Irish version seems to consist of two Old Irish texts first written down in the early ninth century and, in the eleventh century, "clumsily joined together by a compiler" (Professor Murphy's adverb). Certain episodes were presumably added by the compiler in Middle Irish, mostly relating to single combat between some of the heroic characters.

But in most respects the two versions of the *Táin* are similar: the Old Irish version more natural and direct, the later manuscript text better organized and more literary.

The basic tale of the *Táin Bó Cúailnge* relates how a single youth held up an army of Connacht invaders while awaiting the arrival of his fellow Ulidians, who were delayed because they were suffering from the "nine days' illness." Some anthropologists equate this malaise with an ancient couvade ceremony, in which men of some races took to their beds while their wives were in childbirth. The Connacht king asks an exile from the Ulidian forces who is guiding the invaders, "What manner of man is this that can inflict injuries on an army?"—a question that conveniently enables the narrator to explore the boyhood deeds—already heroic—of the brave youth, Cú Chulainn.

As the saga meanders along, similarities in concept have been noted with primitive Indo-European beliefs and also with the Greek *Iliad*. The *Táin* is the best known of countless heroic sagas, all pretty much in the same pattern. But after the last of the Irish Kings, the fashion changed from heroic sagas to romantic tales, and the Irish literature of today began to take form.

The lore of the early Irish romantic epics centers about a character named Fionn Mac Cumhall (or Umall), and of his son Ossian, whose name is now used to identify the entire cycle. Many embellishments had been grafted onto the original folk tales about Fionn, notably by Scotland's James Macpherson, who in the eighteenth century published his *Fingal* and *Temora*, supposedly translated from epic poems written by Ossian in the third or fourth century. But Macpherson's epics seem to have been largely figments of his imagination, although loosely based on the sagas of Fionn and his friends. At least they attracted a select audience of enthusiasts including Napoleon and Goethe. (In our own time, of course, we have books of the same type, like *The Day of the Jackal*.)

Indeed, in the seventh and eighth centuries Irish scholars fashioned a history of Ireland modeled on biblical history and on that of Greece and Rome. This "Irish synthetic history"—a fabric tracing Irish origins all the way back to Adam—ultimately included mention of Fionn; today, however, the synthetic history is recognized for what it is, and Fionn's activities are drawn from the original traditions.

It is now widely held that Fionn and his loved one are the Celtic progenitors of Tristan and Isolde, and Fionn is credited with being the first lover to test the suitability of a maiden to be his wife by plying her with riddles. Professor Murphy points out that the frequency of the elopement theme in Irish tradition has convinced scholars of the Celtic origin of the Tristan legend.

In the eleventh and twelfth centuries Irish balladry blossomed; one of the earliest was supposedly addressed to Saint Patrick, some say by Ossian's followers or one of the other members of Fionn's Fiana. An eleventh-century Cú Chulainn ballad delivered to Ireland's greatest saint has served as a model for Fionn ballads generally.

The early modern ballads, noted for their poetic excellence, are directly descended from the romantic Fionn tales. Narrative in form, they may be classed under headings such as ballads of magic visitors, invader ballads, ballads of internecine strife, pursuings and rescues, elopements, foreign expeditions, monster slayings, and hunts.

Poems of the Fionn cycle, written of course in Gaelic, flourished in both Ireland and Scotland, during the sixteenth and seventeenth centuries. Even today Gaelic speakers still pay their respects to the Early Modern Ossianic ballads of the Fionn cycle, as their ancestors did in the fifteenth century.

Today, even in the farther reaches of the Dingle Peninsula, it is difficult to pass many hours without some discussion of the glories of Irish literature and tradition, without some reference to those great names—as familiar to the Irishman in the road as the names of automobile manufacturers are to the American in the street—names like Jonathan Swift, Burke, Goldsmith, Sheridan, Thomas Moore, George Moore, Oscar Wilde, Shaw, Yeats, Synge, and of course Stephens, O'Casey, Joyce, and Behan. And such gifted latter-day writers as Frank O'Connor and Sean O'Faolain are known and celebrated the length and breadth of the land.

Our road to the peninsula's tip took us past some Bronze Age forts, as well as some square forts—round walls, with beehive-shaped buildings—built about 475, at the time of the early Christians. The Gallarus Oratory, a diminutive church whose interior measures 15 feet by 10 feet, stands like a lonely sentinel in the middle of a field, where it has maintained its watch for more than one thousand two hundred years. One must stoop to enter the tiny church—its entranceway is only 5 feet 7 inches high—and its interior is no place for a claustrophobe to spend more than a few minutes. The most remarkable feature of the oratory is its construction of unmortared stones, carefully fitted together in such a way that the building is completely watertight, as it has been since it was first erected on this Dingle plain. It is the only remaining corbel-built structure on a rectangular base, and was placed at such an angle that the rain could not penetrate the interior. If there were a group of pocket-sized wonders of the world, the Gallarus Oratory would certainly be among them.

It is from this area along the shores of sparkling Dingle Bay that the inhabitants today still stoutly believe that their own Saint Brandon sailed on a voyage of discovery that ended in America, sometime during the sixth century, thus antedating the achievements of Leif Ericson and Christopher Columbus by a good margin.

The dramatic view of the sea from the coastal road suddenly included our first sight of the Blasket Islands, six sizable chunks of currently uninhabited islands that rise abruptly out of the sea just west of the tip of the Dingle Peninsula. But they were not always devoid of life. For many years they were home for a modest number of families—totaling 150 to 200 persons—

Gallarus Oratory

that comprised, in the words of E. M. Forster, a "neolithic civilization" all its own. The Manchester *Guardian* has stated firmly that the Blasket Islands have contributed more to the great body of Irish literature than any other area comparable in size.

After a careful sampling of the wares of the excellent bookshop in Dingle town, I purchased two Blasket Island works that have become classics in Ireland: *Twenty Years a-Growing*, by Maurice O'Sullivan, and *The Islandman* by Tomás Ó Crohan, both published by Oxford in English in translation from the original Gaelic. Even in translation, the spirit and sensitivity of the islanders in their rough surroundings, and their encounters with the "mainlanders" on the peninsula, come through to the reader with considerable clarity.

Synge—Forster points out in an introduction to the former work—described the island life from the outside, "and very sympathetically, but I know of no other instance where it has itself become vocal, and addressed modernity." This, then, is "an account of neolithic civilization from the inside."

Like O'Sullivan, Ó Crohan was born and bred on the Great Blasket, the largest of the clutch of islands and jagged rocks that make up the Blasket group.

"I was born," he wrote, "on St. Thomas's day in the year 1856. I can recall being at my mother's breast, for I was four years old when I was weaned.

"My father was a middle-sized man, stout and strong, [whose] kin were from Dunquin. He married into the Island. My mother's people were from Ventry. They were both willing to take one another. They hadn't the way that some couples have that makes you want to take a stick to them to make them marry! They settled down in a little cabin to live on the produce of the sea, and they had a bit of land, too; and both of them were well gifted to make the best profit out of sea and land. There were no asses in the Island in those days, only a creel on the back of every man—and of every woman, too—that is to say, every woman that wasn't a pet or a sly knave who would rather starve than work.

"My father was a marvelous fisherman and great man for work. He was a stonemason and boat's captain, and handy at every trade. He often did a hand's turn for other folk, for in those days most of them were little better than a drove of asses in a field. It was a great year for fish, that year. . . ."

O'Sullivan's mother died when he was six months old, so he was shipped to the mainland, to Dingle, to spend the first years of his life, early in this century. Returned to the island and reunited with his father as a young schoolboy, Maurice had a good working knowledge of English, and was baffled by the Gaelic of the island folk. But he soon picked up the language and learned to love his native heath.

"It was a fine, calm, sunny day," he recalled in his book. "My father had gone at the sparrow's chirp, lobster-fishing to Inish-vick-illaun in the west and was not to return till Saturday.

"'Would you like to go up to the hill with me?' said my grandfather, putting the straddle on the ass to bring home a load of turf.

"'I would,' said I.

"We went up the road, my grandfather with a stick in one hand, the other holding his pipe in his mouth for lack of teeth.

"When we reached the top of the road we had a fine view between us and the horizon to the south—the Great Skellig and Skellig Michael clearly to be seen, Iveragh stretched out in the sunshine to the southeast, not a puff of air nor a cloud in the sky, herring-gulls in hundreds around the trawlers which were fishing out in the bay, larks warbling sweetly over the heather, young lambs dancing and playing tricks on one another like school children let out in the middle of the day.

"We walked on until we reached Hill Head: 'Look where your father is lobster-fishing,' said my grandfather, pointing west towards the Inish. 'Oh, it is grand to be up in that island on such a day as this. Do you see the house?'

"I stopped and looked. 'I do not,' said I.

"'Look carefully at the middle of the island and you will see the sun sparkling on something.'

"'Oh! Is that it? I dare say you were often there.'

"'My sorrow, I spent a great part of my life going out to it, and it is little the shoe or stocking was worn in those days, not even a drop of tea to be had, nor any thought of it.'

"'What used you to have?'

"'Indian meal, oatmeal, potatoes and fine fish from the sea; and they left their marks on the people. Little sickness or infection came to them. Arra, man, it is the way with them now, they have shoes on them as soon as they can crawl, not to mention all the clothes they wear, and for all that they are weak, and will be. Would you believe that it is many a day I left the house at sunrise, myself and Stephen O'Dunlevy, Pad Mor, and Shaun O'Carna, for we were the crew of the one boat, dear God bless their souls, they are all on the way of truth now.'

"As he spoke, the tears fell from the old man and he stopped for a while as if to put from him the catch at his heart.

"'Well,' said he, drawing a long sigh, 'would you believe it, we would have nothing on leaving the house but five or six cold potatoes and we would not come home until the blackness and blindness of the night? Where is the man who would stand such hardship now? Upon my word there is none.'

"'I doubt it. And what need you to be doing in the run of the day?'

"'Killing seals and hunting rabbits. And if so, my boy, we used to be envied when we came home with our spoils, for I tell you, little Maurice, there were many here at the time who could not stand that hardship.'"

And like all the islanders, both authors finally—late in life—left the island to spend their last years in the easier atmosphere of the peninsula. (Some of the islanders emigrated to the United States.) But the bulk of the authors' lives was spent on the Great Blasket, in tiny houses built into the hill to protect them from the powerful winds that regularly swept across the island. Here they learned about life at its most primitive: with only the clothes on their back in most cases, and living on mutton, home-baked bread, and when available lobster, fish, and seal meat. But to provide a family with a meal a day was a constant battle with the elements, usually hostile.

The language of the islands was almost exclusively Gaelic; only a handful were bilingual. Like the language, the life was largely medieval. The pastimes were singing, dancing, storytelling, and conversation. The dances were the hornpipe, the jig, the four-hand reel, various country figures, and a descendant of the quadrille. The literature, preserved by oral tradition, was made up of ancient legends, some older than *Beowulf*, poems and songs of the seventeenth and eighteenth centuries, and an abundance of folklore.

Both O'Sullivan and Ó Crohan drew their inspiration for the writing of their books from a translation of Maxim Gorki's *My Childhood* that found its way to the island, and both were motivated purely by a desire to provide a record of life on the islands for posterity.

During the great Irish famine of 1840–50 the population of the islands doubled, as the peasants fled the interior of the Emerald Isle and made for the coasts in search of food. By 1951 only five families numbering twenty-one persons remained on the Great Blasket, the last of the islands to be inhabited. All have since left.

Today, standing on a hill near the tip of the peninsula and looking out over the nearer Blaskets, I found it difficult to believe that life of any kind had ever existed on their bleak, mountainous expanse; actually, I learned, sheep ranged the hills in some numbers on all but the smaller peaked eruptions of earth rising out of the sea.

Here at the tip and in Dunquin, a tiny village north of Slea Head, the feeling of isolation is overwhelming, but it is felt—if to a slightly lesser degree —in all parts of this primitive southwestern area of Ireland.

In Dunquin I looked up an acquaintance of Padraig's named Seumas, a weathered patriarch who seemed wistfully interested in the offer of a little whiskey, but finally turned it down in favor of a pint of bitter at a local pub.

"Change?" he echoed, in a thin, reedy voice. "Faith, and this is God's own country, and why by all that's holy would He be after wantin' to change it?"

On a high bluff overlooking Dingle Bay and, beyond, the limitless Atlantic, a neat but flimsy uninhabited schoolhouse—built for the filming of *Ryan's Daughter*—provides a perfect lookout point for an impressive view of the majestic sweep of land and sea. It wasn't hard to imagine the bay alive with *curraghs*, the fragile canvas-bottomed boats that skimmed like frisky water bugs across the phosphorescent surface with their cargoes of fishermen and freshly caught fish.

And the land itself at this extreme end of the peninsula—a few windswept mountainous humps and a series of bluffs hanging over the sea—has not changed since the time when refugees from Ireland's interior, caught in the famous potato famine of the mid-nineteenth century, made their way along the peninsula on the way to the sea and to the Blasket Islands, where several varieties of fish and seal meat could be substituted for the edible tuber that has long been a staple of the Irishman's diet.

The grassy highlands of the Dingle Peninsula are no less green than the well-watered "wet" green that is a trademark of the Emerald Isle; the area is more sparsely settled than most, even in Ivernia, the district that comprises the whole of the two counties of Cork and Kerry.

The topography of this corner of Ireland is craggy, but the soil itself is fertile. At every hand, I was advised that life is a hard one for the inhabitants of the Dingle Peninsula, but thanks to the determination they are born with they are surviving. The natives have long since become accustomed to the eternal beauty of their land and sea, but to the visitor the luminous quality of the colors of earth and water in the sharp, clear, northern light provides a sense of very special pleasure. In *Ryan's Daughter* many moviegoers considered the scenery—faithfully reproduced in color—the star of the film.

Returning to Tralee along the peninsula's idyllic southern coast, we passed still more ring forts and megaliths and arrived at my hotel, the Earl of Desmond, a modern inn surrounded by cows and sheep, to find its banquet hall occupied by the guests at a wedding reception. Reflecting on Seumas's sentiments, I found it no shock to discover that the dances the wedding guests were performing, with great gusto, were the jig and the four-hand reel.

At dinner that night the serving girl, a rosy-cheeked colleen, heaped more vegetables and potatoes on my plate—certainly no trace of a famine now —than I had ever seen in one place before. The Irish diners on all sides of me qualified as the heartiest eaters I had observed in any part of Europe. Yet they seemed in excellent physical condition—the result no doubt of a goodly amount of exercise daily. For the descendants of Brian Boru, who defeated the Vikings on the island in 1014, are an active race—even the old-timers are still busily working the soil at advanced ages that would give retired American office workers a start.

What with Eire's uncrowded, unpolluted, hospitable atmosphere, the time for leaving the old sod is a sad one. More than one departing visitor at Shannon Airport has been literally moved to tears at the prospect of ending an acquaintance with Ireland.

Even though the leprechauns seemed to be in hiding or on strike along with the electrical workers, the aura of the supernatural was always present. Long after the plane's wheels have left the strip at Shannon Airport, thoughts of Ireland keep flooding back into one's consciousness. There is no other corner of Europe I know that possesses the same haunting, lyrical, soul-cleansing quality.

Maastricht

Maastricht is a restful place, a city truly representative of the Old World, with its own distinctive background. A promised land for enthusiasts of barge- and small-boat travel, this well-watered terrain is irrigated principally by the river Maas. Like Egypt's Nile, it rises in the south and flows north, making all manner of liquid connections with canals and other streams.

Maastricht is a small steel-engraving of a town, precise, meticulously designed, perfectly proportioned, and containing a wealth of carefully executed detail.

$\mathcal{T}$here are precious few parts of the world left that have not been discovered by indomitable tourists in search of the last unspoiled spot on earth. Even the New Hebrides, an idyllic backwater in the South Pacific thought of by some as paradise, by others as hell on earth, is now the seat of the most modern, twenty-first-century-style hotel, replete with all the trappings of luxury living, set in the heart of one of the most primitive societies still extant on this globe.

In Europe especially—long the favorite continental playground for travelers —it is virtually impossible to uncover a small corner where one is in no danger of encountering one's next-door neighbor from Oshkosh, Wisconsin, or Sausalito, California. But there is just such a charming, absorbing area only an hour's drive from Brussels, a slightly longer trip from Cologne, and what is really a short jaunt from Paris. Further, it is truly a historic area, featuring some lovely countryside, several incomparable art museums (although not of the gigantic variety), a small but unique natural history museum, some dazzling old churches, a great restaurant—one of the best in Europe, in my view, and certainly a candidate for the best outside France —and the most fascinating, frightening, and unbelievable complex of interlocking caves I could have imagined in my most vivid dream.

This is the Maasland, a region composed of portions of the Netherlands, Belgium, and Germany, where the people speak a variety of Dutch dialects, a French dialect with a Celtic and German character, known as Walloon, and of course German. Not exactly an undiscovered part of the world, but certainly one not yet inundated by waves of tourists.

At its center is the charming, comfortable city of Maastricht, the oldest and most southern community in the Netherlands. Lying in the eastern end of the country, flanked by Belgium on one side and Germany on the other, Maastricht is not Dutch as Amsterdam and Rotterdam are Dutch; there is a distinct Latin strain that sets its people and its culture apart from the rest of the Netherlands. Its history, going back to the Roman occupation, includes lengthy periods in which the land was settled successively by several tribes of Franks—Charlemagne's principal residence for years was at Aachen, now in West Germany, just thirty kilometers away.

From his palace, he instigated an emphasis on cultural life that had lain dormant since the Roman days; he had, in fact, long dreamed of reviving Roman civilization on a grand scale. This Carolingian renaissance left its mark on all of Maasland, its art and culture generally—and gave them a distinction not shared by other medieval movements.

This imposing chronology has left its imprint on the Maastricht of today. One feels oneself moving about in an ancient city still, in spite of the occasional modern building; but these inevitable touches of the twentieth century are never obtrusive, never placed in a context that might destroy the symmetry of the centuries.

I first happened on Maastricht, on the banks of the Maas, some seventeen years ago, after a drive across the Netherlands from Amsterdam and Rotterdam; the ostensible purpose of this trip to the lesser-known, inland part of Holland was a visit to the Kröller-Müller Museum, a low-slung, modern structure dedicated chiefly to the works of Vincent van Gogh and set in an immense, 22,500-acre national preserve where in some areas stags, wild boar, and other unusual fauna roam freely. The Hooge Veluwe is a park of matchless beauty and repose, located at Otterlo, near Arnhem. In addition to a modest collection of other masters (Picasso, Braque, Mondriaan, Seurat), the pale, unblemished walls of the Kröller-Müller are devoted principally to the works, paintings and drawings, of van Gogh—272 of them at the time of my visit, including some of his greatest. This handsome collection, housed in the midst of this wild but carefully manicured wooded terrain, is the result of the foresightedness of Mrs. H. Kröller-Müller, who had the good sense to listen to the advice of a certain H. P. Bremmer—to buy van Goghs at a time when the deceased artist was an unknown and his paintings sold for anything the buyer cared to pay. Today, there is a newer temple dedicated to van Gogh in Amsterdam, but to me—and I'm sure to other van Gogh devotees—the Kröller-Müller in its giant park is the true shrine.

Continuing on from Arnhem, it was an agreeable drive south to Maastricht, a city that took me completely by surprise. I have been promising myself to return for all the intervening years, for it is one of my favorite places of its type in all of Europe, and finally—recently—I kept my promise.

Unlike the larger cities of the Low Countries to the west and those of Germany to the east, where the life tends to be more hectic, Maastricht is a restful place, a city truly representative of the Old World, with its own distinctive background, zoological as well as cultural. And its people are refreshingly alive—friendly, quick-witted, communicative, and buoyant. Some ascribe the undeniably more relaxed mood of Maastricht, compared with other Dutch centers, to its extreme southerly position, a quality shared by southern cities in many countries.

This low-lying land, which was the bottom of the sea going back 70 million to 140 million years ago, has been occupied at least twenty times in its more recent history, including forces of Romans, Franks of several varieties, Spaniards, Austrians, Dutch, Belgians, French, Germans, and finally Americans (in 1944). The philosophical Maaslanders became indifferent to this succession of occupants, and in fact even today pay little regard to the borders that separate the area into parts of Belgium, Germany, and the Netherlands.

A promised land for enthusiasts of barge and small-boat travel, this well-watered terrain is irrigated principally by the river Maas, which is called the Meuse farther south, in Belgium and in France. Like Egypt's Nile, the Meuse/Maas rises in the south and flows north, making all manner of liquid connections with canals and other streams on its way to the sea. This is sometimes referred to as the Scheldt/Maas/Rhine delta. In the primeval ooze of prehistory, this region was a playground for reptilians like the Mosasaurus; even in less ancient times it furnished an agreeable locale for duck-billed platypuses, bears, marmots, tapirs, monkeys, beavers, elephants with giant tusks, rhinoceri with several horns, and other species no longer found in this part of the world as well as those long since extinct.

An exception to the unrelieved flatness, a hill called St. Pietersberg (140 meters high) contains the record of this prehistoric life; in its interior, in a giant honeycomb of underground passages, rest the fossilized remains of sharks' teeth and the petrified bones of reptiles. Lying just south of Maastricht, this tableland of marlstone, a form of sandstone, was formed some 150 million years ago, as a result of the accumulation of the remains of shellfish and other crustacea.

The head of a fossilized Mosasaurus, or Meuse lizard, whose overall length was twenty meters, was taken back to France by Napoleon, that collector extraordinaire, in exchange for six hundred bottles of good wine. This story is regarded by many as apocryphal, as Napoleon rarely gave away anything, much less six hundred bottles of good French wine. Some say it was two hundred bottles. Well, maybe fifty.

At any rate the great French leader paid a visit to the cave system of St. Pietersberg on July 31, 1803, a date duly inscribed in the sandstone, along with the names of other distinguished visitors: Don Alvarez de Toledo (in 1570), the Duke of Parma (1579), Sir Walter Scott (1840), Frederick Lamont (undated), and during World War II the well-traveled, ever-present Kilroy.

The caves of Mount St. Peter, which now include more than twenty thousand intersecting passages, were described by the Roman historian Pliny in A.D. 50; he noted that besides affording shelter for soldiers and civilians alike the caves, with their soft but enduring walls of marlstone, were an unending source of building material—for the past two thousand years the local inhabitants have busied themselves sawing blocks of marl, for use in the construction of houses, churches, and fortifications.

About 1700 a fort was built on the north side of St. Peter's hill; it was connected to the caves by a spiral staircase, used by the troops of several nationalities when under siege.

My own visit to Mount St. Peter was made in the company of a qualified guide who has memorized the plan of the passages. He and his fellows continue meeting at regular periods to keep their memories jogged, for it is not difficult to lose one's way very quickly in the maze of seemingly identical paths.

Armed with a suddenly fragile-looking gas lamp, we moved into the total blackness and began inspecting some of the messages on the walls. The name of Don Alvarez de Toledo was barely decipherable in the limited circle of light, since the inscription is now positioned near the ceiling, the tunnels having been dug out considerably since 1570.

"Pilots and smugglers found these caves very handy," my Dutch guide told me. "You can walk right through to Belgium without meeting a customs guard. Or a soul. *If* you know the way," he added thoughtfully.

I asked if anyone had ever lost his way and failed to find an exit. "Oh yes indeed," he said mildly. "For one example, four monks entered in 1640 fixing the end of a thread at the entrance. But the thread broke." He paused to let the situation sink in. "They were found much later, starved, without any fingers."

We passed an ambitious charcoal sketch of the Crucifixion in the sandstone, an ominous conception in a shadowy location, and turned a corner into a passage that sloped downward. "Just to give you an idea of the feeling you would have," said the guide suddenly, "you stand here and I'll go back around the corner with the lamp." He retreated up the passage and turned the corner, leaving me standing in the pitch dark. There were no footfalls in the soft stone. After a moment I laughed self-consciously and said, rather loudly, that I could imagine the feeling, all right. But there was no reply. I started back up the path the guide had traveled, first stumbling into the

Caves of Mount St. Peter

tunnel wall, and finally made what I judged to be the corner. But there was no light, nothing but total blackness and absolute silence. I must admit to feeling slightly uneasy but assured myself that there must be some simple explanation. I recalled that before entering the caves I was told that the worst decision anyone who was lost could make was to move. So I nearly slid down the uneven path to approximately the position I thought I had last held when the guide left.

Still no light, not a pinpoint, and still no sound. "Hallo," I shouted. No reply. I stood absolutely still, flexing my fingers, and tried to contemplate my next move if the situation didn't change. A number of groups, I recalled having been told, could wander in just this section of the caves, the Zonne-berg, without ever encountering one another or even being aware of one another. Besides, for my visit the gates had been opened especially and the guide and I were the only ones in the underground network at this time, I reflected. There would be no groups going through until the following day sometime.

I heard a faint whoosh, and immediately recalled having been told that twelve varieties of bats, of the fifteen found in the Netherlands, inhabit the caves. As in battle, I found, in a situation like this one's senses operate at peak efficiency. I assessed the position and couldn't bring myself to believe that the guide, who had wanted me to see the caves so I could write about them, would simply abandon me, but I admit to a slight but growing feeling of unease as the minutes passed.

Finally, of course, the guide reappeared; the extra time, he explained, was to let the feeling really sink in. It certainly wasn't difficult to imagine the sense of helplessness if one were alone and lost in the caves.

During World War II it was estimated that some fifty thousand could find refuge from bombing and shelling in the caves. Plans were made to accommodate the local inhabitants, but the Germans didn't attack Maas-tricht. In preparation for an emergency, the Church of the Caves was dug out of the stone, with a row of stations of the cross stretching away into the dark. Two babies were born in the subterranean passages and later baptized at the church.

Farther on we came upon an area devoted to a mushroom culture, with water piped in; the constant temperature of 10 degrees Centigrade and the high humidity (90 percent) are ideal for the growing of the edible fungus, as well as the ghostly white cardon, a variety of artichoke, and the chicory plant.

"Here is where the Austrian mercenaries took refuge," my guide said, as we turned yet another corner. "Back in the eighteenth century the local powers hired Austrian and Italian soldiers to help them fight the French and others. Today, the NATO forces in Belgium have their eye on the caves for possible use in an emergency.

"When the Allies marched into Maastricht in September 1944, the people took to the caves again, once more without necessity. Some Americans know the caves well, as General Simpson's Ninth Army was headquartered in Maastricht for a time."

I found myself walking alone in the dark again, but this time it wasn't more of the same treatment; my guide had simply stopped to inspect something in the wall. (The gas lamp lighted a really limited area, I noted.) His discovery was a fossil—perhaps a sea hedgehog, he guessed. At certain points in the network of passages fossils of many kinds and shapes can be spotted in the walls and ceilings, encased in the soft stone.

"In a way this is really the strongest fortress in Europe," the guide continued. "In its time these caves were completely equipped, and a besieged garrison could hold out here for some time. We'll probably pass by a field hospital, ovens, a well, and even troughs for cattle."

His use of the word "probably" jarred me a bit, and I asked if he ever had any difficulty knowing where he was. "Not really," he said. "We keep going over all the possible combinations of routes in our meetings."

And had he ever lost his way or lost a member of a group who hadn't kept up with the rest? "Never," he said reassuringly. "Most visitors stay very close to the lamp."

A few more corners and the soft light of a damp autumn day greeted us at the entrance. My guide extinguished the lamp, locked the grillwork gate, and offered to drive me back to town. A few yards away from the cave mouth, a casual traveler would have no idea that this honeycomb of passages exists inside the slight bulge of earth called Mount St. Peter.

The sense of history is strong in Maastricht; aside from its reptilian and amphibious prehistoric period, the visitor is aware of the city's dramatic past, dating back two thousand years to the Romans' fording of the river Maas (Trajectam ad Mosam) and settling in the community they knew as Mosae Traiectum. The landscape was dotted with Roman villas, and the Appian Way of the North, from Cologne to the Channel ports, passed through Maastricht. The most important arrival in the Roman city was that of Bishop Servatius, subsequently elevated to sainthood, who converted most of the inhabitants to Christianity. He was buried in a cemetery paralleling the road just outside the walls of the city in 384, but his memory in Maastricht is evergreen; the sixth-century church of Saint Servatius built over his sepulchre is now—since 1229—within the expanded city, just off the main square, the Vrijthof; it ranks on my own private list as one of the more memorable in Europe.

The cathedral was reconstructed largely during the eleventh and twelfth centuries, although parts are older. Its style is chiefly Romanesque; a chapel in the northern end of the transept, the work of North Italian craftsmen, is in its simplicity a pure example of this style of architecture.

But its choir, added later, was built in a decorative style that showed Rhineland influence. The Emperors' hall, in the upper story of the western division, is called one of the most beautiful Romanesque halls in western Europe. Throughout the structure, chiefly at the top of capital columns, Maasland art is represented—encompassing the wide range of designs of Romanesque art but also including depictions of biblical events and contemporary figures in scenes from daily life: stone carvers at work, a domestic group, a fight, grape pickers, and others.

The golden reliquary shrine of Saint Servatius (known in Maastricht as Sint Servaas) is shaped like a house, the Saint's abode in the New Jerusalem (Heaven), with carved relief figures of the Saint and two flanking angels on the front. The reliquary measures 175 centimeters in length, 49 in width, and 74 in height (weight approximately 200 kilograms) and while the most spectacular and the most hallowed art object in the group is only one of many memorable precious works related to the shrine, referred to locally as the Golden House.

Maastricht is a good museum town; my two favorites are small, cozy, rather specialized, and uncrowded—at least that was the case at the time of my last visit. The Museum of Natural History contains fossils of the Pleistocene, Miocene, and pre-Cambrian periods as well as skeletal remains of reindeer, mammoth, and bison. But its prize exhibit, what with the Mosasaurus head being in France, is the reconstruction of an ancient giant turtle, most of it remarkably well preserved.

The Bonnefanten Museum features, in the center of its principal room, a scale model—about 19 by 22 feet—of the old Maastricht of 250 years ago; the houses are two inches high, the trees slightly overlarge, and the churches in proportion to the houses. This replica, unfortunately, is the property of France and was on loan by the French government at the time of my visit. It will be replaced by another similar exhibit currently in the planning stage.

On the way back to my hotel on foot, I passed—quite by chance—through a charming block of houses restored meticulously in the style of the sixteenth century. This was a welcome breath of the past, after walking through the center of the business section with, among the assortment of shops, numerous toy stores (more plentiful, I thought, than in Geneva) and sex shops (as abundant as in Stockholm, Paris, or on New York's 42nd Street).

After a full morning of moving around town on foot, I returned to my hotel, the du Casque, nursing a growing appetite and decided that, convenient though it was, the hotel's excellent restaurant—perhaps the best in town—was no match for the attraction the gastronomic delights of the Château Neercanne had for me that day.

Giant sea turtle

This is the establishment I mentioned that is number one on my personal list of favorite European French restaurants outside France. It's a short drive from the Vrijthof through agreeable countryside; on our route the cab driver took me past the town's fortifications, before which—he informed me— d'Artagnan (or the man who served as the model for that Dumas hero) was killed just three hundred years before.

The Château Neercanne, also known as the Château de Nedercanne, and sometimes Nederkan, is perched on the side of a hill in Holland, with its luxuriant gardens just down the slope in Belgium. Across the driveway from the building's entrance, which is at the back of the structure, is an opening to a ten-mile-long cave, which houses near its mouth the castle's stock of vintage wines. The host, Hubert Stassen, who greeted me at the door, led me inside for a brief look round. NATO, he advised, had also earmarked his cave for contingency use, and has already installed an emergency phone system.

Replica of old city of Maastricht

In the attractive bar, while awaiting the arrival of the hour for the luncheon service, I was presented with the house apéritif, called a *pousse rapière*—composed of seven or eight parts champagne and one part Armagnac. The resulting mixture was almost as celestial as Paul Bocuse's inspired concoction at Collonges-au-Mont-d'Or, seat of one of France's greatest restaurants. Over my second *pousse rapière*—it seemed even better than the first—I studied the menu with an eye to an excellent, not too rich and not too expensive lunch, with just one principal course. The carte du vin, as always, made intriguing reading: a bottle of Château Yquem '66 was priced at 100 guilders (just under $32), a Puligny-Montrachet '69, an imposing white burgundy, was offered at 37 guilders, and a St. Veran '71, a white beaujolais, at 25 guilders. One of the best Bordeaux, a Château Margaux, was available at 35 guilders a bottle; since I was opting for fish I ordered a Pouilly-Fumé from the Loire valley, which brings 26.50 guilders a bottle and 14.25 the half.

The prices listed above include of course the duty that must be paid on wines coming from abroad. Actually, the list leaned rather heavily on the products of Alsace and on those of Germany. Although there are a handful of vineyards in Holland I saw none listed on the *carte*, and I have yet to taste a Dutch wine.

I was lunching alone, and the host agreed with me that half a bottle would be ample for my needs (especially after three or four of those irresistible apéritifs). No attempt to force the larger, more expensive bottle on the slightly vulnerable client. I appreciated his restraint. "I never try to press a full bottle of wine on a single diner," said de Heer Stassen. "It destroys his afternoon or evening."

The Château's dining room is unostentatious, extremely agreeable, and the tables impeccably laid. I enjoyed the view of Belgium outside the window, as the waiter poured my consommé. "The management has changed," he told me when I had commented that I had dined at the same table fifteen and a half years before. "The former owner, Theo Koch, retired and turned the place over to his nephew, de Heer Stassen. But many of the waiters are still here."

The *consommé double* featured bits of white chicken and carrots, an auspicious if simple introduction to a carefully measured, excellent repast. The service was just as expert and unobtrusive as in former years, and the food seemed better than ever. My trout, from the nearby river Jeker, was garnished with an unforgettable sauce Hollandaise. But why not! I decided. It should be good, for was I not now really in Holland? (North and South Holland are actually provinces of the country, but the word Holland is used freely to indicate the Netherlands generally.) I am always a little surprised to find a specialty bearing the name of a region available in the area itself, ever since I tried to order Vichyssoise in France. They never heard of it. It is now possible to find it at the hotels George V and Plaza-Athenée, and a few other American enclaves in Paris, but it's no match for the good thick New York Vichyssoise, which turns out to have been a concoction devised by the chef of the old Ritz-Carlton Hotel in Manhattan.

A platter of cheeses—a native Limburger (this was, after all, the province of Limburg), an Italian Gorgonzola, and two French entries, a ripe Brie and a perfect Chèvre, a goat cheese—made it unnecessary for me to agonize over the selection from among a bountiful variety of cheeses of five or six nations. Petits-fours and chocolates rounded out the meal. The Pouilly-Fumé had been chilled to just the right degree—it was not served ice-cold as is the practice in some restaurants—and the entire meal was fully satisfying. My host arrived promptly with a house offering of Armagnac, which gave my superb Dutch cigar a special flavor.

He asked if I had had any mushrooms (unfortunately I had not), as the Château is very proud of its own mushroom culture in the inner recesses of its cave inside the hill adjoining the building.

As I savored the Armagnac, the chef, Guus van Mieghem, appeared, bearing a small aromatic packet; it proved to be his own special spice powder, intended for use on his own personal mushroom dish.

I don't know what the ingredients of the powder are, but they certainly provided a pungent perfume for the interior of my valise all across northern Europe and back to the United States. Van Mieghem did not volunteer the contents of the spice powder, but he did offer the recipe for his mushroom specialty.

"Take 200 grams of cultivated mushrooms," it read, in French and in Dutch, "heat them with fresh butter and chopped scallions for about five minutes. Then add pepper and salt and season with the spices herewith

(2 teaspoons), 3 cloves of garlic; stir while it cooks; incorporate half a liter of double cream, let it cook at low heat, stirring the bulk; then sprinkle with parsley. The cooking is finished when your cream has become firm. Serve in a bowl or in a baking dish. *Bon appétit.*"

The recipe is entitled Champignons de Canne à l'Escargot (4 pers.) or Mushrooms from Canne in snail sauce. (Canne is nearby in Belgium; Neercanne is in Holland.) Equipped with the powder, I will be able to prepare it in my own kitchen, although not with Canne mushrooms.

The furnishings in this exclusive auberge are simple but tasteful, and its terraces are an attractive vantage point for viewing the surrounding countryside, including the Albert Canal which winds its way through the verdant fields on its way from Antwerp to Liège.

The combination of good food and drink, imaginatively prepared, the uncrowded country, unlimited quantities of good fresh air, and a well-decorated, comfortable inn has always seemed my idea of heaven on earth, and nowhere is this as true as at the Château Neercanne.

After luncheon, I was invited on a drive through the area by the former director, now retired, of the Maastricht office of the VVV, the Dutch Information Service. Our first stop was at Valkenburg, a vacation region for the Limburgers, where a "mountain" rising 1,093 feet high gives the eye something different to gaze upon than mile on mile of perfectly flat land. In most countries this slight protuberance of earth would go unnoticed, but in Limburg it's a mountain, and the inhabitants flock to it eagerly as though it were one of the seven wonders of the world.

Our first real objective, after driving through some miles of fertile farmland, was the American Military Cemetery at Margraten, which Mat, my volunteer guide and driver, insisted that I should see. Southern Limburg is not far from the Belgian Ardennes, where the famous German thrust of December 1944 was made, and many of the 8,301 American soldiers buried in neat rows of graves fell there. Margraten is one of fourteen formal American Military Cemeteries for World War II dead on foreign soil (there are eight for World War I), and is of course the only one in the Netherlands. It lies at the extreme southern tip of the country and is, as Mat said proudly, a very impressive sight, with its orderly rows of white crosses in a perfectly landscaped preserve, its chapel, and its modern memorial building. Mat is unreservedly pro-U.S. and still expresses his gratitude, in emotional terms, for what American fighting men did for his country in the Second World War.

Our afternoon drive was delightful; even on a brisk November day one was convinced of the lush fertility of the land. As we drove, and at tea at a roadside restaurant, Mat rambled on about the ancient town of Maastricht, which is, quite obviously, very dear to him.

Holland, he pointed out, did not have one Golden Age, but several. Two separate Romanesque periods mark the beginnings of Maasland art that survive to this day. The first, in the eleventh century, was highlighted by a plain and monumental style; the second, in the first half of the twelfth century, featured artwork abundant in detail and decorative sculpture. In addition to the Cathedral of Saint Servatius, a second great Romanesque church in Maastricht is eminently worth visiting: the church of Our Lady, representative of both Romanesque periods. The nave, transept, and choir are excellent examples of the style of the latter, twelfth-century phase. This was the glorious age of the Maasland goldsmiths and metalworkers, who became renowned throughout the civilized world of that time.

A hundred years later the Gothic period began; its architecture was notable for a blossoming of sculpture and a continuing profusion of metalwork of all kinds. In this last phase of the Middle Ages, the late Gothic influence spread over all the Netherlands; fifteenth- and sixteenth-century churches sprang up throughout the country, and the vista across the flat landscape was studded with inspiring, majestic steeples, symbols of the newly acquired power of the burghers.

Numerous art treasures of a fresh quality appeared (this was the age of Hieronymous Bosch), and wood sculptures in magnificent detail—which reached their zenith in this period.

While classical Gothic architecture in the sense of the French cathedrals is exceedingly rare in Holland, many public buildings, including town halls, were erected in this time—an indication of the burgeoning prosperity of this era. The town hall in Maastricht, constructed to serve two mayors who held office at the same time, features twin staircases leading from the sidewalk, starting as one, branching off to left and right, and rejoining at the building's doors, forming a diamond shape. Each mayor took pains to use his own side on all occasions. Inside, a vast central hall separates two sets of identical office rooms. I did not have the opportunity to visit each room—there were meetings in progress in some—so I cannot say if the furnishings and décor are identical on each side of the hall.

The Renaissance provided a short interlude between two great periods of Dutch cultural life: the Gothic and the classic baroque of what is called Holland's Golden Age. The Dutch Renaissance was at first featured by imitations of the work of Italians, but gradually Italians who had come to Holland to work gave it a legitimacy of its own.

The great "age of Rembrandt" (and Frans Hals, Vermeer, and so many others) had its beginning just about the year 1600, at the very start of the seventeenth century. Trade flourished, and Dutch fleets were embarked on the course of discovery and expansion of empire in far corners of the globe. As the center of world trade at the time shifted from the south to the cities of Holland, Maastricht found itself in the center of the stream.

Great paintings were legion, with the Dutch atmosphere and climate accurately reflected in the leaden gray skies of the seventeenth-century masterpieces. Etchings and engravings also appeared in quantity, and the art of the silversmith and furniture maker thrived. This was truly the greatest Golden Age of all of Holland's golden ages.

The creative cultural life of the Netherlands, Mat concluded, tapered off during the eighteenth and nineteenth centuries, and into the twentieth, although any period that encompasses the life and works of Vincent van Gogh, Piet Mondriaan, Kees van Dongen, and Karel Appel can hardly be called sterile.

All this cultural ferment had its impact on Maastricht; in addition, the superimposition, in this most southerly city, of sophisticated Latin overtones on the stolid but jolly Dutch character and characteristics makes for an interesting, and unique, mixture.

The natives of Maastricht today are colorful in appearance, and by consequence most shop windows are also bright and uplifting—in contrast to the city's buildings, medieval and ancient, which are a grayish-brown, set, in deep November, against skies that are an almost-matching dull gray. But curiously there is a sprightly feeling about Maastricht, even on the grayest days. The service personnel, at my hotel and in the restaurants and shops, was attentive and cheerful. Excepting only on the sandstone walls of Saint Peter's caves, the traveler will find no graffiti anywhere in the spotless town itself, and the usual urban crush of automobiles and accompanying smoke fumes is considerably diminished by the preponderance of bicycles—a Dutch trademark—the standard means of transportation for thousands of the young, the middle-aged, and the elderly. On Sunday, at midday, the voices of the male choir, the nationally celebrated Maastreechter Staar (or Mastrichter Star), from the Concertgebouw just off the Vrijthof, lend a festival touch to the weekend throughout the year.

Maastricht—a small, steel engraving of a town, precise, meticulously designed, perfectly proportioned, and containing a wealth of carefully executed detail—is well worth working into one's European itinerary.

$\mathcal{D}ubrovnik$

Dubrovnik has the appearance of an artist's conception on an architect's worktable—a model city come to life. The walls, in more primitive form, were begun during the Middle Ages; as they stand today, they are the product, mostly, of the fourteenth and fifteenth centuries, with later additions through the seventeenth. They are largely responsible for the city's independent status over a span of nine hundred years, four hundred of them as a sovereign state. With their numerous bastions and towers and nearby forts, the fortifications must have seemed impressive indeed to covetous powers eying this desirable Adriatic "pearl."

*D*ubrovnik, the medieval walled city on Yugoslavia's Adriatic coast, is—according to some—a state of mind. And since no two minds are necessarily alike, there are differing views on the subject.

It is perhaps to be expected that a literate Irish opinion and a literate English assessment do not coincide. George Bernard Shaw, a critic of all he surveyed, put it succinctly: "If you are looking for heaven on earth, go to Dubrovnik."

Countering this unqualified endorsement, England's Dame Rebecca West, who felt tied to Yugoslavia as by a spiritual umbilical cord, said to her husband some years later: "I can't bear Dubrovnik."

He quickly protested. "Dubrovnik is exquisite, perhaps the most exquisite town I have ever seen."

Dame Rebecca parried: "Yes. But all the same I don't like it. I find it a unique experiment on the part of the Slav, unique in its nature and unique in its success, and I do not like it. It reminds me of the worst of England."

Her husband agreed diplomatically: "Yes, I see that, when you think of its history," then returned to his own premise: "But let us give it credit for what it looks like, and that too is unique."

At this, Dame Rebecca apparently mellowed and admitted, in her massive two-volume *Black Lamb and Grey Falcon*: "He was right indeed, for it is as precious as Venice, and deserves comparison with the Venice of Carpaccio and Bellini, though not of Titian and Tintoretto.

"It should be visited for the first time when the twilight is about to fall, when it is already dusk under the tall trees. . . ."

It was with these thoughts tumbling about in my mind that I approached Dubrovnik. I saw it first on the horizon just at dusk, from the deck of the motorship *Tiziano,* a well-scrubbed car and passenger ferry which had brought me from Bari, across the Adriatic at the Achilles tendon of the Italian boot.

The walled city stood out on its promontory against the mountainous background, as dramatically lighted as any theater technician could have wished. The ramparts that encircle the old city were constructed beginning in the Middle Ages and continuing to the seventeenth century, and except for some earthquake damage have survived till this day; coming closer to the city one had exactly the same view of this magnificent bastion as sailors on passing ships have had for a thousand years. The sight of the walled city from the sea is an image that will never fade; it is well worth making the pleasant seven-hour crossing from Bari in order to see Dubrovnik first from this vantage point.

The *Tiziano* circled close by the walls and passed on to the deep-water port of Gruž, a few miles from the city. Dubrovnik can be approached from abroad directly only by boat, from Greece and Italy, and by plane, from Rome; driving by car or by train one must proceed through the interior of Yugoslavia. Whatever point of entry you select, you will be given a visa, after some formalities, on the spot. Aboard the *Tiziano*, the immigration officer opened his shuttered window a good hour and a half before we were scheduled to put into port. Everyone was asked to surrender his or her passport; then the shutter was slammed against the counter, and presently two police officers arrived and entered the booth by a back door. Although the passenger list on this trip was light, the muttering went on behind the shutter for well over an hour and continued even while the ship was being made fast to the quayside, giving rise to a variety of black, pessimistic thoughts about what lay ahead.

Finally, some little while after we had berthed, the shutter abruptly flew open and we were handed our passports without a word. Customs inspection of luggage—a cursory look in my case—took place on the quay and passed very quickly. On the taxi ride from Gruž to Dubrovnik, the soft lights in the stone houses on the hillside winked on as we passed, and when we reached the hotel it was already quite dark.

I had chosen to stay in the Grand Hotel Imperial, built at the end of the last century by the Austrians, who controlled the Dalmatian coast at that time. It was a happy choice, for it proved to be situated just a five-minute walk up a hill from the west gate of the city, and facing an unbelievably dramatic-looking fort (Lovrijenac), perched on a summit overlooking the ramparts and dominating the vast stretch of sea.

From my balcony, the deepening cast of the light combined with the light-colored stone of the fort so that it almost seemed to be illuminated; it gave me the feeling that the scene before me was an oversize stage setting.

The hotel, listed in Category A, is a comfortable, full-blown resort hotel unmistakably of the nineteenth century, with ample, high-ceilinged rooms —recently redecorated—and flanked by a garden that added just the right touch of instant *gemütlichkeit*. The whole effect was one of gaiety; at any moment I half expected to hear a string trio break into the "Merry Widow Waltz."

But finally the note of schmaltz was not sounded; the clerks at the reception desk could never have been mistaken for Austrian with their stern faces and the cryptic, carefully measured remarks they made. Not that they didn't try to perform as they supposed hotel clerks should greet visitors intent on spending their money and swelling the country's treasury.

The young lady behind the desk was very pretty—blond, with a rosy complexion, and strong cheekbones. But as I studied her features approvingly, she scowled and adopted her Madame Commissar manner—her standard mien for the duration of my stay except for one brief moment when she dropped her guard, on the occasion of my giving her some U.S. postage stamps from my incoming letters.

In fact the entire establishment was staffed by persons who had the appearance of having been schooled just recently for their various roles. Across from the driveway entrance to the hotel proper is a small building housing a casino; on the three occasions I paid a visit to the gaming rooms there was not a customer in sight. Admittedly I looked in each time early in the evening and it was off-season. The resultant tableau had the look of what someone thought a casino should resemble—perhaps after seeing an old French movie: a bar near the door manned by an expectant (perhaps anxious would be the word) bartender; then, at the entrance to the main gaming room, a roulette table staffed by a chef de casino, a cashier, and several croupiers dressed impeccably in dinner jackets with—nice touch—one female croupier in a bright red evening dress over black boots. All were poised for action, but with the self-conscious attitude of the subjects of a nineteenth-century photographer equipped with camera, tripod, and flash powder.

I would have liked to see them all in action to see how well they had learned their parts—baccarat was also promised on the posters—but I was loath to rearrange this daguerreotype for the sake of a few minimal bets on the red or the black. Besides, there is something rather melancholy about being the only player at a roulette table. It is one thing to have the odds against the player, as always, but it is another to be, in addition, out-numbered. Before leaving after my third visit I did buy a drink at the bar, to the relief of the barman, who rewarded me with a grateful smile.

I hope, for the sake of the Yugoslav treasury, that the action is a bit livelier than this during the season, which stretches from May to November. My visit was made during the latter month, and I was able to take ad-vantage of off-season prices; my large room, with a balcony overlooking the garden with its palm trees, Fort Lovrijenac, and the sea, and a commodious bathroom—nineteenth-century style, but with twentieth-century plumbing —cost me, with full pension (three rather good meals), the equivalent of $6.60 a day.

At that price one would allow for a few disappointments without com-plaining, but I found my stay in Dubrovnik as agreeable as any I have enjoyed in any European city. The weather was superb—warm but with an offshore breeze—and the city itself was clean and fascinating. Nothing about it, by the way, reminded me of England, either the best or the worst of Dame Rebecca West's homeland.

The people were friendly if a bit stiff at first, especially those persons in positions of some authority, who acted as though they were constantly re-minding themselves that they must be on their best behavior for the bene-fit of foreigners. In sum, I am inclined to agree with George Bernard Shaw's estimate: a bit of heaven on earth.

Of all the medieval city-states, Dubrovnik found and preserved its own identity, at the center of constantly shifting political and racial movement around it. Even the major earthquakes in the area failed to demolish it or its spirit.

That spirit is directly related to the people's thirst for independence, a preoccupation that might almost be termed an obsession. The centuries of the city's independence are reflected in the strong, determined faces of its inhabitants; even today, though they live in a nation that has an unchallenged central government, it is quite obvious, even to a recently arrived visitor, that they consider themselves citizens of Dubrovnik first, Yugoslavia second.

During the great days of its sovereignty, Dubrovnik, then a city-state, was ruled by a rector, its highest-ranking personage, who served for only one month before being replaced and who could not reassume the post for at least two years. He was supported by an inner council of eleven members and a senate of forty-five, who had substantial decision-making powers.

But this heady stretch of freedom came to an end in the early years of the nineteenth century. It was sudden and swift: Austria, which had gained control of much of Dalmatia (which also encompasses Dubrovnik), ceded to France almost the whole of that coastal province. The army of Napoleon had requested the right of passage through Dubrovnik in order to seize neighboring Kotor from the Russians.

Without waiting for an answer, they occupied the tiny city-state on May 28, 1806. On January 31, 1808, the French occupation officials announced an act abolishing the State of Dubrovnik.

Many of the people of Dubrovnik, warm-hearted, outgoing, and accustomed to dealing with many nationalities, did not dislike the French at first, but their conscription fiat and the new taxes they imposed soon made them universally resented.

The *coup de grâce* was administered to Dubrovnik's independence at the Congress of Vienna in 1815. Before the congress convened, Dubrovnik's nobles met secretly, to mount a last attempt to recover her freedom. In a meeting in a palace at Rijeka Dubrovačka, they drew up a request for representation at the forthcoming congress, for the purpose of pleading for a restoration of the Dubrovnik state. The request was refused, and Dubrovnik passed under the control of Austria.

I am devoting a bit more space than usual to Dubrovnik's history, for it is a contributing factor in the spirit of its inhabitants today; some knowledge of that history is a necessity for the appreciation of that unquenchable *esprit*.

To the loss of independence, the Dubrovnik nobles reacted in a manner that is surely unique: they vowed not to marry or have children because they felt dishonored and determined to make certain that no progeny of theirs would live under an occupying power. Thus the old aristocracy died out completely.

To the people of Dubrovnik, the Austrians were a different matter from the French. Although they gave the appearance of being benevolent rulers, they soon resorted to their old Hapsburg trick of pitting the subject racial groups against one another. Throughout their Adriatic territories, Italian was made the official language wherever Slavs were in the majority, and where the Italians were most numerous the use of German was made mandatory.

But in fact, the Austrian rule was generally benign; they found the climate agreeable, even in winter, with no fog. Even today Dubrovnik is pollution free, with mild temperatures in winter and no uncomfortable excessive heat in summer. The nearby beaches are in the main sandy and well kept. Evidences of the Austrian presence during about a hundred years abound; so too do visual reminders, via many of the buildings in the surrounding hills, of Serbian and Turkish habitation. Ancient Greek and Roman ruins are not plentiful, but there are some, carefully preserved, some little distance from Dubrovnik.

With the collapse of the Austro-Hungarian Empire in World War I, Yugoslavia became a kingdom at war's end. Its recent history is more familiar: in the Second World War Yugoslavians split into a number of groups, the strongest being the partisans, led by Marshal Tito (Josip Broz), and the Četniks, commanded by Draja Mikhailovích. Their loyalties to the two warring power blocs shifted at various times, but after the rupture of the German-Russian pact and Hitler's invasion of the Soviet Union, the battle lines were more clearly drawn. Tito and his partisans fought on the side of the Allies, while the Četniks, whose principal enemy was Tito's force, inevitably gravitated to the German-Italian orbit.

After the war's end, Tito was in complete control; he unified the country as it never had been before.

Today, while the spirit of Dubrovnik is strongly independent, the city has firm, sympathetic ties with the rest of Yugoslavia. Marshal Tito himself, a Croatian (that republic extends from the north of Yugoslavia down the

Dalmatian coast and includes Dubrovnik within its borders), regards the city as a special jewel and visits it at least once or twice a year. Sometimes, after a state visit by a foreign dignitary in Belgrade, often with a side trip to Brioni, the chief of state's island retreat in the northern Adriatic, Tito will accompany his guest to Dubrovnik for his departure from Yugoslavia. Thus, the visitor's last thoughts about the country will be filtered through the agreeable images and the incomparable scenery and climate of Dubrovnik and its environs.

The history of the city is a series of remarkable achievements—unquestionably unique, as Dame Rebecca put it. In my first trip down the hill from my hotel, thence across the drawbridge (over what is now a pleasant park), through the city's Pile, or western, gate, and down into the walled city and the promenade known as the Placa or the Stradun, Dubrovnik's main street, I came at once to the local Information Office. At the door, looking speculatively at the strollers, stood Gino Sukno, a veritable fount of information, and I was soon on the receiving end of a recital of the town's past, present, and —in Mr. Sukno's view—its future.

Motorized traffic of all types—except for an occasional delivery van—is forbidden within the walled city, so we sauntered leisurely along the Placa, stopping before each storefront to enable me to study the native products exhibited in the display windows.

"This old city of Dubrovnik is one thousand three hundred and forty-five years old," Sukno said authoritatively, without preface. "It has thirty-one thousand inhabitants, four thousand of whom live here in the old city. There are several casinos in the expanded area of the city," he added abruptly, giving me an appraising glance.

I told him about my first visit to the casino attached to my hotel.

"The Imperial?" he said approvingly. "That's much more interesting than some of the new tourist hotels along the beaches. Especially at this time of year. It was built in 1897 by the Austrians, and the Austrian navy had a school there for a while.

"The Duke of Windsor when he was Prince of Wales stayed there one night in 1934 and loved it," he went on without pause. "After the Germans took over from the Italians here in 1943, Hermann Göring used to drop by at the Imperial whenever he felt he needed a little sea air."

We stopped in at one of the coffeehouses along the Placa for a pastry and coffee while he summed up the city's history in capsule form.

"For a large part of its life, Dubrovnik has been an independent republic, and a gateway between east and west. It has always been a thriving seaport— the goods that were brought here by ships of all nations continued overland to Constantinople and the Near East." Sukno—one of whose parents, I guessed, must have been Italian, to account for the Gino—speaks five languages fluently, and has a working knowledge of several others.

He went on spewing out facts he had obviously memorized some time ago; I'll telescope them here.

Yugoslavia—*yugo* means south—formally became the land of the southern Slavs and a kingdom in 1918, at the end of the First World War. But it has been inhabited by a number of races at least as far back as the Neanderthal Man, whose remains have been discovered near Krapina, north of Zagreb, in the country's northern reaches. Refugees from the Greco-Roman city of Epidaurum (now Cavtat), just twelve miles to the southeast of Dubrovnik, first settled on a small island that is now the southern part of the walled city of Dubrovnik. The narrow channel between it and the mainland was subsequently filled in, and today is the promenade called the Placa, which— running from east to west—divides the old city into halves, both now part of the mainland.

But in those early days, in the seventh century, the Roman inhabitants of Illyrian ancestry who had lived in Epidaurum occupied the islet south of the channel and spoke Latin, while the northern part and the mainland thereabout was settled by southern Slavs, who spoke Serbian.

Dubrovnik, I know from having spent a half-hour with the first booklet on the city I had purchased, was named from the *dubrava,* or oak groves, that surrounded it. The Byzantine Emperor Constantine Porphrogenitus is said to have referred to the founding of Dubrovnik in the mid-tenth century, and its name was said to have been mentioned by a Bosnian monarch in 1189. Nevertheless, until the end of the First World War, the city was known as Ragusa; a seventh-century geographer of Ravenna referred to the city as Ragusiam, and it flourished, as Ragusa, for centuries. But finally that name was considered "too Italian" though it is Illyrian, and Dubrovnik, its slavonic name, was formally settled on. (There is an interesting town in

Sicily named Ragusa, to further complicate matters, as most Italians today persist in calling Dubrovnik Ragusa, too.)

During its early development, the city-state came under Byzantine influence, following the occupation of the area by Slavs and Croatians. One of the popular legends, still current, has it that Orlando (the Italian name for the knight Roland) fought against the Saracens, as one of Charlemagne's paladins who led the expeditionary force that conquered and occupied northern Dalmatia. The fact that Roland, the hero of Ronceval, had died fighting the Basques in the Pyrenees has not diminished by one whit the enthusiastic acceptance of the legend of his antics in what is now Yugoslavia.*

As we sipped our strong coffee, Gino Sukno skimmed quickly over the centuries from the tenth onward, with the developing city-state being dominated first by Venice, then by the Croato-Hungarian kingdom, and at intervals by the Turks. (Although tribute was paid to the Turks, the Dubrovnik elders succeeded in keeping them out of their city.)

Through it all, perhaps partly because of its sturdy defenses and partly because of the strength of its trade with both east and west and the size and mobility of its merchant fleet, Dubrovnik maintained at all times a good measure of independence; when that began to show signs of diminishing, it was—the rector and the nobles who helped rule the city knew—time to find a new protector.

The passionate appetite for an independent status has been a characteristic of Dubrovnik's citizens for a thousand years, and by now it is shared—in varying degrees—by the natives in other parts of Yugoslavia.

"The saying today goes like this," said Sukno, selecting a particularly luscious piece of pastry and lapsing into a Yugoslav equivalent of the Twelve Days of Christmas: "We are today a country with seven borders, composed of six republics, populated by five nationalities, speaking four languages, practicing three religions, employing two alphabets, and sharing one wish—to be independent."

For the proud people of Dubrovnik, the heritage of independence is a prime factor in their lives. As the power of Venice declined, that of Dubrovnik increased; her ships traveled throughout the Mediterranean and beyond,

* As in many legends, the hero really moved around, faster than anyone in the jet age.

to the shores of England and the Low Countries and finally to America. For a less determined people, the violent earthquake of April 6, 1667 might have occasioned the end of the republic. But the citizenry fell to, rebuilding where necessary, and the life of the republic continued, albeit somewhat less serenely. Although its walls had been ruptured, three-quarters of its buildings destroyed, and two-thirds of the population killed, Dubrovnik fought off repeated attacks by the opportunist Venetians.

But the delicate task of balancing its relations between hostile power blocs was becoming more difficult, or perhaps the patricians who governed Dubrovnik were not as adept as their forebears. At any rate the nobles no longer enjoyed the full confidence of the people, and there was grumbling on both sides.

Finally the occupation by the French heralded the death of free Dubrovnik. Still, its independent spirit seemed to be assimilated by the new nation, Yugoslavia, especially after World War II.

"Don't forget," Gino reminded me, over our third coffees, "our leader Tito really gave notice of our intention to be an independent country in 1948 when he split with Stalin and succeeded in keeping the Russians from retaliating with military force."

As we resumed our stroll along the Placa, I inquired delicately into the subject of life under "independent Communism."

"The people are happy," he said with conviction, gesturing at the passing promenaders on the cobblestoned street. "You don't see any beggars here, is it not so?"

I agreed that I had seen no beggars.

"Everyone who can work works. There is no unemployment. And no crime," he added, eyeing me carefully.

I changed the subject. "I see quite a few churches here. How does the government feel about the practice of religion?"

"Well, you know Communism stands for atheism. We don't believe in God. But the government is generous and allows those who want to worship God to do so. About fifteen or twenty percent of the population, mostly older people, keep up their religion. The young are almost entirely atheists."

"So that one day before long the churches will be empty?" I asked.

He shrugged. "Sometimes the older people take very young children to church. But as they grow older they usually give it up. If you're a church-goer you can't go into politics or have any relation to the government."

We had returned along the opposite side of the Placa and stood before the Franciscan monastery, across from Gino's office. After he had made his departure, promising to show me some of the principal points of interest on another day, I entered the church and was struck at once by the harmonious mixture of Eastern and Western overtones. It was completed in the fourteenth century, but the steeple was a later addition, as was its largely baroque décor. Its tall campanile is topped by an attention-arresting cupola.

Adjoining the hall of worship is a small, enchanting cloister—a series of delicate, slender arches supported by graceful pillars, each bearing a different capital adorned by either a human or animal head, in the Romanesque style, surrounding a small garden featuring a statue of Saint Francis standing atop a stone birdbath. An upper cloister of great simplicity is in the Gothic tradition. The monastery has its own library, with many rare volumes, and a historic apothecary shop, containing many old-fashioned jars and retorts; it is descended directly from one of the oldest such shops in Europe, founded in 1317.

Returning to the church the following Sunday, I found a large con-gregation filling every corner of the main hall. Since there were relatively few tourists in the city at the time of my visit, I could only conclude that the practice of religious worship is very much alive. Contrary to Gino Sukno's observations, there were quite a few young people, in their teens and twenties, in the assemblage.

In this country that is predominantly atheistic, there seem to be a great many churches, at least in greater Dubrovnik, where fourteen churches, in-cluding two monasteries and one synagogue, vie for the believer's patronage. Within the walled city the most notable, in addition to the Franciscan and Dominican monasteries, are the early eighteenth-century baroque church of Saint Blaise (also known as Blasius), Dubrovnik's patron saint, on the square at the eastern end of the Placa; the Cathedral of Our Lady, also in the eastern end of the walled city, rebuilt after the earthquake of 1667; the tiny Renaissance church of Saint Saviour, squeezed between the Franciscan monastery and the city walls (sixteenth century); the Jesuit Church of St. Ignatius; the Serbian Orthodox Church; and Saint James's Church, the only purely Romanesque building surviving in Dubrovnik today. All were worth visiting.

The area surrounding the city, including the islands and islets along the coast nearby, is equally studded with steeples and the ruins of exquisitely fashioned monasteries of the twelfth to the seventeenth centuries.

In line with my custom of viewing the points of interest at a leisurely pace, I postponed visits to other museums and fell in with what seemed to be the favorite leisure activity in Dubrovnik: walking up and down the Placa, also known as the Stradun. Its shop windows seemed never to cease fascinating the Serbians and Croatians, shop windows filled with displays of pigskin luggage, other leather goods, carved wood handicraft items, lace and embroidery, untanned leather Bosnian slippers, local brasswork of Turkish design, and everywhere—in shops of all kinds—postage stamps, mostly from Communist countries in Europe, although Grecian issues were well represented.

The strollers on the Placa scrutinize with unconcealed frankness those approaching in the opposite direction; this openness is a part of the charm that seems to be shared by the local inhabitants. They can be by turn jolly or somber, but usually their sad moods tend to disappear quickly. Those shopkeepers or salespersons who speak only Serbo-Croat resort to gestures, when questioned by foreigners, and make themselves understood in quite a high proportion of cases.

The largest contingent of foreigners, judging by my fellow occupants in the Imperial Hotel, was Italian, who are of course neighbors of the Yugoslavs. The hotel has a very attractive bar, just off its public sitting rooms; it was filled every day of my stay, from early morning till dinner time, by the same group of Italian businessmen, who discussed their affairs in a high-decibel, volatile manner and drank, usually Campari, throughout the day. (I could gather, with my limited Italian, only that a considerable investment was involved.)

German is the most comprehensible foreign tongue (dating from the Austrian occupation)—not including languages spoken in other parts of the country, such as Slovenian and Macedonian—and Italian is understood by some. English was spoken and understood at my hotel by all the employees I came in contact with except the chambermaid, who used German with gestures, but in the city itself the distinctive cascade of English syllables was a rarity.

One English-speaking resident whom I came to know during my stay in Dubrovnik was a young waiter of perhaps twenty-five or twenty-seven years, though the ages of Yugoslavs, who generally take excellent care of themselves and live longer than most peoples, are hard to judge. I had first met Marko aboard the *Tiziano* en route to Dubrovnik; he had been on a short vacation in Italy, following the closing for the season of the restaurant where he worked, very close to the Grand Hotel Imperial. "A really good restaurant," he had said firmly. "You should try it next time you're in Dubrovnik."

It was called the Mimosa, or Mimoza, and catered to foreigners. Of course on my visit to Dubrovnik on that trip I never had an opportunity to try it; besides, I was so intrigued by the price of the pension plan at the hotel that I found myself eating there more or less regularly, except for snacks and a very few late-evening meals.

At the Imperial the food was on the heavy side, with special emphasis on potatoes *and* spaghetti (canned, I fear) to accompany the meat dish. A delicious yogurt was a staple of each meal, sometimes at beginning and end. I wondered why it tasted so much better than yogurt I had had elsewhere, and suddenly remembered having read somewhere that the yogurt in Bulgaria, one of the country's neighbors, is the best in the world but for what reason I had forgotten. The wine, on the other hand, was almost medicinal in taste. After the heavy main course, the salad, light and fresh, was always welcome. Then for dessert, having already had my ration of yogurt, I invariably chose the compote of fruit, which was always the same: three wrinkled undernourished prunes. But unusual though they were, the meals were satisfying. I certainly never left the table feeling underfed.

Marko and I met again, without prearrangement, on the Placa, where one encounters anyone resident in or visiting Dubrovnik. Like most of the natives I met, Marko has an outgoing personality. Over a glass of local brandy— rather raw on the throat, but warming on arrival in the stomach—Marko readily admitted that he was not a Communist, nor was he a member of any church, although—he quickly added—he did not disapprove of the exercise of religious beliefs.

"You don't have to look very hard to find capitalists here—they are everywhere," he said. "Persons working for themselves, employing others, and owning their own seaside villas.

"But Socialism as we have it here in Yugoslavia is the best thing for us. Without it we would never have been able to hold onto our independence. Marshal Tito," he said, with a reverential nod toward the photograph of the leader hanging on the wall over the cashier's post, in the classic Communist tradition, "he is a very wise man."

Then, after waving for our glasses to be refilled, he said emphatically: "Really," as though he imagined I would not be inclined to believe him.

"I do not remember the war personally, of course, but I know from my family and friends that Marshal Tito really saved this country." He spoke with great sincerity.

On the subject of religion and religious worship, which seems to come up quite often in conversation in Dubrovnik, Marko observed: "My parents are Eastern Orthodox Catholics. They go to church regularly. But most of my friends and I don't believe in God and don't attend church."

Marko, who is a mixture of national strains including, among others, Serbian and Macedonian, has the same strong spirit of independence so characteristic of his countrymen. What the chief of state has accomplished here is the binding together of a nation, composed of disparate elements, that is truly independent of both East and West. This self-sufficiency is reflected, in miniature, in Dubrovnik, which has developed through the centuries a perfect wholeness, physically and spiritually.

But however independent, Yugoslavia is still a Communist—thus totalitarian—state, with all the strictures and inhibitions that implies. On the occasion of my second meeting with Gino Sukno, who, like the clerks in my hotel was a government employee, his manner had changed substantially overnight. Apparently he had had some thoughts—either his own, or someone else's—about my stated intention of writing about Dubrovnik; his enthusiasm of our first encounter had changed to a reserved attitude, and his offer to guide me to some of the city's more interesting sights was not repeated. It was evident that in spite of the stated friendliness between Yugoslavia and the United States there existed still a deep-rooted suspicion on the part of many, particularly government functionaries.

It was during my stay in Dubrovnik, in fact, that two edicts were promulgated, suggestive of a slight but perceptible shift in the wind coming from Belgrade, the nation's capital. First, the custom of certain youths to dress in cast-off American army fatigue jackets was brought to an abrupt conclusion by government order, and second, the American television series *Peyton Place* was replaced, without prior announcement, by Britain's *Forsyte Saga*. This substitution was made, it was declared, on moral grounds; *Peyton Place* was simply not suitable fare for decorous Yugoslav audiences.

As to world news: Sukno assured me that during the season some fifteen foreign newspapers were on sale in Dubrovnik; in my own, off-season peregrinations in and around the city I found an abundance of newsdealers but only *Corriere della Sera*, of Milan, among foreign papers, and the magazines *Der Spiegel*, of West Germany, and *Jours de France*, of France, available to residents and visitors. On departing the country, at the airport serving Dubrovnik, I did find a copy of the *International Herald Tribune,* published in Paris, and had trouble holding onto it, after several other Americans spotted it in my hand.

Sukno claimed there was no attempt at censorship, but a Yugoslav man in his forties, encountered leaving the Dominican monastery at the far end of the walled city, said that one newsvendor's "Finish" meant not merely that the papers were no longer available because the season had ended but rather that the state was less and less tolerant of having the foreign interpretation of world events accessible to its citizens.

In the area of the arts, happily, the country is far from chauvinistic; performances of a variety of plays, ballets, and musical compositions by nationals of many countries are within easy reach of visitors during the season. At the dramatically situated Fort Lovrijenac, rising majestically above the sea— the centerpiece of the view from my balcony—*Hamlet* is performed in an unmatched setting during the annual festival.

Perhaps the most satisfactory way to appreciate the wholeness of Dubrovnik is to walk in a leisurely fashion along the walls, a winding promenade some 1,940 meters long, with the walkway ranging from 1½ to 6 meters wide. Some unparalleled marine vistas vie with constantly changing perspectives of the old city: Dubrovnik has the appearance of an artist's conception on an architect's worktable—a model city come to life. The symmetry

Festival theatre

of the stone buildings and the dim, yellow lights in their windows as dusk descends provide an unmistakably Old World feeling; it is quite an easy matter to forget that one is indeed living at this moment in the last quarter of the twentieth century.

The walls, in more primitive form, were begun during the Middle Ages; as they stand today, they are the product, mostly, of the fourteenth and fifteenth centuries, with later additions through the seventeenth. They are largely responsible for the city's independent status over a span of nine hundred years, four hundred of them as a sovereign state.

With their numerous bastions and towers and nearby forts, the walled fortifications of Dubrovnik must have seemed impressive indeed to covetous powers eyeing this desirable Adriatic "pearl."

The walled city had to be substantially rebuilt after the Great Earthquake, as it is still known today; as one walks along the Placa the Renaissance style of the original city is suggested by the retention of the original plan and appearance of the buildings, with a number of baroque innovations superimposed.

The eastern end of the Placa is set off by the sixteenth-century Sponza Palace, the city tower, and the bell loggia; facing this consortium of distinctive structures is the eighteenth-century Church of Saint Blaise, replacing a fourteenth-century edifice on the same site destroyed by fire in 1706. A few steps farther south, to seaward, are the Rector's Palace and, beyond that, the Cathedral.

This concentration of outstanding architectural achievement combined with relics of earlier epochs is worthy of a liberal portion of any visitor's time. The Sponza Palace, whose delicate colonnaded arcade gives directly onto the Placa, was built in the early sixteenth century in a Gothic-Renaissance style with stone carvings in the spirit of many of the façades and arches of Dubrovnik. Once used, successively, as a custom house, mint, state treasury, and bank, the Sponza subsequently served as a forum for literary societies in an era when the upper floors saw service as a granary. Today the Sponza Palace (the Italian word *spongia*, literally deposited matter, refers to the alluvial soil) is a museum devoted chiefly to the "National Liberation Struggle" and is a repository of the Historical Archives of the Republic, where evidence of all facets of Dubrovnik's life is preserved.

Numismatists will find here a record of the city's currency, preceding today's dinar (which is not negotiable outside the country). The first document to include mention of the local currency is dated 457. In 596 the legal tender in Dubrovnik was a copper coin bearing the head of the Greek Emperor, and by the beginning of the tenth century the mint was in full production turning out Minca (copper pieces) honoring Prince Pavlimir, the Slavic King. The developing numismatic history of the city-state was recorded in the Charter of 1272, when it was ordered that dinars of silver should supplement the Minca. In 1337 the mint was modernized, and new issues were authorized by the government; at the start of the fifteenth century new coins bearing the large letter R (for Ragusa) were minted and circulated widely. When Napoleon's troops took over and the French occupation began, the old mint ceased functioning and Dubrovnik has never again had its own currency, a blow to the pride of its independence-minded citizens.

At right angles to Sponza Palace and facing the Placa, which terminates at this point, is the city tower with its bell loggia, recently rebuilt to correct a dangerous list caused originally by the Great Earthquake of 1667. When the tower was finally reconstructed in 1928–29, someone hit on the idea of having an electric clock below its more conventional clockface, giving the time in numerals (10 03, for example) which change every minute. It is

somewhat startling to come on this modern timepiece in the tower surrounded by the buildings of seventeenth-century Dubrovnik, but it is one of
very few discordant notes observed during numerous visits to the old city.

The Church of Saint Blaise, opposite Sponza Palace and facing on Luža
Square, was built—like many Dubrovnik buildings and fortifications—
by an Italian, in this case Marino Gropelli of Venice, in an eighteenth-century
reincarnation of this house of worship. On the high altar stands a fifteenth-
century sculpture of Saint Blaise, depicting him holding in one hand a model
of the ancient town of Dubrovnik. It is one of the most noteworthy of many
statues of the patron saint scattered about the city. (Another worth the
visitor's inspection is a copy by Yugoslavia's esteemed sculptor Meštrović,
above the western, Pile Gate to the walled city.)

On the square named after Gundulić, the nation's heroic poet—just a few
meters south of Luža Square—one comes first on the Rector's Palace, seat
of government of the republic as well as the residence of the rector, plus all

Dubrovnik from Mount Srdj

government offices, rooms for receptions, quarters for the guards, and the state prisons. It also, unfortunately, included an arsenal, responsible for two rather devastating gunpowder explosions during the fifteenth century— a situation roughly comparable to storing a hydrogen bomb in the basement of the White House.

The building, constructed on the site of a twelfth-century castle destroyed by a gunpowder explosion, was designed by Onofrio della Cava, an Italian who constructed the city's waterworks system. (Two public fountains, small gems of architectural skill, still provide water, at either end of the Placa, and have become landmarks—known as Onofrio's Small Fountain, at the eastern end of the Placa, and Onofrio's Large Fountain, at its other extremity.) The Palace's arcaded portico was rebuilt in Renaissance style after the second of the explosions already mentioned. Some give credit for the attractive arcade to Salvi di Michieli, others to Michelozzo Michelozzi, a Florentine. It was definitely an Italian.

Lest I give the impression that the "look" of Dubrovnik was created by Italian architects exclusively, let me hasten to add that the city has a distinctly Slavic appearance overall; the walled city encompasses an area of buildings constructed of silver-gray ashlar and, except for the churches and palaces, they are of uniform height and topped by red turnip-colored tiles. The stone streets are immaculate; no garbage is in evidence to offend the senses, as is the case in many other aging cities.

Completely rebuilt following the earthquake of 1667, a date as indelibly inscribed in the minds of Dubrovnikans as 1066 is to the English, the Cathedral of Our Lady of the Assumption, an Italian baroque structure, does not match in magnificence the former, Romanesque church commissioned by Richard Coeur-de-Lion in 1190. The story, passed on as oral history from generation to generation in Yugoslavia, goes as follows: during a severe storm at sea, the English monarch made a vow to the Virgin Mary that if he ever felt solid earth beneath his feet again he would build the most beautiful church possible on the spot in her honor. (His spiritual descendants are the fog-blanketed air travelers of today who make various vows in exchange for a safe landing—vows that are invariably forgotten once the fog clears.) The spot where he was shipwrecked was a beach on the island of Lokrum, just off the coast opposite Dubrovnik, whose citizens prevailed on him to build his monument to the Virgin instead in their city, where presumably more worshippers would be able to admire its beauty. A sizable number of the paintings in the old church were saved and currently adorn the walls of the Cathedral, along with a truly impressive polyptych of the Assumption by Titian, transferred from the Church of Saint Lazarus in Ploče, just east of the ramparts.

In the Cathedral Treasury, adjoining the church, the most spectacular of its exhibits is the golden reliquary of the skull of Saint Blaise in the form of a Byzantine crown, studded with enamel medallions of saints; a similar golden reliquary of the head of the city's patron saint also dates from the twelfth century. Other masterpieces by Dubrovnik's gold- and silver-smiths, including a silver cross allegedly containing part of the cross of Calvary, are supplemented by some fascinating examples of early metalworking. In the course of admiring an early-Byzantine icon commemorating the birth of Christ, I learned that the building had three locks, with one key each having been distributed to the Archbishop, the Rector in Office, and the Secretary of the Republic, thereby insuring that no one could enter without the other two.

Retracing my steps and continuing on past still another splendid monastery (this one Dominican) to the east gate, beyond, in the sun-drenched suburb of Ploče, stands a large lazaretto, used as a quarantine center and during an epidemic an area for isolating infectious cases. Merchant seamen who were suspected of bringing a contagious disease from abroad were often lynched, Eric Whelpton notes; otherwise, Dubrovnik was ahead of its time, abolishing trade in slaves in the thirteenth or fourteenth century. Torture was also outlawed, and the rights of the individual were, to a degree, respected.

My sightseeing had taken me deep into the luncheon period, so I hurried back to the Placa and searched out the excellent, tiny fish restaurant on one of the narrow side streets just off that main thoroughfare. It had been highly recommended by a taxi driver who had been to London and spoke English passably well. The menu offered a variety of fish and shellfish dishes; the Adriatic equivalent of halibut I chose was well prepared and obviously very fresh. Dubrovnik is a commercial fisherman's heaven, certainly.

The Placa, with its squares at either end, is truly the center of life in Dubrovnik. In the suburbs adjoining the city one may find modern hotels, equipped with their own beaches and casinos, but only within the walled city, roughly thirteen hundred yards in diameter, does one find the real atmosphere of Dubrovnik, along with evidences of its unusual past. (Since the Great Earthquake of 1667, the city has been untouched physically; even World War II virtually passed the city by, and left no discernible mark.)

The coffeehouses along the wide promenade do a brisk business, not least the Central Café, facing the eastern square, near Onofrio's Small Fountain and the Pillar of Orlando (Roland). Here, on its ample terrace or in its large interior, the natives meet to exchange gossip or, as in the case of students, discuss their academic prejudices. The poet Gundulić is the hero of many daily literary forums, while the mathematically and scientifically oriented youths refer often to Ghetaldi and Bošcović, two of the city's most honored scholars. In the seventeenth century the former published an algebraical work that included a number of postulations later proclaimed by Descartes. In addition, the local people claim, he succeeded in setting a ship in the bay afire by the use of reflectors, in the manner of Archimedes in Sicily.

As they take their ease over strong Turkish coffee in this agreeable coffeehouse overlooking, on its other side, the Old Port, one can see in their faces the fierce national pride that has been inherited from their forebears, the citizens of the Republic of Dubrovnik, which may have set some sort of record for continous independence. Even though I could not understand what they were saying—the principal language is Serbo-Croat—it was obvious that they are an alert, sensitive people, with a keen intelligence.

Serbo-Croat sounds a difficult tongue for a westerner to master. The natives have come to expect that visitors will not speak their language; in fact, they readily admit that it, like their currency, is of no use whatever outside their country.

At night the Central Café is filled with music; on one of the evenings I dropped in for an after-dinner coffee the place was pulsing to the beat of a Yugoslav rock group—one of the few jarring notes encountered in my stay in Dubrovnik. The musicians were dedicated and performed with great precision, as though this were a mathematical exercise; I was somewhat embarrassed, just as I have always been, privately, embarrassed on hearing American jazz played by a European combo, no matter how technically expert.

On a sparkling sunny afternoon I searched out my English-speaking taxi driver friend to find out if he had time for a trip around the area encircling Dubrovnik. For a really comprehensive view of the countryside and seaside, one should make a tour of the hillside behind the old city. It can be done by bus, leaving from just outside the Pile Gate, or more comfortably and with greater freedom of movement by taxi. I chose the latter. The day was sunny, warm, and almost cloudless—a typical November day, I gathered, in this Nirvana—so it was possible to enjoy a maximum view toward the horizon. The driver spoke acceptable English, and much better German; with the help of both we managed to converse during the ride. (Since my English is much better than my German, the dialogue finally evolved into questions on my part being asked in English with the driver's replies in German.)

Soon after our departure from the Pile Gate, we had an excellent view of the Minčeta Tower along the northern ramparts. Built in the fifteenth century by the talented Florentine architect Michelozzo Michelozzi, it is a stirring monument of towering strength facing the steep slope of Mount Srdj to the north, not far beyond which—hundreds of years ago—lay the front line of the Turkish forces. The Tower has become a symbol of Dubrovnik and, along with the superb loggia of wide arches in the front of the Rector's Palace, for which he is given credit by most, has left Michelozzi's mark on the city for posterity.

We climbed steadily toward the crest of Mt. Srdj and another fort, the Imperial, built by Napoleon's soldiers in the early nineteenth century to protect the area from the Russians and any other aggressors who might venture into the district with designs on the picturesque southern Dalmatian coast.

The one-hour drive took us through villages that one could imagine existing only deep in the Balkan interior—villages that had changed hardly at all for hundreds of years. Except for the addition of electricity and a paved road, these towns and villages were just as the Turks, Russians, Montenegrins, and Napoleon's French troops found them as they swept across the countryside. Abruptly, completing a sharp turn in the road, we would come upon the most magnificent views of the sea and the offshore islands. Nowhere short of the South Pacific have I seen such vistas of an earthly paradise. The most expert color photographs do not do justice to the scenic delights of the area.

Back in the walled city, for an afternoon coffee and pastry, I embarked on a series of visits to a few of the museums, but I soon realized that I would not have the time, and perhaps not the energy—even over a span of several days—to see all, since Dubrovnik seems to have even more museums than churches. For a couple who gravitate separately—one to churches, the other to museums—this is an ideal city to visit. Among the principal museums I did manage either to inspect at first hand or look into there are: the Cultural and Historical Museum in the Rector's Palace, an Ethnographic Museum (old costumes, and handicrafts of the region), the Rupe Museum (containing archeological, lapidary, and folk art sections), the Museum of the Socialist Revolution, the Maritime Museum, the Art Gallery (mostly works by the prolific Dubrovnik Renaissance school), the Museum of Old Icons, the Natural Sciences Museum, and the Aquarium (a living museum), among others.

In this community of buildings, one can learn almost all there is to know about Dubrovnik's political, social, and cultural history, with special emphasis on its ruling class and its seafaring exploits. In the Rector's Palace I examined the first town statutes, written in 1272, portraits of assorted nobles, senators, and rectors, the clothes they wore (carefully preserved in glass cases), and on the walls remnants of the décor of the rooms in which they worked, ate, and slept. The traditions and successes of the Ragusan maritime might are proudly kept in the city's Maritime Museum. The bulk of the republic's archives, housed in the Sponza Palace, provided another absorbing hour, followed by a hasty inspection, just before closing, of the history of the National Liberation.

But its museums, churches, and ramparts are only a part of the distinctiveness that Dubrovnik holds for the visitor. Its people—fierce, proud, hospitable, gay, and somber by turn—so obviously savor the experience of living that their enthusiasm is contagious, even to the most cynical. The citizens of this historic city seem to find delight in the most inconsequential objects and in the most casual encounters. Unlike many other Europeans, and like small children, they seem to be completely guileless.

A traveler who visited "Ragusa" just before the French Revolution said of them:

"They have more learning and less ostentation than any people I know, more politeness to each other, and less envy. Their hospitality to strangers cannot be exceeded. . . ."

And so they are today.

Syracuse

— ⟡ —

The Greek theatre is reputed to have been in its time one of the finest in the entire Grecian world. The auditorium is carved into the rock in a large semicircle, with a diameter of 151 ½ yards. This classic structure, like many others throughout the island, is set in a hillside overlooking the sea. In this sanctuary the dramatic works of Aeschylus and Euripides were performed, some twenty-five centuries ago; in more recent times the classic plays have been presented on holidays and in festivals, usually in Italian. . . . Here on the heights of Greater Syracuse, it is virtually impossible not to feel the spell of the ages.

$\mathcal{S}$icily, the largest island in the Mediterranean, separated from the European mainland by two miles of rough water, is the fulcrum of the Mare Nostrum, the sea that lies between Europe and Africa and borders on Asia. In that strategic position, it has been coveted from all sides by countless power-hungry monarchs and conquered and claimed by a good many of them.

Its history, as turbulent as the waters of the Straits of Messina, which pass between it and Italy proper, and as explosive as the eruptions of Mount Etna, on its eastern coast, includes occupations by invaders representing a great variety of nations, so that today's "Sicilian" is a mixture of more races than any other European. Successors to the prehistoric inhabitants were Sicans, Elymians, Sicels, Greeks, Phoenicians, Carthaginians, Romans, Goths, Byzantines, Lombards, Germans, Arabs, Berbers, Franks, Herulians, Norsemen, Persians, Tartars, Sudanese, Jews, Vandals, Slavs, French, Saracens, Normans, Swabians, Spaniards, Bourbons, as well as assorted drifters with still other backgrounds from the entire Mediterranean basin and beyond, before the arrival of Garibaldi and his band of patriots, who helped turn Sicily into a part of a unified Italy. It has been suggested that the island's domination by powers based beyond its shores is responsible for the rise, in modern times, of the Mafia, which claims to represent the "natives" and exercises a local, unofficial control independent of the Italian state.

The island lies just off the tip of the toe of the Italian "boot," and Sicilians are fond of saying that the Italian boot has been kicking Sicily for generations. Travelers taking the express from Rome, which is loaded aboard ferries at San Giovanni for the short trip across the straits to the city of Messina, have a close-up view, to starboard, of Scylla and Charybdis, the rock and whirlpool respectively of the Greek legend that prompted the phrase "caught between Scylla and Charybdis" as an expression of extreme danger without hope of salvation.

It seemed inconceivable that, in this age of thirty-mile-long bridges not to mention voyages in outer space, a narrow strip of water like the Messina straits had not been spanned by a bridge. The political gulf between the two bodies of land is, it seems, much wider than the straits, but that is not the only reason. Standing beside me on the deck of the train-ferry was a young Italian from Bologna, Dr. Giulio Panza, who teaches at the University of Bari, on the mainland's Adriatic coast; it seemed at the time perfectly logical that he should be able to supply the answer.

"Besides the political considerations, which are very complex, there is," he said, "a very practical reason: the two land masses which almost meet are constantly moving slightly, but in opposite directions. What material, other than rubber, would be appropriate for building the structure?"

The youthful doctor and his vibrant Italian wife, who is also a professor, proved to be ideal companions for an appreciation of the Messina area. Dr. Panza, it developed, is a seismologist and seems to be magnetically attracted to locations where the earth's surface is likeliest to crack. (He recently spent a year's tour of duty at UCLA in southern California, a seismologist's dream.)

I was directed to put a pin on the map between Ragusa and Modica, in the southeastern corner of the island—virtually destroyed in the powerful earthquake of 1693—another pin between Messina and, on the mainland, Reggio Calabria, where 84,000 persons died in the earthquake of 1908, a third pin between Vulcan and Stromboli, a fourth pin between Pompeii and Herculaneum, buried in A.D. 79 by a massive eruption of Mount Vesuvius, and a final pin between Naples and Cumae. The line connecting these pins traces the major geologic fault line of a land mass once thought to be continuous.

Dr. Panza was intent on examining the areas on the island where other, lesser fault lines occur. My own objective was Syracuse, almost due south on the island's east coast, fronting on the Ionian Sea. To reach that gem of a city the train winds along the coast past Taormina, the picturesque resort perched partly on the bluff overlooking the blue-green sea and partly along the beach, and past Catania, eastern Sicily's largest city, which lies beneath ever-threatening Mount Etna. Finally, after a ride of more than three hours from Messina, one arrives in Syracuse. The city's finest visual glories are certainly not wasted on the area where the train traveler disembarks to find himself, especially in the evening, in what appears to be a Sicilian version of a ghost town, with one disreputable-looking bar still open and no taxis in sight. But this initial disappointment serves only to heighten the enjoyment of the splendors to follow.

Cicero proclaimed Syracuse the finest Greek city in the world—perhaps the loveliest of all cities. It was one of the favorite sites for contemplation for Plato, Goethe, D. H. Lawrence, and Ruskin. Saint Paul passed this way, and Julius Caesar is said to have celebrated the third anniversary of his consulship in and near Syracuse, partaking liberally of the wine of the region; Archimedes and Theocritus were born here (the former was also killed here, by a Roman soldier), and Aeschylus found it an inspiring place.

The process of Hellenization of Sicily has, of course, been chronicled in detail by Thucydides—including the final fatal Athenian naval expedition which had been mounted with an eye to the subjugation of the entire island, with Syracuse as its particular target.

In brief, anyone addicted to walking in the footsteps of history will be enthralled with a visit to Sicily and, in particular, to Syracuse. And walking is by far the best way to explore the city. The island of Ortygia, with a narrow channel separating it from the larger expanse of Syracuse adjoining it, is the site of the original settlement of Corinthians in the eighth century before Christ—although Thucydides and certain archeologists are certain that the Sicels inhabited the place at least a century before. Today, thanks to the shattering earthquake of 1693 which caused such devastation, a Greek relic of the fifth century B.C. stands beside an eighteenth-century baroque structure; the whole of the island is an assortment of Greek, Roman, Byzantine, and Norman architecture and craftsmanship, with evidences of Spanish and Arabic influences—all confined in a small space, much as though Ortygia were a warehouse whose custodian had crammed a collection of pieces, of varying ages and degrees of preservation, willy-nilly into the smallest possible area, without regard to size or order.

The Cathedral, on Ortygia's Piazza del Duomo, just off the Porto Grande, is a true amalgam of three distinct epochs: originally a Greek temple, a shrine of Athena, in the fifth century before Christ, it was remodeled as a Christian church in the seventh century after Christ, and redone again in the early eighteenth century in the southern baroque style of its present incarnation. Here God has been worshipped, through the ages, under the names of different deities. (In Grecian times, by the way, only the priests were allowed inside the temple—the congregation did its worshipping alfresco.)

Impressive fifth-century B.C. Doric columns from the original edifice dominate one side of the Cathedral, which in its seventh-century A.D. construction reversed the major entrance of the building from that of the Greek temple. Its majestic interior combines in its decoration a Spanish mood, with its lacy wrought-iron gates, with a Norman front fashioned out of a Greek marble block. The outer door has a Saracen feeling, and the whole—with its ancient Greek columns—has a disjointed effect that is fascinating to the student of the layers of history represented here.

Across from the Cathedral stands the National Museum, reputed to contain one of the finest archeological collections in the world; here the patient visitor can immerse himself or herself in an absorbing study of the advances of civilization from prehistory on. Perhaps no other one place is so appropriate for looking backward across the span of ages as this museum in this particular city on this embattled island. From the original Temple of Athena nearby, various classical forms, not least the seductive statue, minus head and right forearm, of the celebrated Venus Landolina, have found repose in the museum.

Ortygia is really tiny, so its treasures are only a distance of a few strides, one from another. Just down from the museum, fronting on the Porto Grande, the larger of Syracuse's two harbors, is the fountain of Arethusa, the legendary water nymph whose ancestry is clouded in conflicting versions of the tale of how she had spurned the river god, Alpheus. Its bountiful supply of fresh water is mentioned by the ancients, and Admiral Nelson, bringing his large fleet into the Grand Harbor before attacking and defeating the French naval force at Aboukir, felt at the time of his stopover at Syracuse: "surely, watering at the Fountain of Arethusa, we must have a victory." And so he did.

In his appraisal of historic Sicily, Alfonso Lowe, of England, relates that the spring of clear water was turned to salt following one of the island's many earthquakes, but "by the beginning of this century cups were provided for those who wished to drink from it." Briton Peter Quennell notes that "her fresh springs mingle with the salt of the sea." The ancients believed that

Arethusa, in her flight from the river god took refuge beneath the sea and changed herself into a fountain, whereupon the river god found her, thus accounting for the plentiful supply of fresh water. (I saw no cups, and did not drink.)

At any rate, her fountain—in a large circular pool—is carefully railed off; its occupants, mostly carp, lead a protected if not very private existence among the papyrus reeds. A few swans and ducks make the pool headquarters, and, depending on the season, migrant quails are said to descend on their way from Europe or Africa or return for a watering stop in the manner of Admiral Nelson. (Lowe reasons that since *Ortyx* is Greek for quail, the migrating fowl that landed on Ortygia must have been quail, which used other nearby islands for their stops, and that the name Ortygia relates to quail.)

The streets of Ortygia—alleyways, really—are narrow and twisting, but invariably at the end of each one will find oneself at the seafront—either the Porto Grande or the Porto Piccoli, both of which offer colorful harbor atmosphere, the size of the ships and boats corresponding to the relative size of the particular port, with as a backdrop the pale blue vastness of the Ionian Sea.

Ortygia is variously described as ancient and modern, for while its history dates back to the Greek occupation of the area it boasts fewer vestiges of that period beginning eight centuries before Christ was born than the extension of the city across the canal, on what is often referred to as the "Sicilian mainland." Indeed, the appearance of Ortygia is a curious mixture of Greek (a few mutilated columns in approximately their original state, and also the narrow front of the so-called Temple of Diana, which, authorities say, was more probably a Temple of Apollo), Roman, Spanish, Arab, and Norman architecture—like a busy back lot in Burbank, California, in the golden days of Hollywood film production. On Ortygia, however, the buildings are not simply façades, as was the case at the studios.

At one point, following a Roman takeover of the area, Ortygia was off-limits as a place of habitation to "Syracusans"—then a mixture of Athenian, Spartan, Carthaginian, and other more aged stocks.

Perhaps the most spectacular view Ortygia affords is from the area surrounding the post office, a "modern" structure undoubtedly built within the last century, with a niggardly amount of window space giving its interior a cavernous feeling and depriving the postal workers of the exhilarating sweep of sea visible once outside the main entrance. A short walk along the canal to the bridge that spans it, and one is ready to return to the "Sicilian mainland."

Since Ortygia was too small to serve as a location for the construction of major stadia, much less for catacombs, the most massive evidences of Greek and Roman habitation in Syracuse are to be found in the more extended part of the city across the bridge. But before venturing on that swing of Syracuse's chief attractions, I decided to drop into a trattoria, chosen at random, for an inexpensive meal in the native style. Its one simple room, devoid of any attempt at decoration, featured at one end a table bearing an assortment of some of the dishes available on the brief menu: fish, cold meats, a variety of fruits and vegetables, and a tempting Italian salad.

The principal dishes—mostly various forms of pasta—were prepared in a back room. All the diners in the restaurant, all presumably workmen, were engrossed in the consumption of pasta, of one kind or another, so the problem of what to have for lunch was greatly simplified. The fettucini I selected was excellent: obviously homemade by someone with considerable experience. The house red wine, however, I found harsh—not to be compared with even an ordinary Chianti on the mainland of Italy. But the fettucini was an agreeable surprise, not that it should have been in other circumstances (I was once served the very worst spaghetti in my experience—a lifetime of eating spaghetti—in Milan).

I made a mental note to return to this trattoria, with its unpretentious, inexpensive menu and its attractive view of the harbor (the Porto Grande) with, in the foreground, ships from Russia and Malta berthed along the quay. The combination of the agreeable atmosphere of the trattoria, its interesting patrons (with a variety of facial characteristics), the simple but satisfying food, and the sounds and smells of the harbor induced a certain languor and made it difficult for me to resume my journey on foot through the historic city. Two cups of espresso helped strengthen my resolve, but just after reaching the main street that crosses the bridge over the canal, the Corso Umberto, while carefully studying the flow of motorized traffic headed for the bridge, I walked into a horse pulling an open carriage; its driver cried out in astonishment and seemed genuinely concerned about my well-being. He also gently reassured his horse, a smallish member of his breed, just about my height, and was not at all angry or annoyed, as would have been the case almost anywhere else in the world. I straightened my jacket and patted the horse's nose in apology. The driver smiled winningly and asked where I was bound. When I replied—the Greek and Roman ruins —he suggested that I hire his vehicle, since the way was steep—no exaggeration, as I was shortly to discover.

We darted in and out of streets and avenues, proceeded up the Corso Gelone past my hotel, and started a circular climb toward the area of the most interesting Greek and Roman remains.

A left turn on the Viale Paolo Orsi brought us quickly to the Viale G. Emanuele Rizzo and the winding way up to the plateau where the Greek theater and the Roman amphitheater are situated. Our horse slowed from a canter to a walk, and Lucio, whom I had hired simply as a driver, attempted manfully to fill in as a guide as well, in a mixture of heavily accented Italian and a few words and phrases in French and English.

As we climbed alongside and behind and above some very ancient-appearing stones I gathered that we were passing a Greek cemetery and then one of a number of latomies (quarries) we were to encounter on our route. We also paused for a look, in one of the quarries, at the "Ear of Dionysus," with a seventy-foot-high aperture, a man-made construction of stones so placed that the tyrant then in power, sitting in a concealed niche above, could listen to the talk of his political captives, with the sound magnified many times by the arrangement of the stones. The theory that it is a natural setting, as some believe, is belied by the presence of tell-tale chisel marks. It is popularly supposed that this facility did indeed furnish the tyrant with vital information useful in dealing with his enemies and political opponents, setting an example, in the practices of eavesdropping, that has come down to us through the centuries.

Although we had not yet reached the summit of this particular rise, the view across the new city, and the island of Ortygia, the miles of coastline to the south, and a limitless expanse of sea was spectacular. After a brief pause, which provided me with a few moments for reflection on the quarries, where the Athenian prisoners in the rout of 415 B.C. were interned, and gave the horse a chance to recover his breath, we moved on toward the entrance to the Greek theater, unquestionably the city's number one attraction. Here Lucio's equanimity deserted him upon learning that the guards, employed by the state, were on strike and that there would be no chance to enter the arena that day. (As is the custom in Europe generally, the strike was to be of only one day's duration.) I didn't catch all of Lucio's harangue delivered to the single individual delegated with the task of making certain that no one violated the strike, but I did make out a reference to the anger of the gods who would consider this deprivation of the rights of foreign visitors as sacrilegious. The picket, if that's what he was, remained impassive throughout the tirade; finally, Lucio, having recovered his composure as swiftly as he had lost it, climbed back up onto the driver's seat and we rode on to the Roman amphitheater nearby.

Here we met a similar situation, but of course it was less of a surprise. Lucio attempted to recapture the spirit of his bravura performance at the Greek theater but his heart wasn't in it. He seemed obviously crestfallen; after all, he had convinced me to hire his services and vehicle to come here, and now there was no reason for the trip. Furthermore, he added, as a guide of sorts and a knowledgeable man-about-Syracuse, he should have known about the strike. He seemed truly remorseful, but there were of course no offers to cancel the fee we had agreed upon. Nor was he too embarrassed to ask whether he could conduct me to this point again when the strike was ended. I told him I'd think about it.

Before starting down the hill toward my hotel I asked if there were anything else of interest in the area that wasn't on strike. His brown eyes flickered before I had finished speaking. Of course! The most celebrated of the Syracusan catacombs were relatively close by, and since they were attended by clergymen—Franciscans, he thought—they certainly shouldn't be on even a wildcat strike.

While he was stirring up his horse to a slightly faster pace along the level stretch of road heading, I calculated, east, he rambled on *con brio* about the merits of Syracuse's catacombs versus the Roman ones. According to Lucio, the former—some of which I was about to see, he assured me confidently— are apparently more extensive than their more famous counterparts in Rome.

Every pronouncement that Lucio made was delivered with such winning charm that I instinctively felt that he must be exaggerating; each time I was surprised to find his statements substantially correct.

It was two forty-five P.M. when we reached the entrance to the grounds of the early medieval cathedral and the catacombs of San Giovanni; a sign on the door in the walled enclosure announced that the Franciscan monk who served as guide would be available from three o'clock. A few minutes before the hour he appeared at the door and seemed to feel put upon to have to conduct me through the underground tunnels and to view what remained

Cathedral of San Giovanni

of the cathedral. Lucio was not keen on joining me, indicating that he had little interest in the site, like most natives who are unimpressed with the marvels of their own communities.

Throughout the promenade through the catacombs, the good friar wore a distracted look as he rattled off the names of the saints who had been buried here. Quite obviously he had trod this path so often that it no longer occupied his attention at all; nor was he surprised or pleased by his guest's reactions to the impressiveness of the size and well-planned design of the chambers and the routes of access to them.

In fact, the only moment of animation he showed came at the end of the tour when I thanked him and handed him a 1,000-lire note ($1.71)—more than he usually received, I gathered. As I left, three bearded youths in blue jeans and tattered shirts arrived, and his face fell, dissolving quickly into its customary trancelike attitude.

The catacombs themselves are well lighted and accommodate six-foot and taller westerners with room to spare. The shelved resting places are neatly arranged, and the passages intersect in ample, circular rotundas. This burial ground, the friar told me, dates from the fourth to seventh centuries A.D., although there are evidences that similar passages existed in the area in the pre-Christian epoch.

Ruins of the early medieval cathedral are combined with a western façade, with its justly celebrated rose window, and porch, part of the fifteenth-century restoration of the building; in the garden there are a few remarkably well-preserved column bases. Below the base of the church is the crypt of Saint Marcian, who—tradition has it—was dispatched from Antioch by Saint Peter to found the first Christian community in the world in Syracuse in the year 44.

At a roadside refreshment stand a friend of Lucio's, an English guide at the Greek theater who had the day off thanks to the strike, added a bit more detail; he said the early Christians, like the Saracens later on, showed a tendency to use the same places of worship that their predecessors had chosen. Thus, fourteenth- and fifteenth-century Norman fragments survive alongside sixth-century Christian pieces, on a site that had previously been occupied by a Temple of Bacchus and, it is claimed, before that by a Temple of

Dionysus, although this is mostly speculation. In any case, this church of San Giovanni remained *the* Cathedral of Syracuse until the bishop Zosimus moved his see, in the seventh century A.D., to the fourth- and fifth-century church on the Piazza del Duomo, on Ortygia island, then the only area of Syracuse free of Saracen rule.

The small chapel in which the Crypt of Saint Marcian was housed is certainly one of the earliest surviving centers of Christian worship in the world, according to Lowe and his partisans. The altar used by Saint Paul during his brief sojourn in Syracuse stands just a few feet in front of Saint Marcian's tomb.

Altogether it was an edifying and humbling experience; on the leisurely jaunt down to my hotel in Lucio's carriage I felt that it was just as well that the Greek theater and Roman amphitheater had to be left to another day.

Just as fear, for example, cannot be maintained over an extended period, so I believe that after a few hours of exposure to antiquity, brilliant art masterpieces, or meals prepared by master chefs, a certain numbness sets in; as an English acquaintance once put it, once the mind boggles it cannot continue boggling indefinitely. His remark is most apt in the case of Syracuse and its treasures.

The Americans I had noticed in the bar and restaurant of my hotel, which seemed to cater to commercial types, were not in Syracuse to go sightseeing among the Greek and Roman ruins, I learned one evening soon after my arrival. They were interested in only one commodity—oil, a substance dating back to prehistory whose value increases with each passing year. Thus the search for deposits beneath the earth's surface and beneath the sea as well knows no bounds, or boundaries.

The strike of the state-paid employees at the ruins on the hill above Syracuse gave me an opportunity to pass some extra time in the pleasurable atmosphere of the Porto Grande. But it ended as abruptly as it had begun, to be followed by a demonstration of students on the Corso Gelone near my hotel. These appeared to be majoring in mathematics and were calling attention to the fact that they had insufficient classroom space and inadequate facilities. One of the American oil company "prospectors" who inhabited the hotel said sympathetically: "These students really have something to complain about. When I think of those American kids carrying on, and the modern buildings and superb equipment they have at their disposal—well, I think they have a hell of a nerve."

The demonstration was small and nonviolent, consisting mostly of the exhibition of placards and a great deal of horn blowing. The reappearance of a smiling Lucio as the protestors moved on signaled the end of the strike, and I readjusted my schedule to accommodate an immediate visit to the Roman amphitheater, which Lucio classed as the most impressive and the most complete in Sicily.

Although I gathered that he had not spent too much time in pursuit of a formal education, Lucio seemed to have a fairly good groundwork in the island's history; to his mind, the Punic Wars in which Romans and Carthaginians vied for power on the battleground of Sicily constituted the island's most glorious period.

We agreed on the Roman amphitheater as the next stop on our carriage tour—he because he seemed genuinely partial to the Romans, their civilization, and their life-style ("That Caesar! Magnifico!"), I because I had from the beginning planned to reserve the Greek theater as the climax of my stay in Syracuse. (Incidentally, I might explain that I decided to use the word Syracuse throughout, even though the city is today known as "Siracusa," for this Italianate designation does not ring fittingly with relation to the ancient Greeks and their habitation of the area.)

By now a rapport of sorts had sprung up between Lucio and me, but he never confided to me the results of the quickly ended strike: what gains, if any, had been won by the employees. Information of this sort, though of no real significance, is obviously considered "private," and the discreet Sicilians, who treasure secrecy as though it were a divine gift, are loath to dispense facts of this kind to curious, loose-tongued foreigners. I personally suspected that like so many short European strikes this one turned out to be just an extra bit of vacation for the workers.

The road we followed runs along a ridge above the amphitheater, to which we descended carefully on foot. The Romans felt obliged to erect their major structures alongside or not far from a Greek theater or other architectural wonder—perhaps because they hoped for some of the Greek greatness to rub off on their own less noteworthy effort. This Roman amphitheater, which specialized in the presentation of gladiator and wild animal acts, dates from the time of Augustus, but was restored in the third century. Some of the blocks of marble lying about bear the names of the proprietors of the seats they helped form.

The remains of the amphitheater did not detain us for long, to Lucio's disappointment, and we pressed on—past a huge altar (of Hiero II), another quarry, and a cemetery—to the Greek theater, reputed to have been in its time one of the finest in the entire Grecian world.

The auditorium is carved into the rock in a large semicircle, with a diameter of 151½ yards, compared with one of 109 yards in the Athenian theater. This classic structure, like many others throughout the island, is set in a hillside overlooking the sea; the first eleven rows of seats were covered with marble and reserved for local functionaries and important guests from abroad, but because of the position of the elevated stage it was the ordinary citizens in the tiers farther up who had a spectacular view of the stage with the coastal area and the shimmering sea behind it.

It is estimated by Baedeker that there were at least fifteen more tiers plus a colonnade behind and above the forty-six tiers of seats still visible. As in the nearby Roman amphitheater, it is still possible to make out inscriptions in the more select part of the auditorium, but here they were made beginning in 238 B.C.—notably the names King Hiero II, Queen Philistis, Queen Nereis (Hiero's wife and daughter-in-law respectively), and Zeus Olympios.

In this sanctuary—now silent except for the ripple of a light breeze—the dramatic works of Aeschylus and Euripides were performed, some twenty-five centuries ago, by all-male casts; in more recent times the classic plays have been presented on holidays and in festivals, usually in Italian. In ancient times, the festivals lasted several days, with each play being given only once, and with each day's program including as many as three tragedies balanced by a comedy and a satyr play. The spectators, says Lowe, though free to applaud or condemn the performances, were expected to behave in a manner befitting a sacred edifice.

In the comedies, David Barrett points out that the actors customarily wore tights over heavy padding and a tight tunic cut very short so as to reveal an artificial phallus. "In *Peace*," he adds, "the leading character, who flies up to heaven astride a dung-beetle, uses his phallus as a kind of joy-stick or tiller." In *The Wasps,* another character "offers his to the flute girl as a hand-rope by which to pull herself up on to the stage." There is no record of how these comic bits of business were received, or whether the required decorum in the audience was maintained.

The stunning structure in Syracuse seems to have escaped the fate of some other Greek theaters, like the one in Taormina, where the front rows were cut away by the Romans for their wild animal and gladiator offerings.

Standing among the majestic rocks on this hillside that has overlooked so much history in the making, Quennell felt himself in a "windswept lunar emptiness." Here on the heights of greater Syracuse, it is virtually impossible not to feel the spell of the ages.

This lovely city, which had been besieged, invaded, and even destroyed, and governed by a great variety of races, has remained aloof, in recent years, from the administrative affairs of the island, content to rest on its epic past, stretching more than twenty-five centuries, and on its reputation, at various times during that span, as the greatest and finest city in the civilized world.

Salzburg

———— ❦ ————

———— ❦ ————

As one stands facing the swiftly flowing river, the view after dark has fallen is pure magic. Dominating the scene on the heights above the town is the brooding fortress erected in the eleventh century by the Prince-Archbishop reigning at the moment. The monster on the mountain, bathed in its gangrenous light, had a hypnotic effect; it was hard to tear one's eyes away from the sight.

here is a certain place at the edge of a footbridge on the right bank of the river Salzach where the whole of Salzburg —through the centuries—comes to life right before one's eyes, just as clearly and poignantly as a Mozart concerto performed by the Festival House orchestra under Herbert von Karajan. The footbridge parallels, not many meters distant, the main vehicular bridge across the river, the one that leads on the right bank into the square that is highlighted by the church and seminary of the Holy Trinity and by the Landestheater, one of the most *gemütlich* structures in a land of *gemütlichkeit* rampant.

As one stands facing the swiftly flowing river, the view after dark has fallen is pure magic. To the far right is the brightly illuminated, Gothic Mülln, one of about forty churches in the city proper; a cluster of churches to the left includes Saint Peter's, the Salzburg Cathedral, and the Franciscan church, and behind them—dominating the scene on the heights above the town—is the brooding fortress erected in the eleventh century by the Prince-Archbishop reigning at the moment, lighted in a misty green that would make Count Dracula turn even greener with envy. I have never seen a green quite the color of the Festung HohenSalzburg, sitting atop its mountain in the dark and peering suspiciously down at the town below. It is not a garish green, nor of course an emerald green; I would call it a bilious green except that that description does not connote the fascinating mixture of subtle color and massive fortifications that give the visitor standing transfixed at the footbridge a visual representation of the Middle Ages before his eyes. The monster on the mountain, bathed in its gangrenous light, had a hypnotic effect; it was hard to tear one's eyes away from the sight.

This is the Salzburg ruled—through the centuries—by the Prince-Archbishops, temporal as well as spiritual sovereigns of the area, among them one who had a Roman basilica torn down in order to build another on the site that would be architecturally more to his liking, and another Archbishop ruler who literally drove Mozart, the city's most illustrious son, out of Salz-

River Salzach

burg by being so miserly with his minuscule court grants to the composer-performer for his work.

Today, the Archbishop is in charge only of his subjects' spiritual lives, and in Salzburg that role has much more meaning than in many Western countries. On my first night there on my most recent trip there were well over a thousand of the faithful standing in the square outside the Cathedral in a driving rain to listen to a concert issuing from the opened windows of His Holiness's Residence. The Europeans—especially these Salzburgers—have something that we Americans seem to have lost; I couldn't imagine even a handful of Americans standing in such a rain for almost an hour to hear anything.

Except for the forbidding presence of the fortress, Salzburg is all gaiety, light-heartedness, and high spirits. The people are happy—no somber thoughts about the state of the world seem to intrude—and their perfectly preserved city is a toy setting. Many of its buildings, in fact, have the appearance and feeling of dollhouses, slightly enlarged to accommodate six-foot-tall visitors. The people seem oversized; I had the same impression of being at large in a children's play world as I had in Neuilly-sur-Seine, France, where

I lived for a time, while riding the toy train that runs through part of the Bois de Boulogne; the train is dwarfed by its full-grown passengers who are barely able to squeeze into the tiny seats of the coaches. But the pleasure experienced was never to be duplicated in an ordinary, full-sized-train ride.

The atmosphere of unreality—for happiness and good-fellowship are unreal in this world of the late twentieth century—is underscored by a steady accompaniment of concertos, sonatas, operas, and masses performed by expert quartets, full orchestras, and choirs. For Salzburg today is most notably a city of music, befitting the birthplace of Wolfgang Amadeus Mozart.

The next morning I stood, shoulder to shoulder, with a throng of Salzburgers in the Franciscan church to listen to his "Krönungsmesse"—an exalting experience; we were assembled literally just around the corner from the narrow five-story (plus ground floor) house in which the composer was born on January 27, 1756, on a little street on the left bank called Getreidegasse.

It is difficult to reconstruct a composer's life and its trials out of material remains; his legacy to the world of course is his music. Otherwise, there is, in the house on Getreidegasse, an area roped off where his cradle stood, his first small violin, the clavichord on which he first picked out tunes, and his piano, along with numerous portraits of himself at various ages, as well as of his father—who pushed him along in his career as relentlessly as the mother of any Hollywood child star of the 1920s and '30s—and of his mother and of his sister, who performed duets with him in his early days as a musician.

There are other, more edifying monuments to his genius, such as the Mozarteum on the right bank—for student musicians and directors—with its own respectably accomplished orchestra. And, of course, the Festival Hall, across the river on Mozart's own left bank, where at Easter and in August Salzburg becomes the musical capital of Europe, if not of the world.

But there are dissident currents here, as there are in any place of ferment —and Salzburg is a city in musical ferment. An agreeable, bearded, forty-year-old composer named Klaus Hochmann, who lives and works near Zurich, was telling me in the Café Tomaselli, one of the most frequented of the *gemütlich* cafés specializing in coffee *mit Schlag*, that Salzburg is no longer the place to hear Mozart, in his estimation. In Augsburg, Germany, yes, or in Vienna, or in a number of other cities one could well hear Mozart performed better.

"Von Karajan?" A wry face and a wrinkled nose. "He is a conductor who is good only for surface things—like Wagner. Did you ever hear him try to do Mahler?

"Only Karl Boehm and one or two others, including your Leonard Bernstein, really understand Mahler. I heard Bernstein conduct Mahler once in Vienna. After a short rest early in the piece he kicked out with his foot for the effect he wanted. The orchestra was stunned."

Hochmann was in town for the performance in a few nights' time of his composition "Concertino for Percussion and Woodwinds" to be given by a percussion group of the Orff-Institute at the Mozarteum. Meanwhile, he was passing his time like so many Salzburgers, sitting in their favorite café, drinking coffee and eating kuchen, and reading the numerous newspapers hung on racks for the customers. (The Germans and Austrians are, I believe, the most voracious newspaper readers on earth; as a result there are so many different papers published one can't count them all.)

Incidentally, despite Herr Hochmann's estimate of von Karajan, that conductor has a reputation in Salzburg as secure as Toscanini's at his peak. In Salzburg Mozart and von Karajan go together like coffee and whipped cream.

On another visit to the Tomaselli, to which I became accustomed to dropping in, I encountered at the table I chose a cheerful, brown-haired, sparkling-eyed Austrian girl who undertook—in a mixture of German and English—to advise me on how to pick from the *karte* the items that gave one the most for the money involved. (Since the tables at Tomaselli's are invariably all occupied by someone, it is the custom simply to sit down at any vacant place. Thus one acquires acquaintances quickly.)

After several coffees *mit Schlag* (pure cream) we made a tour of half a dozen of the principal churches, as well as a few lesser shrines. Anna was very knowledgeable on the religious history of this ecclesiastical city: there are, she told me, thirty-six Roman Catholic churches, one Protestant, and one Jewish synagogue, not to mention various seminaries and monasteries. Her estimates of the various Prince-Archbishops of centuries ago—some of them obviously villains—were firm and deeply felt.

The Cathedral, which dates from the eighth century and was rebuilt and reconsecrated in the early seventeenth, is probably the most impressive house of worship, commensurate with its rank, but my favorite was the Franciscan Church close by. (I seem to gravitate to Franciscan churches in spite of the fact that my father studied for many years to be a Jesuit, in Austria, stopping just short of taking his vows—a break for me—and I too was schooled by the Jesuits, in the United States.)

Anna's enthusiasm kept mounting with each new visit; in Saint Peter's cemetery, she told me proudly, there is a waiting list of applicants. One headstone marked the grave of Major General Harry Collins, commander of the 42nd Rainbow Division during World War II. He fell in love with Salzburg (no difficult feat), was made an Honorary Citizen, and was given a plot in Saint Peter's. (Even the cemetery had a certain air of *gemütlichkeit* about it.) Collins died in the United States, but according to his wishes his bones were returned to this Austrian retreat.

Perhaps the secret of Salzburg's charm is the feeling engendered in the breasts of its visitors of a return to the wonderful, carefree, uncomplicated world of childhood. Not a deliberate, artificially created fantasy complex like Disneyland and Disney World but a genuine, unselfconscious atmosphere of childhood attitudes that has existed for generations. I never actually saw a copy of a gingerbread house, but I would not have been at all surprised if I had come upon one, along Getreidegasse or one of the narrow streets giving off it.

Salzburg is a city of many narrow streets, particularly on the left bank, so walking is the accustomed manner of getting around, as many of the most interesting buildings are located along them. Anna looked game for another thirty churches or so, but it had been a tiring two hours. I suggested splitting a bottle of Grüner Veltuner, a local white wine, at my hotel. She was still bubbling over with information, and though she had a date to meet her husband shortly she agreed.

My hotel, the Goldener Hirsch (the Golden Deer), is easily the most picturesque and certainly the oldest in the city, lying just down Getreidegasse a few doors, on the same side of the street, from Mozart's birthplace.

This six-centuries-old building has been an inn since 1564 and has borne its current name since 1671. It has of course been restored several times, according to the dictates of the increasing demand for comforts in later centuries, and rooms have been added in the building next door. But it still retains the charm, and many of the accouterments, of the original structure.

The hotel is of three stories above the ground floor, and there is an elevator tucked away in the recesses of some recently built walls. But one usually mounts to the first floor by the stairway from the lobby. About halfway up, the stone ceiling slopes at a low angle across the stairway, dating back to the days before the building became an inn. The Salzburgers must have been a short species in those days; "Anno Domini 1407" was painted on the bulge at the precise spot where I banged my head every time I used the stairs. One was not allowed to forget how old the structure was. (Every time I shaved I half expected to see "Anno Domini 1407" imprinted on my forehead.)

The distinctive wine—not too fruity, thus not a typical Teutonic type— loosed a new burst of information, largely ecclesiastical but more comprehensive, from Anna. The fortress, I learned, had its furniture taken by Napoleon, one of whose chief reasons for waging wars seemed to be the treasures he could seize. Archbishop Leonhard, in the 1500s, she added, reminded the peasants who was boss by having the sound of the bull—a great booming organ—swell out over the city from the fortress at four and eleven A.M. and at six P.M. It proved to be not a particularly good idea, though, for the peasants—perhaps because of their irritation at the noise— revolted in 1525. . . . The catacombs cut into the Monks' Mountain, a conglomerate of stone adjoining a monastery, date from the third century A.D. . . . The mountain's façade, and the monastery's conformation, was altered by a landslide three hundred years ago. . . . It was Archbishop Wolf Dietrich —at the end of the sixteenth century—who disliked the Romanesque style and destroyed the Basilica, which displeased him. Dietrich, whose mother was a Medici, also had many medieval buildings torn down, so that he could replace them with Italian Renaissance structures. He was responsible too for the construction of the Mirabell Palace. At his death, he was buried— not in the Cathedral with all the other Prince-Archbishops who had preceded him since the Middle Ages—but in a special chapel called Saint Gabriel's in Saint Sebastian cemetery. . . . Finally, Anna confided, if there were only three churches one could visit in Salzburg they should be the

Cathedral, Saint Peter's (Romanesque in 1122 when it was constructed but transformed into baroque in the seventeenth century), and the Franciscan church already mentioned.

All this, I suppose, I could have discovered in a guidebook, but it was much more agreeable hearing it from Anna, her refreshing desire to share her knowledge of Salzburg's history stimulated by the pleasant wine. Then she was off—her departure as abrupt as our introduction had been—leaving me to find out for myself whatever else I wanted to know about her native city.

I did learn that the population was 126,000, that the principal attraction for traveling treasure hunters was its Mount Dürnberg, ten miles from the city, and its salt—which was of top value. There had been countless struggles for the mountain among the Bavarians, the Salzburgers, and the Austrians—who sometimes held opposite sides of the peak. The fortress overlooking Salzburg, I was told, had boasted some of the most sumptuous private rooms in Europe as well as some of the best equipped torture chambers. (I was denied a chance to see Festung HohenSalzburg close up since the funicular was not in operation at the time of my visit.)

As I walked through the narrow but straight streets of the left bank, I was made aware again and again of my friend Anna's observation on the fact that the streets—even the short back ones—were so arranged that at each end there was a framed, well-composed view of an aspect of a church, a flower shop, a coffeehouse, or whatever.

Getreidegasse, for example, the street that includes both Mozart's birthplace and the Goldener Hirsch Hotel, as well as a profusion of shops selling everything from lederhosen, native handicrafts, leather goods, silver, jewels, porcelainware, boots, dirndls, and Tyrolean hats to whiskey, is so narrow that from my room, in the old part of the hotel, I felt I could reach out the window and touch the building on the other side.

As if to compensate for the narrowness of the streets on the left bank, the right, where the newer part of town is situated, is a pattern of broad avenues with a feeling of airiness, punctuated by the Mirabell Garden, a formidable expanse of formal gardens highly regarded by the citizens of Salzburg who are inordinately concerned with the appearance their city makes on the eye of the beholder, native and visitor alike. The pride they take in their community and its aspect is apparent in every part of the city, in whichever direction one looks.

Setting foot on the right bank at the end of either the principal vehicular bridge or the footbridge nearby, one is in a matter of seconds in one of the city's most charming squares, the Makartplatz. On the far side is the Holy Trinity Church, a baroque edifice, one of the finest works of the Austrian architect Johann Bernhard Fischer von Erlach; to the left is the Landestheater, a neat, decorative structure with an especially pleasing appearance, and behind it, along Schwarzstrasse, lie the Marionette Theater and the impressive Mozarteum. At the Landestheater, on one of the evenings of my most recent visit to Salzburg, I attended a well-honed performance of Molière's *Tartuffe*—in German, of course. Some of the nuances of the Comédie-Française version in Paris were lacking, but even in German it was remarkably faithful to both the spirit and the letter of the original. The largely local audience (again, my visit was not in the high tourist season) seemed delighted with it.

This avenue, Schwarzstrasse, running off the square to the left, was familiar to me from a previous visit to the city, when I had stayed at a perfectly comfortable modern hotel on the right bank (the Goldener Hirsch having been full) and spent most of my time walking to and from the left bank— at least twice a day. For, in addition to the buildings mentioned and the Mirabell Palace and gardens, this side of the river is the center of the business community, and I was not in Salzburg to do any business. In some of the offices in the area beyond the Mirabell preserve one even detects faint intimations of the twentieth century in this city that still bears evidences of the Roman age, along with the medieval German atmosphere, superimposed by a layer of the Italian Renaissance, and over all the seventeenth-century Italian baroque additions.

To return briefly to the Schwarzstrasse: all three of the establishments that adjoin one another—the Landestheater, the Marionette theater, and the Mozarteum—specialize in performances of the works of Mozart (*Le Nozze di Figaro* is one of the local favorites), especially during the festival season.

There is no official precise count of the number of residents of the city who are directly concerned with its most prominent citizen of all, but what with musicians, conductors, choristers, student composers and musicians, librarians, guides to Mozart's various working and living quarters, plus the staff to support this group it must constitute a sizable percentage of the population. Every day—even in the middle of winter—one can find a recital of concertos, an opera, or a mass of Mozart's being performed somewhere in the city.

The December day was damp and chilly, and I had the good fortune to spot an almost hidden bar-and-coffeehouse that accommodated about half a dozen customers at a time. As I entered a young man and woman were talking animatedly with the proprietor, or the keeper of the bar, about an upcoming recital; I gathered they were students at the Mozarteum, situated diagonally across the street. The remaining four customers were reading newspapers with great concentration. The coffee was exceptionally fresh, and the warmth—both the atmosphere and the room temperature—provided just the intimate climate—one part good-fellowship, one part intense enjoyment of the subject under discussion (in this case music), and a third part comfortable surroundings—all that is embodied in the German word *gemütlich*, which can safely be applied to this beautiful city in its entirety.

The bar-coffeehouse, whose name, if any, I never did discover, was a perfect setting for reflection on the success of the Salzburgers in maintaining the character of their city through the centuries—even into the jet-plastics-synthetics-polluted-computerized age of today, an age, happily, that is still alien to Salzburg. It was an appropriate place too to reflect on the difficult, far-from-happy life of Mozart, who was determined, against considerable odds, to make his mark as a composer. Just across the nearby Makartplatz, adjacent to the Holy Trinity church, is the house where he spent eleven of his thirty-five years of life; it is now used for the presentation of outstanding chamber-music recitals for limited audiences in an intimate atmosphere.

Mozart's father, Leopold, the guiding spirit behind young Wolfgang's rise in the musical world, forsook his post in Augsburg, Germany, to become court composer and assistant conductor of the Orchestra in Salzburg. But his son heartily disliked Archbishop Hieronymus, who ruled the city, and seemed intent on keeping the young composer-performer, whom he had appointed Hofkapellmeister, from acquiring the recognition that should have been his in Salzburg. Wolfgang's various tours of Europe, stretching from England to Italy, were undertaken partly to escape from the control of the Archbishop; even so, with all the concerts he gave to overwhelming ovations he was barely able to earn enough to live on: he was constantly out of money, with no wood for his fire, and no money to buy any, at a point when he was well along in a successful career.

At thirty he had already lived a full life: he had started composing at seven, made his first European tour between the ages of seven and ten, wrote his first full-length opera at thirteen, became Koncertmeister, and resumed his exhausting and unremunerative tours of a number of European countries.

At thirty-two, weary and poverty-stricken, he wrote to his father: "I swear on my honor that I cannot bear Salzburg and its inhabitants. . . . To me their speech and their manner of living are quite unendurable. . . ."

Most of his resentment, of course, was caused by the Archbishop's policies. In spite of all Mozart's tribulations, the compositions—concertos, cantatas, sonatas, masses, operas—flowed from his hammer piano in a stream that ended only with his death, on December 5, 1791, at thirty-five at the height of his powers. At the time many felt that he had been poisoned by an arch rival, Antonio Salieri, a successful composer who made Vienna his base. Quicksilver, or mercury, was supposedly the agent used to dispatch Mozart.

His father Leopold was convinced that Salieri had used underhanded methods to gain supremacy over his Salzburg rival, and Mozart himself, on his deathbed, is supposed to have muttered that he had been poisoned, but without mentioning any names. But Harold Schonberg, the music critic and historian, points out that modern medical tenets have established that Mozart had kidney trouble, and doubtless died of uremic poisoning.

In Mozart's time, Salzburg must have been a pleasant place indeed, in spite of the unsympathetic Archbishop Hieronymus Count de Colloredo. As W. J. Turner, writing in 1938, points out, in *Mozart: the Man and His Works*: "The small towns of Germany and Austria have always given better value for the same money than has ever been obtainable in any English or American town or city. Further, in the eighteenth century in Salzburg no part of a man's income went in dog-licenses, wireless sets and licenses [an English tax on sets in use], movies, automobiles, or any other of the new pleasures of the twentieth century; nor was it then necessary to travel twenty or thirty miles from one's home in order to get air to breathe and find a little unspoiled nature."

Well, the sparkling air in Salzburg, coming off the mountains, is still as pure as it was thirty-five years ago, and unspoiled nature exists in abundance. Life in Salzburg today is still an invigorating, healthy experience—especially if the resident or visitor is sports-minded: skiing on incomparable runs on the nearby Tyrolean peaks, mountain-climbing—all summer and winter sports are practiced within easy reach of the city.

And life in Salzburg is uncluttered by the demands of twentieth-century existence; there is little interest in television, and the automobile is virtually useless in Salzburg's more interesting quarters.

But as for Mr. Turner's statement about better value for the same money: I was shocked to find that six and a half years after my last visit, Salzburg was no longer an inexpensive hideaway. At an attractive bar (with no entertainment) a Scotch on the rocks cost the equivalent of three dollars plus on my most recent visit; a pot of coffee good for two cups brought one dollar, with the tip extra, in the coffeehouses. And at a not outstanding restaurant, where everything was à la carte, I spotted what I thought was a bargain—hors d'oeuvres at the equivalent of sixty cents. It quickly developed, however, that each individual item on the tray (one very small piece of cold asparagus, for example) went for that price. But then every country in Europe, save for one or two, was in an inflationary spiral on that trip.

Except for these elevated rates (a temporary condition, one hopes) in the cost of food and drink, Mr. Turner is still right: the visitor receives value galore for his currency during his stay in Salzburg.

I have neglected so far to mention a splended new Conference Hall, a profusion of lovely gardens, in addition to Mirabell, especially those at the Paracelsus Kurhaus (where one drinks the curative waters of the springs— or takes a mud bath), named after another famous inhabitant, who has been called Europe's first "modern" doctor; a neat, compact zoo; and, in the surrounding area, lakes, mountain streams, and an assemblage of handsome "palaces"—actually the equivalent of intermediate-sized French châteaux.

In this idyllic setting visitors can golf, play tennis, and ride cable cars up to the Alpine peaks. This pastoral charm made the Salzburg area a natural choice as the locale for the film *The Sound of Music*.

Of course the leitmotiv is Mozart and music, but the city's architecture, representative of various of the more intriguing centuries, particularly as mirrored in its ecclesiastical structures, is worthy of equally close attention.

The rule of the Prince-Archbishops really had its origins in the seventh century A.D.—about the year 680—with an Englishman named Wynfreth, who later became Archbishop of Mainz in Franconia, of which Salzburg was then a part. He subsequently installed another of his countrymen, John, as the first Bishop of Salzburg. Early in the eighth century an Irish bishop named Virgil succeeded him, and forty years later the next chief prelate was raised to the rank of Archbishop. They shortly became primates of Germany and were absolute rulers of the area.

Thanks to that celebrated rearranger of the map of Europe, Napoleon I of France, Salzburg lost its independence at the beginning of the nineteenth century and fell under the control of Bavaria. It became part of Austria in 1816; its civil officials, no longer concerned with affairs of state and competition with great powers, concentrated on making their city a cultural shrine, encompassing all the arts but with special emphasis on music. That they have succeeded in such large measure is a tribute to their single-mindedness of purpose; there is today no other cultural font of city-wide proportions to compare with Salzburg.

The two-score churches that decorate the landscape of the city provide a broad range of architectural styles available for inspection by the diligent visitor, sometimes several styles in the same structure. In fact, Salzburg is unusual in having such a wide variety of architectural periods represented in such a compact area. In some places churches of different centuries stand side by side: in a few squares in the city everywhere you turn there is another church—as plentiful as hair-dressing shops or cafés in Paris.

Of this plethora of churches the one regarded as the keystone by the natives is not the Cathedral but the Abbey of Saint Peter, part of the monastery complex that is described as "the cradle of Salzburg." It also has the distinction of being the only German monastery to have been continuously in existence since the seventh century. In the ornamented abbey Mozart's C Minor Mass was heard for the first time, on October 25, 1783, with the composer himself conducting and his wife Konstanze singing the soprano part. During the festival each year the C Minor Mass is performed in the Abbey, and on the eve of the day he died, December 5, Mozart's Requiem Mass is sung here.

Early in the seventeenth century the Romanesque ceiling was removed, and the former flat roof was replaced by a vaulted one. During the eighteenth century, in line with the European fashion, Saint Peter's acquired a rococo look, which sets off the remains of Romanesque wall paintings dating from the first half of the thirteenth century; those early paintings are still in good condition on the first pillar of the right aisle of the main church.

It is possible to enter Saint Peter's from one of two courtyards; the one adjoining the western wing is the hub on which two new wings were built in this century, primarily to house the new Benedictine College, for members of the order attending Salzburg University. The old courtyard to which the main entrance of Saint Peter's gives access leads one to the Franziskaner-gasse and then through the Cathedral Archway to the airiness of Cathedral Square.

The Salzburg Cathedral has always occupied the same site. The original, built during the stewardship of Virgil, the Celtic abbot and bishop, who reigned from 745 to 784, was burned down; various attempts at rebuilding were made, with notable lack of success, and finally the dashing Wolf Dietrich von Raitenau, elected archbishop at the age of twenty-eight, demolished the remains of the building and started over. As the son of a Medici and nephew of the Pope (Pius IV) he felt he had *carte blanche* to do virtually anything he wished in Salzburg, with absolute powers especially over its ecclesiastical plant.

Architecturally, he leaned of course toward the Italians, and as the seventeenth century began he called in the most important Italian artists and architects of the day to create a cathedral worthy of the city, one so beautiful that it would insure the immortality of his name as long as Salzburg existed.

His name became renowned all right, but not in exactly the way an Archbishop's was expected to be. Early in his reign he had discovered a very attractive young woman, Salome Alt, whom he installed with her children in the Mirabell Palace, which he had constructed partly with that maneuver in mind. He lavished love, affection, and jewelry in large quantities on Salome, and in spite of his elaborate ideas for the beautification of Salzburg, the citizens finally began to grumble about the decline of the treasury and his constant need for more money. He also chose to test his strength with the Elector of Bavaria over some mining rights. Bavarian troops chased him all the way to Italy, brought him back and forced him to abdicate, installing him as a prisoner in the Festung HohenSalzburg, where he spent the last five years of his life. Salome was exiled to a small, dull village, and nothing more was heard of her.

For Dietrich, the turn in his fortunes must have been a deep disappointment, but in a way the crowning of his career with his imprisonment in the historic fortress overlooking the city he attempted to remake completely was a fitting climax to his flamboyant life. No one could say he hadn't ruled with a certain flair.

On a dark night some residents swear they see Dietrich's ghost, bathed in that eerie green, looking down on what he regarded as *his* city.

From the time when the first Cathedral was built on the present site (between 767 and 774), the seat of the Salzburg see has undergone so many permutations, struggles for power, one major fire and at least one lesser one, one air bombardment, and a wild assortment of additions, changes in décor, and unfulfilled plans for a complete overhaul that the mere recital of them all would easily fill a volume of its own. The most recent partial reconstruction was accomplished in 1959, the final touch being an up-to-date mausoleum and a new flight of steps leading down to the burial vault of the Archbishop-rulers (except Wolf Dietrich).

The four-story towers, over 200 feet high, dominate the city in the valley; the marble of the Cathedral's façade is of a striking reddish-white shade. The statues atop the towers, the parapets, and at ground level depict the Redeemer, the prophets Moses and Elijah, the four Evangelists, disseminators of the Divine Word (favorite subjects in Salzburg), and—beside the portals —Saints Peter, Paul, Rupert, and Virgil.

The three bronze doors at the far end of the vestibule were cast as recently as 1957 and '58, giving on to an interior whose ceiling stucco work and designs were executed about 1630. The frescoes above the central aisle and the choir are scenes of the life of Christ: the Passion, the Miracles, and the Transfiguration.

Typical of the mixture of styles in the Cathedral as it stands today is a bronze font, part Romanesque, part Gothic, which one will find in the chapel to the left of the entrance. The four lions that form its feet are of the twelfth century; the font itself—with stylized representations of bishops—

was cast in bronze about 1320, and the cover, with its engraved baptismal scenes, was added in 1959.

The adjoining Residenz, the Archbishop's seat of power, was also thoroughly rebuilt by Dietrich, who possessed all the attributes of a frustrated architect. The huge Carabinieri-Saal, named after his bodyguard, was designed for use as a setting for theatrical productions when open-air performances in the courtyard proved not feasible.

Dietrich never lost an opportunity to leave his individual stamp on the city, and that desire has been respected through the centuries. When the new Festival Hall was built, to supplement the original, the large auditorium, which accommodates more than 2,300 persons, was situated in such a way that the façade of the Old Stables was not demolished or even blocked from view, and thus the portals decorated by the coats of arms Wolf Dietrich bestowed on them are still on display in an advantageous position.

My own favorite among the principal churches of Salzburg is, as I have noted, the Franciscan, which during the rebuilding of the Cathedral served for a brief time in its eminent place. It is not easy to pinpoint the exact reasons for my preference; rebuilt and consecrated in 1223 after the original church that had occupied the site since the time of Saint Virgil, the Franciscan church possesses, to my mind, all facets of what a church should be. Its late Romanesque nave is much as it was when constructed; the choir is in the Gothic style; the façade has a subdued baroque veneer; the altar encompasses dazzling gold panels once adorned by delicate figures of saints paying attendance on a truly impressive Madonna, who survives in nearly pristine condition. The ornamentation includes such unusual disembodied matter as the forms of plants, animals, and monsters. Finally, the inner door at the southern entrance of the church—of the Lombard type, executed in the early 1200s—is of a magnificent red and white marble. As Paumgartner, the late chronicler of Salzburg, notes: it "repays detailed inspection—tiny human heads peep out at irregular intervals from between the shafts, the leaf capitals are alive with animal forms and two warriors have been worked into the vine-leaf frieze."

But despite this extraordinary collection of decorations, the fact is that the Franciscan feels like a church. The nave is dark and somewhat gloomy, providing the perfect locale for introspective thought, while—above—the high altar is washed in an ethereal light that seems to be directed to it by a celestial electrician. It is also, as already mentioned, the perfect church in which to hear a Mozart mass.

The connoisseur of churches will obviously have the time of his or her life in Salzburg; even the cemeteries are of a high order, far above the average in interest. The most cynical cemetery enthusiast will be transported by Saint Peter's, and he will be in a state of enraptured bliss following a visit to Saint Sebastian's, which was laid out in about the year 1600. Eighty-eight sepulchral chapels form a square around the centerpiece—Saint Gabriel's Chapel, where Archbishop Wolf Dietrich von Raitenau's bones are interred. The rotunda of the chapel is supported by Tuscan pilasters; the delicacy of the cupola gives the whole an appearance of simple elegance and an airiness that make it difficult for the visitor to leave. Beyond the arcade on the lawn are the tombs of Leopold Mozart, the composer's father and mentor, Konstanze, his wife and widow, and her second husband, Georg Nikolaus von Nissen, counselor of the Royal Danish Embassy.

But churches, churchyards, and cemeteries, though principal features of Salzburg, do not provide an overriding oppressive atmosphere. The churches explored above should suffice for anyone but architects or members of religious orders, who will of course want to inspect every single house of worship within yodeling distance.

In spite of the reminders of death on many sides, Salzburg manages to be a frothy, gay city. After its centuries of independence, and its brief rule by Bavaria, the city developed a certain carefree spirit when it became a part of Austria, now a provincial city with no need to keep up any pretense of being a sober, serious Great Power.

The proponents of making the city a cultural center, with W. A. Mozart supplying the motivating force, won out without much of a battle over those who wanted to turn this Tyrolean retreat into a health resort. Some vestigial remains of this latter effort are still in evidence today: though it is, as noted, possible to "take the waters" and a luxurious mud bath can be arranged without difficulty, the city is hardly a spa in the league of Baden-Baden, for example.

Contributing to the feeling of gaiety and good will which seems to hang in

A Salzburg horse pool

the air in Salzburg is the periodic Old-World sound of the town's Glocken-spiel, which sits atop the Neubau (new building) on the Residenzplatz, and the sight of the sculptured baroque horses which populate some of the pools—often referred to as horse pools—that abruptly give the town an im-probable look not shared by any other.

Then the people themselves seem to exude a spirit of gaiety and well-being, certainly of friendliness and hospitality, that they transmit to the visitors. Many of the newcomers waste no time in buying their Tyrolean hats; some go all the way with lederhosen and dirndl skirts. And in this atmosphere of good fellowship, it is virtually impossible to feel inhibited or embarrassed about wearing the local costumes.

Along the Getreidegasse, with its wrought-iron signs (including the Goldener Hirsch's golden deer encircled in that medieval fashion) hanging

Getreidegasse

just above the heads of the passersby, the visitors descend on the concentration of shops that make this street the most traveled in town. Although most are not entirely in native dress, all have caught the spirit of Salzburg; there are fewer arguments and fewer scowls and less rude behavior here than one could find in any corner of the civilized world.

Most foreigners with a limited time in the city concentrate their first days on the left bank, working out from Getreidegasse, and leave the palaces till last. Not that they deserve that position, for although they are certainly not comparable in sheer magnificence to their Czarist Russian counterparts, for example, or even to certain castles in Spain, they are well worth the investment of a few days.

The Mirabell, Wolf Dietrich's monument to his love for Salome Alt, is the showpiece of the right bank just behind the Mozarteum and not far from the busy Makartplatz. It was first named Schloss Altenau in honor of the Archbishop's mistress, but his successor quickly moved to blot out the memory of her name and rechristened the building and its lovely gardens "Mirabell." Many architects and landscape architects had their way with the estate, making small changes and pecking away at its original appearance, which had seemed quite admirable to most Salzburgers.

But the truly imposing Palace, with its majestic crown—its pediments capped with delicate vases, sandstone figures, and fanciful silhouettes spaced along its roof line—almost all was destroyed by fire in 1818.

The architect who was chosen to "re-create" the _Schloss_ was a classicist, Clerk of the Imperial Works in Vienna, one Peter de Nobile. His palace was solidly baroque, fanciful but with a certain dignified simplicity—following the line, as Paumgartner puts it aptly, "of good old Kaiser Franz's legendary concept of thrift in art." And despite some inevitable restoration work in the interim that imprint is still visible today.

Since 1947 the Mayor and his deputy have occupied bright, airy offices overlooking a part of the gardens.

To the visitor, the Palace certainly appears to be splendid, in the literal sense of that word, but its moderate size and squat look as one approaches it may provide an initial feeling of slight disappointment. Actually none of the schlosses of Salzburg could be called massive or "grand," on the scale of not only the Czars' opulent palaces but some of the châteaux of the Loire. In fact, one of Salzburg's most celebrated "palaces"—the Hellbrunn—looks on first inspection more like a villa or, at the risk of being disparaging, an intermediate grade school.

But then the Teutonic conception of a castle is generally not that of the visionary architects and rulers of other lands.

This is not to say that there are not lovely, even spectacular, effects to be observed in the Salzburg schlosses. The Mirabell's dazzling Marble Hall, with its marble facings and gold décor, and the white marble balustrade of the magisterial, ornamental Main Staircase, have a regal splendor appropriate for the habitat of the most powerful sovereign.

And both the Leopoldskron and Klesheim palaces are magnificent of their genre. Leopoldskron lies in a verdant setting in the general area of the Salzburg moor, on a small lake once known as the archepiscopal fishpond. It was built, in a graceful rococo style for the reigning archbishop, Lord Firmian, in 1736, and after a few changes of occupant it passed into the hands of Max Reinhardt, at the end of the First World War; it finally became the property of the Salzburg Seminar in American Studies.

The Klesheim, another solidly constructed building with a majestic spirit lacking in most others, is situated in a giant park near the Bavarian border on the Salzach. It was begun with great enthusiasm at the turn of the century in 1700 on orders of Archbishop Thun, based on a design by Johann Bernhard Fischer von Erlach, who could lay claim to having designed more of the outstanding buildings of Salzburg—ecclesiastical and otherwise, not to mention altars and other incidental creations—than anyone else, including Italy's Zugalli, who brought to life a series of striking, smaller churches. He is characterized as perhaps the last master of the Italian period in Salzburg's architectural chronology.

Fischer von Erlach it was who lavished his brilliant talents on Salzburg before being summoned to Vienna, where he achieved a considerable reputation. But his heart and some of his most dedicated work belonged to Salzburg.

In the case of the Klesheim Palace, the building was stopped short of completion by the death of the Archbishop. His successor, Leopold Anton Lord Firmian, took charge of the project and added a series of his own innovative ideas—a ramp, the Firmian family emblem at strategic places, a gatehouse with a tower, and an inner staircase, among others—some of which had been in the mind of the architect when he undertook the commission under the previous ruler. But this was one of the hazards of working for Archbishops in the first place, as W. A. Mozart, for his part, discovered to his sorrow.

The summer house adjoining the Palace was also the work of von Erlach, in one of his capricious moods, a kind of hors d'oeuvre before the main building was begun.

Along the Hellbrunner Allee, an arboreal avenue that leads to the Palace, one passes a number of small but very attractive Schlosses, a few fronting on ponds and lakes. The Hellbrunn itself is a product of the Italian Renaissance, and its gardens were designed in the manner of Italian stage settings. The wholeness of the Hellbrunn—palace and grounds—is credited to that talented architect of what is really still today's Cathedral in Salzburg, Santino Solari. "The original design of the park," wrote Paul Buberl, "is the oldest surviving example of Italian baroque garden architecture and sculpture on German soil."

The interior of the Palace, with its Italianate décor mirroring the Mediterranean culture in this northern outpost, is more interesting than the exterior of the building, but it is the series of gardens that make a visit to the Hellbrunn memorable. Among the abundance of carefully orchestrated foliage, an arrangement of grottos in one area provides a theatrically effective backdrop for some unusual statuary, some of it doubtless also Italian in origin, and even mechanical toys geared to water power. "The Goddess of Love," a clothed Venus, is one of the more popular carved works in this section of the gardens. Several natural "theaters"—miniatures in the form of the familiar Roman open-air semicircular terraced dramatic forums—are almost hidden among the yew trees, and behind the zoo is a natural rock theater, again the first on German soil, designed for the presentation of pastorals among the rocks.

In the area known as the "pleasure gardens" a Mechanical Theater has been a feature since the mid-eighteenth century, a creation of a local mine worker and technician from the "Salt Mountain"—Dürnberg. This

Mechanical Theater and other aspects of the gardens give emphasis to the delightful notion that one is alive as an adult in a marvelously conceived children's world, where no one is evil and pure joy is available in unlimited quantities.

The zoo itself is—in this age of specialization—probably the only one of its kind: devoted exclusively to mountain animals, but not merely the local Tyrolean variety.

Through the entire complex of gardens, grottos, outdoor theaters, zoo, and statuary a network of fountains plays unceasingly amongst the gently stirring arbors.

Some schlosses are really only small villas, as noted, but the closest to a schloss that Mozart ever lived in was a very small villa indeed, called Robinighof, the country home of a family named Robinig, friends whom the Mozarts—especially Wolfgang and his sister, Nannerl—often visited. Wolfgang's habitations are still carefully staked out: his birthplace on Getreidegasse, well preserved; similarly his house on Makartplatz, near the Church of the Holy Trinity on the right bank; and currently the tiny hut in which the revered composer in the last year or two of his life wrote what was to be his most successful opera, *Die Zauberflöte*. Once a prized exhibit in Vienna, the hut is now safely tucked away at the Mozarteum in Salzburg.

Music critics since the youthful Mozart's death have credited him, among his many achievements, with having been a major link in the evolution of eighteenth-century German music; with Haydn, his contemporary, of having been responsible for the development of the sonata and the symphony; in operatic music of having carried forward the work of Gluck and of having prepared the way for Weber. Finish, elegance, and restraint were qualities that permeated all his works, even the slightest.

If a finely tuned perceptive critic like Harold Schonberg, who should be more than a bit jaded by now, can thrill to the music of Mozart performed by random groups in the Kennedy Center for the Performing Arts in Washington, consider what a sensual experience it is to sit back in Salzburg in the modern New Festival Theater that is a miracle of acoustical perfection and listen, on an ordinary, non-festival day, to a concert given by the Mozarteum Orchestra, composed of musicians who are devoting their lives to the music of the master. Or to hear the Coronation Mass as sung at the

Franciscan Church. Or the C Minor Mass sung in Fischer von Erlach's baroque but symmetrically spare Collegiate Church on the Universitätsplatz.

For in Salzburg's theaters, churches, halls, and chambers, the sound of Mozart has a special timbre, and creates special emotions by reason of the surroundings. Here the spirit that Mozart instilled in his music lives on, through the years.

To its most famous native son, and his seven notable operas, forty-one symphonies, thirty string quartets, fifteen masses, and countless sonatas and concertos for violin, clarinet, piano, and organ, Salzburg has dedicated itself in perpetuity.

It is a little as though it were trying to make up for turning him out at the height of his powers, when he was struggling to survive.

A last walk along Getreidegasse and a final look at the brooding, ever-watchful Festung HohenSalzburg. A perfect cameo of a city. Return I must.

Lyon

The churches dominate the old city. The Basilica Fouvière is situated on the spot with the most spectacular view of the region; St. Jean, the seat of the Primate, dating from the twelfth and fifteenth centuries, is located right on the river Saône. . . .

Of all the cultures of modern Europe, the French is, I believe, the most appealing and understandable to one from the western shore of the Atlantic. Perhaps the ideal place to arrive at an appreciation of the civilized quality of France and French life is in a city such as Lyon.

The trip is a three-hour-and-forty-seven-minute delight. One climbs aboard the Mistral, the epitome of modern trains, for a one-twenty P.M. departure from Paris. Equipped with a barber, a secretary, its own newsstand, a boutique, a bar-and-sandwich car, in addition to its restaurant cars, and an art exhibit, the Mistral, named after the wind from the north that sometimes makes life insupportable for the residents of the Côte d'Azur, pulls out of the Gare de Lyon, in Paris, as the minute hand of the station clock rests squarely on four, the hour hand at one, and just as the second hand sweeps past twelve. Before long it is streaking smoothly through the French countryside headed southeast, at a speed just above one hundred twenty miles an hour.

It is a rare occasion when a French train—any train—does not depart or arrive on time. This punctuality and the neat appearance of the fields and occasional villages through which we were passing produced a feeling of order reassuring to a traveler with an extensive itinerary planned.

There had been no need to fuss at the ticket windows in Paris and no waiting; I simply boarded the train with the comfortable feeling that the Eurail Pass I had purchased in the United States for two hundred ten dollars would be good for unlimited travel on any first-class train, and even on some lake steamers, in any of thirteen European countries during the next two months.

Looking out at the distinctive dark-yellowish-colored mustard fields that announce the nearness of Dijon I couldn't help reflecting on the lack of similarity with the scenes one is treated to on most American trains: the shabby slums of cities and a never-ending succession of automobile graveyards.

Over a hot tea and freshly baked croissants served with rich, flowing marmalade I assured myself that we would doubtless arrive in Lyon promptly at 1707 (5:07 P.M.), that I should be in my hotel unpacking by six, and that I could confidently anticipate—after showering and changing—sitting down to a before-dinner apéritif by seven-thirty and to my first Lyonnais dinner of this trip at eight.

As we left Dijon and plunged south toward Lyon I began to grow hungry, in spite of the ample tea I had just consumed. There is something about the word Lyon that causes the brain to react by sending warning signals to the stomach. For once having dined in Lyon, one cannot approach the city again without acquiring a keen appetite en route.

This third largest French city, ranking below Paris and Marseille but above all the rest, was settled by the Romans as Lugdunum in about 43 B.C. but before that, about 500 B.C., there was a Greek colony on the site. The city today has the feeling of an old place: it is not so much a mixture of old and new but rather of old and older. The *vieux quartier* is on a hill overlooking the Saône River, which flows into the River Rhone, en route from Switzerland to the Mediterranean Sea, just a few hundred yards farther downstream. Lyon is noted as the birthplace of Marcus Aurelius and of Ampère, who developed electrodynamics, and for a theater, built at the order of Augustus Caesar, boasting the first curtain to be raised and lowered during performances. In those early days its eminence rested on the fact that it was the capital of Gaul. It should also be noted that Lyon spawned the *guignol* (the Punch and Judy show). After fading into a period of obscurity in the Middle Ages, it is today again a capital—of gastronomy.

Its right to that title is based on the world-celebrated cuisine Lyonnaise, which in turn owes its excellence to the bountiful supply of comestibles of all varieties in the area closely surrounding the city.

The *poulet de Bresse*, for example, is to the average chicken what Dom Pérignon champagne is to bathtub gin. Charolais beef provides the most delicious cuts of beef anyone could desire, and in the category of fruits and vegetables the Lyonnais area is without equal in the quality and abundance of its products.

The expanded region Lyonnais is an area stretching some 67 kilometers (42 miles) to the north and the city of Macon; 155 kilometers to the east, encompassing Talloires; 42 kilometers south to Condrieu; and 87 kilometers westward to Roanne. Within this tract, arbitrarily arrived at but without a hint of gerrymandering, diligent gourmets and insatiable gourmands may choose among five three-star establishments, ten two-star, thirty-nine one-star, and a galaxy of excellent restaurants that have not yet been honored with a star.

In the litany of the Guide Michelin—the index to the best French restaurants—which has become the gospel for epicures of all nations while in France, and which determines the fortunes of all above-average restaurants, auberges, and bistros in the land of Carême and Escoffier, one star—as any Francophile knows—denotes "a good table in its category"; two stars "an excellent table . . . deserves a detour"; and three stars—the accolade supreme —"one of the best tables in France. . . . Is worth the trip."

This gastronomic patina that has given a special luster to the city's reputation was acquired gradually, over a period of several centuries. As the area's superb meats, poultry, fish, and produce were discovered by Frenchmen of other regions, especially Paris, the fame of the cuisine Lyonnaise soon spread throughout the land. The chefs of the district, responding to this esteem for its products, enthusiastically created more succulent dishes, their imaginations functioning at top speed to meet the challenge. It was not long before Frenchmen, titled and bourgeois, were arriving in Lyon from all corners of France. Today that reputation still exercises its magnetic attraction—by now to people throughout the world. And as the quality of the meals increased, the tastes of the Lyonnais—allegedly much more provincial and thus less sophisticated than Parisians'—became sharpened; eventually they became, through a combination of all the above-mentioned circumstances, the most discriminating diners in France.

If it is true, as some hold, that you are what you eat, the composite bourgeois Frenchman of the Lyonnais region is part chicken, part calves' liver, part trout, part thrush, and topped off with a liberal dollop of chocolate mousse. For the more successful Lyon businessman, there would be a few additions to this already ungainly creature: a leg of prime Charolais beef, a morceau of rabbit or hare.

My hotel, like many of the buildings in the business district between the rivers, where it is situated, was built during the past century, mingling with a number of other structures dating from the eighteenth.

This first evening of my visit the area—like business districts everywhere at the end of the day—was deserted; a large, darkened school for boys directly across the street gave promise of insuring that I would not oversleep in the morning. Inside its nineteenth-century shell, the Simplon had been completely redone, with new elevators and up-to-the-minute bathrooms. It was the first time in my experience anywhere that a "soundproof" room proved to be just that. (Except, of course, with the windows open during the night.) It would have pleased Marcel Proust, I thought, to stay here—and appease his hunger for absolute quiet.

Leaving an exploration of the city to daylight hours in the period ahead, I prepared to venture into the inner circle of this headquarters of the culinary world.

For the first evening of my stay I decided to wander through the district near my hotel and pick out at random a modest restaurant where I could dine lightly, in preparation for my assault on the mighty fortresses of gastronomy beginning on the following day. After a good half-hour of window-shopping, my favorite avocation on arrival in a city or town with which I am not intimately familiar, I selected a place to dine—a brasserie with a workingman clientele. The *potage* was watery, but the omelette was of a medium consistency, just to my taste, and the *pommes roties* were a crisp golden brown. A salad and a slice of Gruyère rounded out a good, not great, inexpensive meal.

I resisted the impulse to stop by at a boîte in the neighborhood, to make certain that I would be well rested on the morrow for my first visit to one of the sanctuaries I planned to inspect on this trip.

★　★　★

In this profusion of superb restaurants the most celebrated cuisinier of them all—perhaps soon in all of France—is a fifty-year-old, eighth-generation chef named Paul Bocuse. Reeking with dynamism, he is that rare genus of person who, once encountered, will never be forgot. He has been likened to Napoleon, with a noble face and very short hair lying flat on his head, but to me he has the appearance and bearing of a Roman emperor. Standing in the foyer of his attractive *pavillon* wearing his spotless white chef's outfit, he presents an imposing figure—Caesar rather than Napoleon, I thought, although there are recognizable traces of the personality of the French Emperor.

The analogy is not entirely coincidental; his approach to preparing his

Bocuse

cuisine is as precise as the planning of a successful military campaign. "Everything depends on the order," he explains, fixing his listener with an imperious stare worthy of an emperor.

In Lyon, gastronomic capital of the world of the 1970s, the cuisine has changed since the days of Escoffier and Carême. To Paul Bocuse, the greatest chef of all time was Fernand Point, patron of the famous restaurant La Pyramide in Vienne, not far from Lyon. "He completely overturned the whole concept of French gastronomy of the nineteenth century, with its complicated menus, its prodigious meals," he proclaims.

To appreciate fully what he meant by "prodigious," it is only necessary to examine the menu of a typical Escoffier dinner:

Caviar frais—Oeufs de pluvier (fresh caviar with plover's eggs), *Melon, Tortue claire* (clear turtle soup), *Rossolnick* (a Russian cucumber soup), *Truite au Chambertin* (trout), *Laitances Meunière* (soft roe), *Poularde Soufflée à la Catalane* (chicken soufflé), *Morilles à la Crème* (a small fungus, creamed), *Selle d'Agneau de Galles aux laitues* (saddle of lamb with lettuce), *Petits Pois à l'Anglaise* (small peas), *Pommes Nana, Suprême d'Écrevisses Moscovite* (cray-fish), *Punch à la Mandarine, Caneton de Rouen à la Rouennaise* (duckling), *coeurs de Romaine* (hearts of Romaine lettuce), *Asperges de France* (asparagus), *Biscuit glacé aux violettes* (ice cream cake), *Friandises* (small cakes), *Barquettes à l'Écossaise* (small tarts), *Fraises* (fresh strawberries), *Pêches de Serre* (peaches)—along with various wines, brandy, and other liqueurs.

This was one of the master's comparatively modest meals; for a special occasion, he really let himself go:

Frivolités, Caviar frais, Blinis de Sarrasin, Oursins de la Méditerranée, Consommé aux nids d'Hirondelle, Velouté Dame Blanche, Sterlet du Volga à la Moscovite, Barquette de Laitance à la Vénitienne, Chapon fin aux Perles du Périgord, Cardon épineux à la Toulousaine, Selle de Chevreuil aux Cerises, Sylphide d'Ortolan Reine Alexandra, Suprême d'Écrevisses au Champagne, Mandarines Givrées, Terrine de Caille sous la Cendre aux Raisins, Bécassine rosée au feu de sarments, Salade Isabelle, Asperges de France, Délices de Foie Gras, Soufflé de Grenade à l'Orientale, Biscuit glacé aux Violettes, Mignardises, Fruits de Serre chaude, grandes liqueurs, fine champagne.

As one can detect, it was not only the size of the meal—the number of main courses—that was mind-boggling, but also the variety of side dishes, with heavy emphasis on the sauces and dressings, that made it so hard to walk away from the table without assistance.

Today, thanks to Monsieur Point, who died in 1955, the accent is on simplicity, with a reverential respect for the products of Lyon—the chickens from nearby Bresse, numbered with metal tags in the manner of limited editions of esoteric books; beef from the Charolais region, also adjoining Lyon; and the vegetables that grow in abundance in this cornucopia of France. The fish still are obtainable from certain nearby streams and the Mediterranean, not all that far away, "although," Bocuse says grimly, "one day soon, if nothing is done, the Mediterranean will be so polluted that fish will not survive there. Like Lac Léman, at Geneva, which is just about dead now."

Paul Bocuse arrived at his current estate—that of *patron* of the most re-nowned three-star restaurant of the Lyon region—in a remarkably short span of time. True, like all great chefs—and ballet dancers, and championship swimmers and figure-skaters—he started his apprenticeship early, in his case at twelve; after working for Mère Brazier, a two-star establishment, and putting in six years with Monsieur Point at La Pyramide, he was schooled by his father Georges, who watched indulgently while his son spent a large segment of his time on skiing and wrestling. But père Georges was firm in his conviction that, like all the male descendants of the original chef Bocuse, young Paul would find the attractions of the kitchens too strong to resist. And so it was to be. (In the rigid stratification of French society, a son often has no alternative but to follow in his father's path; thus an eighth-generation chef is not as much of a phenomenon as he would be in the United States.)

On his father's death, in 1959, Paul took over command of the little restau-rant in Collonges-au-Mont d'Or, on the banks of the Saône just nine kilometers from Lyon, expanded its physical proportions and its cuisine as well, replaced the paper napkins with linen, and by 1961 he had acquired his first Michelin star, plus being chosen Meilleur Ouvrier de France, a signal honor that occasioned a flood of visits by journalists and customers. "In 1962 I had my second star," he remembers with pleasure, "and in 1965 my third"—setting a record for the course at that time. Since that momentous Sunday in the spring of '65, Bocuse has worn the mantle of one of the greats of French cuisine. This eminence was officially endorsed recently when he was awarded the medal of the Legion of Honor by President Giscard in a ceremony at the Elysée Palace.

Bocuse is hardly shy in discussing his culinary talents; he speaks with candor but not in an offensive way. "You realize?" he asked incredulously, indicating a copy of the French news magazine *L'Express*. "They compare Bocuse with Carême!" He often refers to himself, refreshingly, in the third person, in the manner of the late Charles de Gaulle, who once achieved a remarkable grammatical gambit by speaking of himself in the first and in the third persons in the same sentence. (When asked about this curious example of syntax, he replied that in the first part of the sentence he had been speaking about himself personally—thus the first person; later in the sentence he had been referring to himself as head of state.)

Bocuse is no less reverential toward himself as Maître Cuisinier. Driving down to the Lyon market early one morning, Bocuse was asked by his passenger about the rumor that he was preparing a book of his heretofore secret recipes. "Why not?" he asked earnestly. M. Bocuse already markets and exports wine and liver pâté bearing his name and doubtless sees no reason why he should ignore another avenue with commercial possibilities for his knowledge and talents.

The title of this best-seller-to-be? "Well, I've been thinking about titles. It's not easy," he said, echoing the words of many authors and publishers confronted with that pesky problem. "But I think I've found one," he announced with a note of triumph.

"Yes?" I asked.

"Bocuse," he replied winningly. "Why not?" ("Pourquoi pas"—an expression he lives by.)

This engaging egotism is only the commercial image that M. Bocuse projects. He is a warm host—considerate and with a real concern for the well-being of his guests and their digestive tracts.

★ ★ ★

The first visit Chez Bocuse calls for a short, but mandatory period of training. The day preceding the big event should be spent in a state of almost complete fasting, if possible. An omelette of two eggs, perhaps, with a single slice of tomato on the side. Black coffee. No wine or liquor.

If the meal at Collonges-au-Mont d'Or is to be luncheon, as it was in the case of my first visit, a very Spartan breakfast is recommended. The usual spare collation of most Frenchmen at the start of the day—strong black coffee and a croissant—is just right. (Some say that the French character has been developed by just this breakfast, taken regularly.)

From the center of Lyon's business district the trip to the village, through daytime traffic, takes about twenty minutes, through the lovely, fertile, gently rolling countryside that borders both sides of the Saône; the river road finally leads to a bridge for a final crossing of the placid stream and there, on the west bank, on a tiny street called Quai de la Plage stands the neat, three-story building, which the present patron has transformed into a modern structure that retains the charm of the original.

My companion and I were welcomed by the patron with an *apéritif de la maison*—consisting of a mixture arrived at by combining the fluid of one bottle of champagne, half a glass of cassis, and half a glass of framboise liqueur. The resulting nectar flowed trippingly on the tongue, and proved the most agreeable introduction to a meal yet encountered on any continent. The patron showed us to a table near the door so that he could sit with us and still attend to the greeting of arriving guests, not forgetting periodic trips to the kitchen to supervise the work of his sous-chefs.

"After lunch you'll meet my wife Raymonde, who works here as cashier," he began, in his orderly way. "My daughter Françoise, who is here sometimes, is married to a good *chocolatier* named Bernarchon." (There are no male apprentices named Bocuse in the kitchen, a fact that makes him sad.)

Formalities disposed of, M. Bocuse addressed himself to the matter at hand—a memorable lunch but built, as he put it, on a cuisine *"plus simple, moins décor."* M. Point's sermons on the desirability of a simplified cuisine, without a large number of side dishes and extra courses, were well remembered by his disciple in Collonges-au-Mont d'Or.

The *potage aux légumes* provided a noteworthy if not sensational start— creamy to a moderate degree and obviously the product of fresh, organically raised vegetables. To follow, a *terrine de ris de veau et de gibier* was suggested along with a *jambon cuit dans le foin* (ham cooked in hay). My companion and I voted for one of each, thereby insuring a taste of each. An omelette fines herbes was soft and delicate.

Our host, who did bear a resemblance to Napoleon at a certain angle, excused himself to welcome some expectant customers; the thought of Napoleon's starving soldiers, retreating from Russia, crossed my mind as I watched, fascinated, the wheeling in of an overladen table of pastries and cream and fruit of every description. Bocuse returned to the table quickly, just as the maître d'hôtel was uncorking a bottle of Beaujolais bearing the appelation Brouilly—a wine that the patron produces himself at a Burgundian vineyard he purchased. Its taste was superior to that of any Beaujolais I had sampled recently.

The moment for the fish course now arrived, and we plunged into the dish that is perhaps the most celebrated specialty of the house—the *loup en croûte*. The Mediterranean *loup*, for the uninitiate, is a type of sea bass, but with a refined taste all its own. Offered encased in a pastry shell in the form of a fish, farci with a mousse of lobster, it easily lived up to its advance reputation; the Pouilly-Fuissé was a perfect complement to the subtly captivating fish dish—an excellent white wine to follow the Brouilly, from its neighboring commune.

Although still recommending the most suitable red and white wines to accompany his delicious meat, fish, and game courses, Chef Bocuse feels that the day is coming when a good fresh red Burgundy, for example, will do for the entire meal. But that day had not yet arrived, fortunately for us and our enthusiasm for the incomparable Pouilly-Fuissé we were enjoying.

Next came a *poulet* of the region: *fricassée au vinaigre de Brouilly—estrade*, mounted among a bank of flowers. It miraculously avoided being an anticlimax. A bottle of Saint-Veran '71, a Haut-Maconnais, was brought for us to sample later, as M. Bocuse correctly chose this moment to show us the more interesting areas of the establishment. "Come into the kitchen," he commanded, "and have a look at how we prepare these dishes." I was delighted at the opportunity to stretch my legs and move about a bit.

Gleaming pots and pans highlighted a spacious, modern kitchen; the volailles de Bresse, plucked clean and ready for the cooks, were laid out in a row, their tags shining, looking for all the world like an advertisement for a French tourist poster: plumes white, heads—above the beak—red, and legs blue. "Just as with a good wine, the phrase 'chickens of Bresse' is an *appellation controllé*," the patron explained. "No one else is allowed to use that name, and for a good reason. They are especially fed to make them the most tender, the best in France."

The cooks were busy preparing a variety of dishes—meat, fish, poultry, game, and soufflés. An orange soufflé au Grand Marnier looked especially tempting.

As we returned to our places, we found, berthed next to ours, the table loaded with desserts—a massive assortment ranging from sherbets to fresh strawberries and raspberries to indescribable pastries and cake and petits-fours and thin mints from the atelier of his son-in-law. I felt incapable of considering the possibility of consuming any of the more elaborate concoctions, and settled for a serving of strawberries and raspberries with just a *soupçon* of the rich cream that accompanies them. Bocuse noticed my hesitation, assured us that we had in fact had a moderate luncheon, and finally succeeded in extracting from us the admission that we did *not* feel that we had overeaten.

"I understand, as Escoffier did not, that my clients wish to *garder la ligne* [preserve the figure]," he interjected; even so—since it happened to be my companion's birthday—we were regaled with a cake of impressive attainments called an Ambassadeur, with a creamy, rum filling. We tapered off with a delicious *tarte aux poires*, petits fours, and some of M. Bernarchon's chocolates. With the desserts, we reverted to the patron's favorite beverage, a good champagne properly chilled. "I really see no reason why anyone should want to drink anything but champagne," he said. "Some wines are excellent, but *nothing* compares with a good champagne."

He meditated briefly on this preference, then reminisced a bit. "Monsieur Point committed suicide by drinking champagne," he admitted. "But then I've known cuisiniers who died at an age younger than his who drank nothing but water."

We left in a happy haze, but not until M. Bocuse had insisted that we return that evening for a light dinner. We must have looked somewhat discouraged or apprehensive or both, for he added quickly: "Just a bowl of crayfish soup really. It's just right. More of a supper."

It was difficult to turn down such an invitation from such an accomplished master of French cuisine, so we didn't try. Besides, it was quite possible that we might not have another such opportunity for some time. "Most of your cake is still to be eaten," he called after us.

"A light supper of soup and cake," we agreed. How could anyone turn down Caesar fixing us again with that imperial stare.

"Seven-thirty," he ordered. We nodded meekly. We had crossed the Rubicon.

As we left, one American diner was overheard saying to his table companion in English (the first we'd heard all day): "Nothing will ever top this meal. I may never eat again."

★ ★ ★

Lyon, happily, is like most French cities a wonderful place to explore on foot. A moderate amount of exercise was clearly in order, before returning to Collonges-au-Mont d'Or. And what more rewarding a way to shake down a Bocuse luncheon than to climb the Fourvière hill for a leisurely look at the remains of the Roman presence.

Besides the Roman theater and the Odeum, which stood nearby, the most important gathering place in the area is the Arena of the Three Gauls, which was on the slope of the Croix-Rousse hill, across the Saône, at a period several centuries before the arrival of the Romans. All Gaul *was* divided in three parts, as Julius Caesar rightly said, and emissaries from all three, including delegates from sixty tribes, convened in this arena in what was certainly the first evidence of a French parliamentary system. This historic ruin, which is still being reconstituted, was also the scene of the birth of Christianity in France—where, in fact, the first Christian martyrs in Gaul met their death.

As always the churches dominate the old city. The Basilica Fourvière is situated on the spot with the most spectacular view of the region; Saint Jean, the seat of the Primate, dating from the twelfth and fifteenth centuries, and the Romanesque church of Saint Paul, of the eleventh century, are located right on the River Saône, along the winding Quai Romain Rolland. The area of the Roman theater and Odeum, and the Palais de Justice, a museum of criminality, are the most notable of the remaining points of interest on the hill.

212

Lyon from the old city

Of all the cultures of modern Europe, the French is, I believe, the most appealing and understandable to one from the western shore of the Atlantic. Civilization, as the French know it today, comprises both a respectful retention of the past and forward-looking designs for tomorrow. Perhaps the ideal place to arrive at an appreciation of the civilized quality of France and French life is in a city such as Lyon, rather than in Paris, which—like New York—is not truly representative of its country.

Lyon proper, which I regard in my mind as the "old city," would be explored in sections as I made my way to one or another of its fine restaurants, for my primary reason for being in Lyon was to visit its citadels of culinary art. Aspects of the new Lyon, too, were to be found spread about the area, like the modern skating rink and swimming pools built for the Olympic Games.

We opted instead for a trip to the zoo in the Parc de la Tête d'Or, to the northeast along the Rhone. It turned out to be quite delightfully old-fashioned—no moats replacing fences here—and it covers quite an expanse of ground, a fact of which we became aware while traversing it from one end to the other. Not a single variety of antelope escaped our attention. It is one of Western Europe's most highly regarded zoos, although it does not rank with the more modern one at Antwerp, Belgium, in my estimation.

We returned to Collonges-au-Mont d'Or in good condition—reasonably well prepared for what lay ahead. Dinner that evening was a modest repast by Bocuse standards, but as we suspected it was not to consist merely of soup and cake. One can beg for mercy only by pleading that one wants to protect one's figure—the only excuse Bocuse will accept. And there was more talk of guarding *la ligne*. According to our host, the new simplified menu is practiced these days throughout the Lyon area, and even in Paris, where he worked for Lucas-Carton, a two-star restaurant today, and Maxim's (three-star) before settling down in Lyon to earn his own *étoiles*.

"No one really wants to spend three or four hours over lunch any more, as they did in the time of Carême and Escoffier, and consume all those courses," M. Bocuse said reassuringly as we sat down to our second meal of the day under his guidance.

The aromatic crayfish soup was all that we had been led to expect; it was followed by an interesting dish—supposedly just enough to taste, but really ample portions—called *un Tablier de Sapeur* (*intestin du boeuf*). A portion of lamb ("from Sahun in the Alps, the best *agneau* in Europe") or a *faux-filet* (the thicker part of the sirloin) were suggested, but we settled for a sole vermouth Noilly with *pois* that were really *petits* and spanking fresh. From here we moved on, with very little opposition, to the cheeses, including a local goat cheese called Cervelle de Canut—a product that had been developed by "the brains of the silk-weavers"—workers in Lyon's principal industry. More strawberries, raspberries, gâteau Ambassadeur, and chocolates rounded out the meal; on the liquid side, we had begun a pitcherful of the tantalizing *apéritif de la maison* that had preceded luncheon, a Meursault Charmes '69 that is worth noting, a good cognac, and constantly refilled glasses of champagne.

"But you haven't really eaten," M. Bocuse protested, although he did not seem to be censuring us with his usual vehemence. "After all," he said, with a trace of admiration, "not very many persons—even Lyonnais—can handle two meals chez Bocuse on the same day!"

While we worked our way through the final bottle of champagne for the evening, our host disclosed some of the details of his operation. For example, he employs sixty *ouvriers* in his luxurious restaurant and in his nearby L'Abbaye, where he accommodates private parties—banquets, marriage feasts, etc. "I make money on L'Abbaye," he admitted, "and I make money on a restaurant I have at the Lyon airport. I make money on the wine and foie gras I market. But on this luxe restaurant Chez Bocuse I lose." He shrugged in that philosophical gesture that the French have mastered. "I refuse to compromise the standards of the meals or of the service. Some men," he explained, "have mistresses. I have a luxe restaurant."

Part of the problem, I learned, is that the patron refuses to charge astronomical prices; he is, in fact, encouraging young Lyonnais to dine at his superb establishment. And when they say, respectfully and honestly, "But Monsieur Bocuse, we do not have much money," the patron charges only what they can afford, and provides the same meals his more affluent guests enjoy.

But even the full price is not high enough to discourage anyone who desires to eat at what may well be the best table in France. "A good average meal, with wine, chez Bocuse," he said, glancing up at the ceiling and calculating, "will run about 120 to 140 francs [about 24 to 28 dollars]. Of course if you order four kinds of wine, you can run it up higher than that."

I reflected momentarily on the meals I'd had at fancy Manhattan restaurants for more than double that amount—meals that could not compare, in any respect, with the fare M. Bocuse offers.

"I buy only the best, even if it costs more. I refuse to settle for meats, fish, or vegetables that are not absolutely top quality." This is quite apparent to anyone who dines chez Bocuse from the moment he takes his first forkful of the first course.

"But come with me tomorrow morning," he suggested with sudden enthusiasm. "We'll visit the market together. I'll pick you up at your hotel at seven forty-five. Done?"

Later that evening at my hotel in Lyon the *patronne* exclaimed: "What? Lunch *and* dinner chez Bocuse! You must be tired, M'sieur. Dining there for just one meal is very fatiguing." She regarded me as though I had just competed in the Marathon.

The next morning she and her husband sprang to attention when the eminent chef cuisinier walked into the lobby. They wore the panic-stricken look a parish priest might have on the occasion of an unexpected visit by the Pope. "Monsieur Bocuse," they murmured reverently in unison. Bocuse bowed regally, and we boarded his van for the short but hair-raising drive to the principal market, in the heart of town.

"Did you sleep well?" he asked anxiously, as though the honor of his establishment were at stake. Reassured when I told him I had indeed, he plunged into a steady stream of comments, not necessarily related, while narrowly missing pedestrians and vehicles. "You know those young people I told you about last night?" he began in his rapid, Lyonnais-accented French. "They may not pay the full price now, but they'll come back when they're older. And they'll be good customers."

Asked about his award as Meilleur Ouvrier de France in 1961, he said: "Well, it's the top prize for someone in my profession. We are in France some ten thousand chef cuisiniers—of a total of maybe forty thousand cuisiniers. The finalists in this competition, where we must prepare a prescribed dish right there on the spot, are less than fifty."

"And you all prepare the same dish?" I asked.

"The same fish," he answered. "That year it was Carp de Chambrun."

"Fifty Carp de Chambrun for the judges to sample?" I persisted.

Bocuse nodded.

"And yours was best," I added.

Again that expressive Gallic shrug that says so much—in this case, You know how it is, or What can you do?

There are several markets in Lyon, some specialized—fish (mornings only), vegetables (afternoons), meats (all day long). Bocuse sometimes visits one or another, but this day, as on most, his objective was the new, covered market, which offers products in all categories.

Bocuse's entrance was something special: to right and left butchers, fish-mongers, fruit dealers, cheese merchants greeted him from their stalls as the Grand Seigneur of the area. "Ça va, Paul?" one of the vendors called as the grand chef passed by. Others waved, shouted greetings from across the hall. Bocuse nodded, striding purposefully ahead in a manner that suggested Caesar moving to the dais of the Roman Senate.

As he paused to consider a product, a salesperson would instantly be all attention. Bocuse pinched some strawberries, but walked on, bought some green beans, quickly moved on to a stall featuring a variety of fish. He poked the dorades Royales with one finger, carefully inspected the rascasse—a spiny, scorpionlike Mediterranean fish without which bouillabaisse is not really bouillabaisse—and finally settled on the rouget.

At a booth displaying cuts of meat, he explained that the Limousin—a beef from central France, in the Limoges area—had a white cast to its color, while the Charolais—his preference—was a ruddy red. As was his custom he picked the latter and swept on without waiting for purchases, which would be delivered to his van when he had finished at the market.

A café and brioche at a nearby counter interrupted the business of the morning briefly, and after greeting the women who served the coffee affectionately he delivered himself of a few further comments as we leaned against the counter—as always without any preamble:

"I've heard it said that you can't find a bad meal in France. I don't go along completely with that opinion, but I do think you'd have to search pretty hard to find a bad meal in the Lyonnais region."

I smiled broadly, causing him to look up and ask what was the matter.

"I just remembered what Curnonsky once said," I replied.

His frown deepened. "And what was that?"

" 'Lyon,' he said, 'is the only town where I did not succeed in eating badly.' " (His construction is typical of the French addiction to phrasing thoughts negatively: "Il ne fait pas chaud" ["It is not warm"]. Never have I heard a Frenchman admit that it was cold.)

"That's a good way of putting it," Bocuse said, smiling faintly. "Even the inexpensive bistros here serve first-rate meals. I hope you plan to try a few," he added.

Assured that I would, he continued: "After we finish here at the market we'll have a relaxed coffee at a café nearby, where we cuisiniers of Lyon usually meet after the market. You know of course that some of the best restaurants in France are right here in Lyon," he added superfluously.

Once his purchases were loaded into his van, we were off to the rendezvous with his fellow cuisiniers. Hesitantly I mentioned the revival of interest in the United States in Brillat-Savarin's *Physiology of Taste*, knowing well that Bocuse, like Carême, was no admirer of that author's achievements in the cuisine.

"Well, yes," he said as we drove off, "one must know a little about the physiology of taste"—pointedly ignoring the name Brillat-Savarin—"but one must also understand something of the psychology of the taster. For after all it is the taster—the diner—we are trying to satisfy."

Ancien cuisinier

He spoke convincingly, and the pupils of his eyes seemed to widen as he looked, piercingly, at this listener. Occasionally he returned his attention to the road—we were again traveling at a goodly clip through the crowded downtown streets. I reminded him that he had been quoted as saying that it was the cook's taste that really counted, not the customer's.

"Yes, of course," he agreed, setting off on a different tack. "You mustn't think you're eating what you feel like eating. You're eating what the cook feels like eating. You're eating according to his taste."

And how, I wondered, do his U.S. customers react to that programming?

"The foreigner is an easy client," he said, "who spoils your cuisine because he finds everything good. We have very few foreign clients."

We were slowing down now to a reasonable rate of speed for heavily traveled city streets, and I assumed that we were nearing the café in question. It would have been hard to pick out, since it was not distinguishable from the great bulk of all the cafés throughout France—a few banquettes but mostly straight-backed chairs, sawdust spread on the floor, and a traditional zinc-topped bar, behind which a large coffee percolator dominated the room. Wine, brandy, apéritifs, and beer were for sale, but the major percentage of its customers came in for strong French coffee.

The patron greeted M. Bocuse effusively, as we seated ourselves in a secluded corner, shortly to be joined by two well-known Lyon restaurateurs —Gérard Nandron (two Michelin stars) and Christian Bourillot (one star).

Bocuse leaned back expansively in his banquette, after introductions had been performed, and announced gravely: "You are now surrounded by the Mafia Lyonnaise. We cuisiniers here in Lyon are friends, not rivals, as you can see. You must dine at their restaurants—you'll be served meals you won't forget." He paused.

"Why not lunch with Nandron tomorrow, and have dinner with Bourillot," he said. It was more of a statement, an order, than a question. Both restaurateurs nodded enthusiastically.

"Good. Done," Bocuse said in his man-of-action style. "Come, I'll drop you off at your hotel."

Nearby we stopped briefly on one of those exceedingly narrow side streets for which Europe is noted. Since a row of cars was parked, illegally, along the curb, we stopped in the one lane available for traffic. Bocuse jumped out, fetched a boyish-looking friend from the interior of a restaurant with the mellifluous name of Léon de Lyon on its façade, and introduced us at the side of the van. "This is Jean-Paul Lacombe, the patron here. I told him you'd be delighted to lunch with him today." (Once you find yourself in Bocuse's hands, it is foolhardy to make any plans on your own.)

There was time for only a quick handshake with this very youthful patron before we were obliged to unblock the traffic we were so effectively tying up. At my hotel, Bocuse said: "I want to show you L'Abbaye. Friday I'll be in Geneva, but come to me for lunch on Saturday. *À bientôt*," and he was off.

★

An hour or so later, when I returned to that narrow street, the Rue Pleney, following a brisk ten-minute walk from my hotel, I was greeted at the door of Léon de Lyon by Monsieur Lacombe; shortly after entering the restaurant I was made welcome by his sister and his mother. His father, he quickly told me, had died six months before, and young Lacombe had been catapulted into the role of patron at the age of twenty-three, perhaps the youngest chef of any so notable an establishment in Lyon and possibly in France. His mother and sister were providing their moral and physical support. "A woman can't be married to a chef cuisinier for twenty-two years without learning something about the business," Mère Lacombe said in a gentle, well-modulated voice.

Jean-Paul and I sat down at a table he indicated and talked for a bit over a Communard—similar to a Kir but made with a Beaujolais. It was superior, I thought, to the usual Kir, the white-wine-and-cassis apéritif first concocted by the famous Communist Roman Catholic Canon in Dijon, and named after him.

"And what was Monsieur Bocuse telling you?" Lacombe asked, laughing.

"Simply that you were already filling your father's shoes with distinction," I replied.

"Giselle, my mother, and Michèle, my sister, share the work, but it's a full-time job, as you may imagine," he said, pouring out two glasses of

Beaujolais, as a waiter served one of the house specialties, a Gras Double. "It's an *estomac du boeuf* and very Lyonnais," he added. Another recommendation of the patron's, the *pieds de porc aux marrons* (pigs feet with chestnut), I decided to leave for another time.

Young Lacombe, I learned, went to hotel school for three years in Grenoble, also in eastern France—the best in France and not far behind, in reputation, to the one in Lausanne, Switzerland. "I learned all phases of the business there, including the restaurant," he said. "It was also a great place for skiing and other winter sports, and I played football [soccer] quite a lot. But now I'm too busy for that.

"Yes, of course I worked here under my father, Paul. No he wasn't Léon de Lyon; the name came with the place when he bought it twenty-two years ago. For a while I served as an apprentice with Monsieur Lasserre in Paris [an esteemed three-star restaurateur] and with M. Vergé in Mougins, in the south [one star]." Two excellent restaurants in two quite different sections of the country. "It's always a good idea," he said, "to serve part of one's apprenticeship away from home."

Another Lyonnaise specialty, *filets de sole au vermouth Noilly*, was deceptively simple but delicious. *"Maintenant je vais vous chercher du vin blanc, une bonne Pouilly-Fuissé,"* he said hastily, excusing himself for a moment. Because of their proximity to the Burgundian vineyards, Lyon restaurants customarily feature Burgundies; throughout my stay I don't remember having one glass of Bordeaux, although it is available on request.

"It's difficult to keep the standards up to those of my father," Lacombe said on his return to the table. He poured the wine and said: "But we're determined to try to do that. A conscientious artisan must concentrate on quality, and here in Lyon we restaurateurs are *sérieux*," he concluded.

On the broader aspects of gastronomy and the cuisine d'Escoffier the engaging young patron preferred to "grow a bit" before venturing any opinions. The cervelle de canut, the local goat cheese originated by the silk weavers, again made an appearance, but the Reblochons from the Haute Savoie proved too alluring to resist. I complimented M. Lacombe on his excellent menu; the lunch, though modest in my case, was entirely satisfying. I truly look forward to another visit the next time I find myself in Lyon.

★

The afternoon passed quickly. Lyon seems to be an easier place to shop for presents (scarves, blouses, gloves, etc.) than Paris, partly because of the relative size of the cities and the difference in numbers of their inhabitants. Two excellent *librairies* (bookshops), stocked with rare eighteenth- and nineteenth-century works, were responsible for the passage of at least half the afternoon.

Fortunately, the restaurant I had chosen for dinner—somehow I had managed to work in one that Bocuse hadn't mentioned and arranged for— is on the Place Bellecour, a central area of the downtown section even closer to my hotel than Léon de Lyon.

Past the florists' stalls in the Place itself and on the opposite side, facing the Place, I easily found Vettard-Café Neuf that evening. I had vowed to dine lightly, but I was soon cajoled by the patron into trying either the *Caneton Truffé, fourée au foie gras*, or the *Poularde en Chemise*. I chose the latter, a chicken that seemed infinitely more tender, thanks to having been cooked inside a skin of pork.

Forty-five-year-old Jean Vettard, who has been in command here these past ten years, has an international outlook on the subject of cuisine, a result of having worked in Germany, England, and the United States (the Chicago Hilton), as well as in his native France. He feels strongly that one should concentrate on the specialties of the country in which one finds oneself; further, that there are in each land superb dishes that do not bear comparison one to another.

M. Vettard is a fourth-generation cuisinier, following in the wake of his father and two uncles. Before taking over from his father, he studied at the famous École Hôtelière in Lausanne. "Today," he said, opening a bottle of Morgon (Beaujolais), which is served cool, "you can still dine as well as—or better than—ever. But the generation after us?" He shrugged. This one seemed to translate into "I doubt it."

"Something is happening in civilized countries all over the world. The spirit of the young has changed. They have no conviction. I have several apprentices in the kitchen here, and only one of them really works, really cares the way I cared when I was fifteen. Maybe there's too much leisure

222

today. There is surely too much nonsense being preached—and quality will suffer."

He switched back and forth from French into English and back to French, the first patron of my stay who did not speak exclusively in French—thanks to his employment in England and the United States. In English I quoted Alain Le Nôtre, of the family of Parisian *pâtissiers* who have inherited the mantle, at least as far as pastry-making goes, of the great Carême. "Quality is everything," Le Nôtre had said. "As we grow, we must take care to preserve it, for once our business ceases to function on the artisan level, it will be in danger of becoming"—and here he hesitated and shuddered slightly —"un snack bar."

The patron concurred. Today, with restaurateurs like M. Vettard, quality is still the ultimate goal, but he agrees with the new concept of gastronomy, drastically altered since the days of Escoffier and Carême.

"The secret of the philosophy of cooking," said our perceptive host of the evening, "is a simple respect for the product and preparing it without masking its flavor.

"And here in Lyon," he added, "we have every type of element we need for a great cuisine."

A memorable evening was concluded with a specialty of the house, a *pâtisserie de Canut*, as well as a *Soufflé glacé de la maison*. The thought of several more days of star-studded meals strengthened my resolve and led me to order coffee without further delay.

★ ★

The avenue that sweeps along the Rhone, obediently executing every twist in direction made by the river, changes its name every few blocks—a practice that exists in the naming of many quais and boulevards in large French cities, notably Paris. Perhaps there are more citizens worth remembering in this manner than there are streets and avenues.

The Quai Jean Moulin encompasses a fairly short stretch of avenue along the river, anchored at one end by the Palais du Commerce and on the other by the fourteenth- and fifteenth-century Église Saint-Bonaventure, so it was a fairly simple matter to locate my target for luncheon on a spectacularly beautiful October day. Gérard Nandron, patron and chef cuisinier of the restaurant bearing his name, a compact two-story building overlooking the river, greeted me at the door, asked if I were well, and invited me in.

Like the other *grand patrons* I had already spoken to, Nandron was quick to deplore the excesses of the cuisine d'Escoffier, a subject he chose for the beginning of our culinary conversation. Son of one of the founders of the cuisine Lyonnaise, Johannes Nandron, handsome, forty-one-year-old Gérard feels that the basic taste of the bourgeois Frenchman is in a state of transition. "No longer does the customer who comes here to satisfy his palate as well as his stomach demand his principal courses garnished with a variety of highly seasoned dishes; he is interested in what might be called a natural taste. It is the *goût* of the products themselves that counts now—without all of Escoffier's condiments and sauces," said the amiable young proprietor as luncheon was being prepared.

"Two main courses are enough even for today's gastronome," he said firmly. The house apéritif, composed of kirsch and jus de framboise, was delicious; I felt it deserved a close second place to the Bocuse apéritif.

M. Nandron, it appears, is more conscientious than his fellows in his solicitude for the general condition of his clients. "Some time ago I took on a medical consultant to oversee the preparation of the meals in order to protect the health of my customers," he said. "No restaurateur benefits by overfeeding his clients. If he wants to keep his customers, he must give them a carefully balanced meal composed of the best products—and not too much! Two principal courses should be enough for anyone," he repeated, as I addressed myself to a Nandron recommendation for the first course, a *terrine laperau* (rabbit). It served its purpose—to lead one into the next course—with its light, piquant flavor.

A white Macon sec was brought, to accompany the delicate *quenelles brochet* (fish balls in the shape of elongated fingers—of pike) that were scheduled soon to arrive.

"In Lyon," Nandron said, gently pouring the wine, "the products are the most honest in France. Neither cuisinier nor diner settles for anything but the best. I remember a vacation trip in Norway with Paul Bocuse and Jean Troisgros [another three-star restaurateur, in Roanne]. We decided to do a little fishing in a clear mountain lake. We each caught a trout—one was superb, another just fair, and the third not good at all. It was, remember, the same lake, the same day, the same altitude, and we used the same bait. It shows you never know. One must be very careful."

The quenelles arrived, served with *écrevisses* (crayfish) in a light but creamy butter sauce, and I congratulated myself on not having had quenelles before these, on this trip to Lyon. They proved a provocative taste experience.

There was no need for M. Nandron to call in his doctor for advice, as I planned to proceed directly to the cheese. Happily, the patron understood my wish. "Here in Lyon," he said, "one does not live to eat, nor simply eat to live. The wisest course is somewhere in between. The future of the grande cuisine Lyonnaise lies in smaller meals of the best quality."

This excellent but modest lunch was concluded with a good chèvre (goat cheese) and a bottle of Beaujolais—the water of the Lyon area. (As this is written, an announcement has been made that M. Nandron will transport the joys of *la cuisine Lyonnaise* to Kyoto, Japan.)

★

Christian Bourillot, a slight, rather shy, forty-one-year-old cuisinier, was my host at dinner that evening in his comfortable restaurant on the Place des Celestins, close by one of the city's most celebrated theaters. He suggested a kir, made in the usual way (white wine and cassis), and opened our discussion with a few observations about pollution in the area and the destruction it is causing.

"There's hardly a lake that isn't four-fifths gone—Bourget, Annecy, Léman [Geneva]—they're all on the way to going dead. And the streams too. Next the fish, if there are any, will be inedible—fish like wonderful salmon that we call Omble chevalier."

Bourillot came to his own one-star restaurant by a route that included working in Paris, Talloires, and Dardilly, near Lyon, and on the transatlantic liner *Liberté* before settling into his present location as chef cuisinier.

As he warmed to the subject of his favorite dishes, his early reticence disappeared. His suggestions for the evening meal consisted of *crêpes au jambon*, a house specialty, a Charolais *contrefilet aux Echalotes*, and *filets de sole au whisky*. Intrigued, I chose the sole, which was indeed floating in a sauce that included whiskey as one of its chief ingredients. It doesn't sound promising somehow, but as served chez Bourillot it was an agreeable surprise. It was also startling to learn that whiskey is also used on his popular (with the French) dessert, *coupe Valérie*—as a sauce on vanilla ice cream!

M. Bourillot, it seems, won the Meilleur Ouvrier de France award in 1968, following in M. Bocuse's path. (This top prize for a cuisinier is presented only once every three or four years.) He recalled the experience with gusto: the forty-four finalists arrived for the grand concours, armed with their own knives. Supplied with the raw material for the dishes they would be assigned to create, all fell to work on the preparation of three courses— a *filet de sole Catalane*, a *poularde chevalière*, and a *soufflé chaud au chocolat*. Four contestants survived for the final vote by a seventy-two-member jury and twelve judges (four previous winners of the award, which an individual can win only once, four *patrons* of quality restaurants in various parts of the country, and four *ouvriers cuisiniers* from different regions). They selected M. Bourillot to receive the award that is the most important single factor in guaranteeing the success of a luxe restaurant. The maison Bourillot has been filled with customers at luncheon and dinner ever since.

★ ★ ★

Promptly at eleven-thirty the next morning, on a perfect, sunny October day, M. Bocuse greeted me at the entrance of the three-story establishment that bears his name. (You may already have gathered that it is my favorite month in France.) The Saône sparkled; it was a day that seemed dedicated

Roman amphitheatre

to the enjoyment of good living. The restaurant was already occupied by numbers of expectant lunchers.

The consuming of the apéritif of the house—that memorable champagne-cassis-framboise combination—had a ceremonial atmosphere; I had the feeling that I was being welcomed by the patron for the first time.

The drive to L'Abbaye, for the promised visit, was achieved in less than five minutes; it is a rambling structure, also facing the river, built originally by the current patron's grandfather. The rooms were large enough to accommodate a banquet of well over fifty guests; Bocuse, apparently not satisfied, gestured vaguely out one window and said casually: "I think I make another room here." I looked out the window indicated and noted that the drop to the river's edge was considerable; still, I'm certain that if M. Bocuse wants to build a room there it will be done.

But the pièce de resistance was saved for the end of the tour of inspection: in an outbuilding, behind L'Abbaye itself, reposed a small part of a unique collection of fifty calliopes, most of them constructed in the nineteenth century. It became suddenly obvious that M. Bocuse must be a frustrated circus performer; overhead were various posterlike illustrations proclaiming CIRCUS BOCUSE and JAZZBAND BOCUSE. One of the larger calliopes (*limonaires*, in my host's spiel) was turning out a march loudly enough to fuel a full-dress circus parade. The figures attached to the front of the instrument were obediently beating a drum and clashing cymbals at appropriate moments, and the flags of France and the United States adorned the roof of the calliope—the latter flag complete with fifty stars, I was delighted to note.

Asked, perhaps superfluously, if he had once wanted to be a circus performer, Bocuse turned to me, nodded, and said soberly: "Always."

On the short drive back to the cornerstone of the Bocuse business, the restaurant known simply as Chez Bocuse, the patron spoke about the vineyard he had bought in Burgundy, the nucleus of his wine-producing and -exporting operation.

"The Abbaye shows a profit," he reminded me. "And so does the wine business. And the pâté. And the airport restaurant. But," he said as we went in to lunch chez Bocuse once more, "even though I lose money here, I wouldn't make money on the others, without this centerpiece."

For the last Bocuse meal on this sojourn in Lyon, I studied the menu and its sixty-seven choices (not including vegetables, cheeses, and desserts). For a starter, I selected a Bocuse suggestion: *soupe à la jambe de bois Henry Clos-Jouve*. The patron explained, in a short brochure that accompanies the menu (translated from the French): "You prepare this in the same way it has always been done in the Lyonnais countryside. You choose a pot of earthenware or copper. Deposit a good hock of beef, which you steep in cold water with salt, onions, and a variety of herbs to give it taste. Simmer slowly over a clear fire. Skim well the bouillon. Once the bouillon is clear, add leeks, turnips, celery. Then add two or three hocks of veal, a shoulder of pig, turkey, partridge, rare lamb, and a strip of rare beef. A half-hour before serving, add some chickens of Bresse and a moment afterward sausage containing truffles and pistachio nuts."

This precise description added weight to my conviction that the Bocuse reputation and the quality of his dishes were a result of his being a true perfectionist. Attention to detail is clearly the key to success as a chef cuisinier. And Bocuse, as the French say, is *sérieux*—translated literally as serious, but also including dedicated, and the effort to do one's absolute best.

As he ordered a bottle of champagne, Bocuse completed his reading on the making of "*à la jambe de bois*": "When it is cooked, stand up a hock straight above the pot so that one will recognize the *soupe*. And one must have some Beaujolais handy and pour it liberally. *Bon appétit*," he concluded.

On Saturdays especially the restaurant fills up quickly, and the patron was often called upon to excuse himself to greet his regular customers. But each time he returned to continue conversing about culinary technique, his ambitions, his hobbies, and his idol, Fernand Point.

He poured himself some Perrier-Jouet and said sadly: "Point was only fifty-eight when he died. But Paul Mercier, his head chef, died at fifty-six, and he never drank champagne. So why not enjoy it?"

As I began on an incomparable *filet de sole aux nouilles*, Bocuse spoke about the hobbies of a three-star chef cuisinier. "I don't have much time to ski any more," he said, frowning. "But I still enjoy practicing as a frogman (*homme-grenouille*)—just for fun, of course."

(But not entirely. I was told later, by one of his maîtres d'hôtel, that the patron had already saved the lives of eleven swimmers, and that his father had saved seventeen.)

"Beyond that," he said, "I like to hunt the duck in Alsace in August, when Chez Bocuse is closed for two weeks."

A platter containing three perfect cheeses—St. Nectaire, Pont l'Évêque, and Fourme d'Auvergne—was set before me as the proprietor expounded his own beliefs regarding food and a good cuisine—beliefs somewhat at variance with those of Brillat-Savarin and Escoffier.

"One can make a very adequate meal with one dish," he said, "as one can make a good meal with only one wine. One may very well keep the same red wine all through the meal, with the soup as well as the salad—yes, even with fish," he added without hesitation. I couldn't help but wonder what kind of reaction that heretical statement would have brought from some of our more prominent wine-and-food experts.

"The gastronome? I think he is the man who knows exactly what he wants—and orders it, without any nonsense."

Then on to a favorite topic: "For me, the apéritif has no use at all. Unless one drinks champagne. I think the best way to drink champagne is before the meal. A glass of champagne is the very best apéritif that exists." Thus, as noted, his own house apéritif has a strong champagne base.

About the masters of the grande cuisine in the nineteenth century: "Well," said Bocuse, his brow furrowed, "an architect who builds a façade badly camouflages his errors with some ivy. Cuisiniers camouflaged theirs with a bit of sauce."

Then, still without a hint of a smile: "And doctors cover up their errors with a little earth.

"A good formula," he added thoughtfully.

The customary overpowering array of desserts was produced, and I lingered long enough to help the patron finish the second bottle of champagne. Finally I bade a sad farewell to M. Bocuse, promising to stop by again on another trip to France. Indeed, Chez Bocuse is, in the words of the Guide Michelin, "worth the trip"—not only from another part of France but worth the trip from the United States. Of all the French restaurants in which I have dined, simply or sumptuously, throughout France, and in the

United States, England, and Japan, none has matched the total experience of dining Chez Bocuse. I shall certainly return.

As for the restaurants of Lyon, I would rate those as a group above any similar collection in any city in France. For even at the smallest bistro in Lyon one dines extremely well.

Before leaving the area I was anxious to try an inexpensive restaurant featuring the typical cuisine Lyonnaise; after several days of one-, two-, and three-star meals, this would, I thought, be a real test. Not far from my hotel I happened on a modest ground-floor dining room, sandwiched between small shops, called Le Condé, open for dinner only, six nights a week. The proprietor was absent, but the maître d'hôtel, or chief waiter really, produced the menu promptly. I studied the imposing list in the dim light at a small table for one along the wall—a staggering variety of choices at unbelievably low prices. First, there was a special for each of the six evenings, consisting of one dish (veal, lamb, boeuf Bourguignon, pork casserole, tuna provençale, duck or chicken) with a vegetable and dessert for 9 francs ($1.80)! The 12-franc menu included a choice among thirty-six entrées (appetizers, in the United States), among twenty vegetables, forty-one *viandes* (meat dishes), and eight desserts—with service and a pitcher of wine included—all for 12 francs ($2.40). The 18-franc menu provided a choice of thirty-seven appetizers, twenty-three vegetable dishes, thirty-two meat courses, a selection of cheeses, dry or cream, and ten desserts. (Wine and service not included at this price.)

À la carte the hungry diner had forty-two appetizers to tempt him, ranging from 2.5 francs for *potage de légumes* or *salade de saison* to 9.5 francs for *Grenouilles des Dombes* (frogs' legs); twenty-four vegetable dishes; forty-one *viandes* prepared in a variety of ways; cheeses, dry and cream; and fifteen desserts. The *carte du vin* offered representatives of all corners of France and while there were no vintages among them neither were there vintage prices.

In order to assess the cheaper menu accurately, I chose the 12-franc dinner, beginning with a heaping bowl of *moules marinières* and following with a *poulet roti salade* (roast chicken with salad), a *ratatouille Niçoise*, and a delicious *mousse au chocolat*, along with a quite passable *pichet* of the house *rouge*.

When I had paid my bill (12 francs, service included), I felt that I had dined well—not, to be sure, as with Bocuse—but a well-prepared meal built on fresh products, and a delight to the taste buds. Certainly it easily outdid many dinners I had eaten in French restaurants in New York at more than five times the prices.

At a few other bistros and brasseries entered at random in the Lyon business district I lunched or dined well, with uniformly good results.

"Cooking is the oldest of all arts," wrote Jean Anthelme Brillat-Savarin in his ornate life's work *The Physiology of Taste*. Adam was born hungry, the renowned eighteenth- and nineteenth-century gastronome and memoirist claims, although he adduces no proof.

The great Carême, perhaps France's greatest cuisinier, did not hold the author in very high esteem; the latter's masterwork, in fact, seemed to give him indigestion. Of Brillat-Savarin, whom he considered just another self-styled gourmet, Carême is reported to have made these comments: "He never knew how to eat. . . . A big eater. . . . He simply filled his stomach. . . . He had a heavy air. . . . After dinner his digestion absorbed him. . . . I have seen him fall asleep. . . ."

But cutting through the celebrated gourmand's rather overblown writings, one does come on some truths pithily put. For instance, Brillat-Savarin notes with pride that "*La Coquetterie* and *La Gourmandise*, those two great virtues which our social existence has evolved from our most imperious needs, are both of them of French origin."

Certainly the torch of the art of cooking seems to have been kept alight in modern times by the French; today it burns brightest of all in Lyon. A stay in that agreeable French city and its environs is a gustatory delight, for trenchermen and moderate eaters alike. One American, who watches his waistline from time to time, summed up his own feelings about the Lyon region thus: "It's a great place to visit, but it must be hell to live there."

Acknowledgments

─────◆◆◆─────

I would like to thank, for their assistance, understanding, and patience, the following: De Heer en Mevrouw van Grinsven-van Oyen, of Maastricht, Herr Richard Schmitz, of Baden-Baden, Mister Donald Francis Sheehan, of Leningrad, Monsieur Paul Bocuse, of Collonges-au-Mont d'Or, a pride of Lyon restaurateurs, the Messieurs Gérard Nandron, Jean-Paul Lacombe, Jean Vettard, and Christian Bourillot, and a mayor, a consul, a lawyer, a few professors, a croupier, a journalist, a judge, a masseur, a composer, a physician, some soccer players, a variety of businessmen, a train engineer, a number of taxi-drivers, some students, a legislator, a congeries of waiters, several maîtres d'hôtel, a handful of concierges, a few reasonable customs officials, a bartender or two, a great many shopkeepers and sales-persons, librarians, and others. God bless them.

Photographs by Novosti Press Agency, Eckhart Breider, Photo-Kühn, Ingeb. Lehmann, Bord Failte, Jan van Eyk, Openbare Werken Maastricht, F. Lahaye, Tanjug, Enit, Gustav Schikola, French Government Tourist Office